A GRANDMOTHER'S ADVICE TO YOUNG MOTHERS ON THE PHYSICAL EDUCATION OF CHILDREN.

BY M. J.,
COUNTESS DOWAGER MOUNTCASHELL.

Revised and Augmented by the Author.

LONDON:
BALDWIN AND CRADOCK.
PATERNOSTER-ROW.
1835.

G. WOODFALL, ANGEL COURT, SKINNER STREET, LONDON.

PREFACE.

This book is really what it professes to be—*the work of an old woman*. In fact no other description of person would have been equal to the undertaking; which, humble as it is, required a peculiar combination of circumstances to insure any prospect of success: and as those old women who have leisure to write, have not always opportunities of obtaining the experience of a nurse, or inclination to study the writings of medical men, the Author has thought it expedient to attempt a work of *real utility*, for which, perhaps, few others possess the necessary qualifications.

Having suckled many children, she has had means of obtaining, from the first source, a species of knowledge which professional men can derive only from the information of women; and by having read with attention most of the best books which have been written on the management of children, she has convinced herself that the subject has not been exhausted.

The object of this work is, chiefly, to instruct young mothers how to *prevent*, rather than to *cure*, the diseases of children: for when maladies assume a dangerous form, and require medical treatment, the study of years is necessary to apply it with advantage. When, at some future time, the progress of science shall have simplified the art of healing, to the general advantage of mankind, the preventive part of medicine will, probably, be considered as the most important; and, in consequence, the number of maladies be diminished.

Long experience, and much observation, have induced the Author of this work to believe, that a great number of the diseases which afflict the human race are effects of imprudence and neglect in the early part of life; and that by constant and judicious attention to the physical education, during the first fifteen years, many of these diseases might be avoided. For this reason she is anxious to diffuse amongst her own sex, a species of knowledge which may enable mothers to educate their children with better prospects of health and happiness; and, perhaps, occasion them to take a greater interest in the welfare of their offspring, by proving how much it depends on their attention.

The disadvantages under which a medical man labours, in his attendance on infant patients, are many, and may be ascribed to various causes; but the greatest is the difficulty of obtaining accurate information from the sick, who are incapable of describing their sensations, and when the principal lights are to be received from some person totally ignorant of the science of medicine. This often renders the task of prescribing for the diseases of children a matter of great difficulty; and the indiscretion of their attendants, frequently, counteracts the good effects of the most judicious advice.

Even where a physician, by being the father of a numerous offspring, may appear to have had the best means of studying those maladies incident to the early years of man, it is impossible he should ever have such experience of the momentary changes to which the infant frame is liable, as may be acquired by an observing mother or an attentive nurse; and which, were it combined with a moderate degree of scientific knowledge, would often prove the surest guide to the medical attendant.

But it too frequently happens that, through the ignorance of those about them, the complaints of children are at first disregarded; palliative remedies are neglected, and the professional man is not consulted until it be too late. In truth, no appearance of indisposition in a child should ever be thought trifling; and though the greater number may not require the assistance of medicine, yet, in those that do, it should be resorted to without delay. It is to little purpose that a physician is called in when the vital powers have been exhausted by the continuance of disease; and still less when only a part of his advice is followed. Such is often the consequence of that sort of ignorance, which it is the object of this work to diminish.

When the best physicians are surrounded with difficulties in their treatment of the maladies to which infants are subject, it is not surprising that many children are lost through the want of a little more knowledge in the women who are constantly about them. Various indispositions are brought on or increased by neglect; and the timely application of simple remedies would often check the progress of maladies which become dangerous through inattention.

It sometimes happens that a long series of

years spent in the service of children, may have given to an old nurse a degree of experience, which, if accompanied with discretion and modesty, would be of infinite value; but, unfortunately, it is usually attended with the inconvenience of her fancying herself capable of prescribing medicines with whose nature and force she is unacquainted, and which, if improperly administered, may occasion the most pernicious effects. The courage of ignorance is always great; the mistakes resulting from it often fatal; and it frequently happens, both in regard to children and adults, that, in cases where the learned and judicious physician considers it prudent to delay his exertions, a vulgar apothecary, or an old nurse, will throw in medicine upon medicine; and, by disturbing the salutary efforts of nature, augment the disease, perhaps to the destruction of the patient.

The excessive ignorance of the generality of mankind respecting every thing which relates to medicine, is productive of many bad consequences: one of these (and not the least) is the power it bestows on a tribe of ignorant pretenders, who infest the earth to the great detriment of the sick; for few persons know how to distinguish between them and those who, by dedicating their time and talents to the researches of science, are enabled to relieve the infirmities of human nature. To choose a physician well, one should be half a physician one's self: but as this is not the case with many, the best plan which a mother of a family can adopt is, to select a man whose education has been suitable to his profession; whose habits of life are such, as prove that he continues to acquire both practical and theoretical knowledge; who is neither a bigot in old opinions, nor an enthusiast in new; and, (for many reasons,) not the fashionable doctor of the day. A little attention in making the necessary inquiries, will suffice to ascertain the requisites here specified; to which should be added, what are usually found in medical men of real worth, those qualities which may serve to render him an agreeable companion: for the family physician should always be the family friend.

Though the design of this work has been merely to treat of *physical education*, a subject which has been much less discussed than *moral*, yet, the strict connexion between mind and body has rendered it impossible to enter fully into the former without touching on the latter:

and it is hoped that what has been said of the moral part of education will not be considered as altogether useless.

The great influence which the conduct of a mother, during the time of pregnancy and nursing, is likely to have on the health of her offspring, has induced the Author to prefix some introductory advice on those subjects; which may possibly be advantageous to the inexperienced, and cannot appear misplaced in a work of this nature.

In these pages will, probably, be found many known truths and many old remarks: but let it be remembered, that the task was undertaken wholly with a view to *utility*, and not to disseminate opinions, or display the learning of the Author; whose object, in fact, has been to write such a book as she would herself, at the age of twenty, have received as a *valuable gift*. Technical terms have been avoided as much as possible, and few medicines recommended; for when many are supposed to be necessary, the opinion of a professional man must be required.

The observations and advice contained in this work are chiefly the result of the Author's own experience; and when they are founded on the information of others, that information has been examined with the strictest attention. The book is the production of many years' study and reflection; and the Author cannot help flattering herself that it will be of some use to those for whom it is designed,—the *anxious mother*, the *attentive governess*, and the *careful nurse*.

PREFACE

TO THE SECOND EDITION.

It is some time since the first edition of the Grandmother's "Advice to Young Mothers" has been exhausted, but various obstacles have prevented the reprinting of it till now; and probably causes of a similar nature have rendered the sale of the book much slower than might have been expected from the intrinsic value of a *really original work, the result of thirty years' reading, observation, and experience; by an independent author, regardless of fame or emolument, but earnestly desirous of rendering her fellow creatures a service, which she felt that an extraordinary union of uncommon circumstances had placed peculiarly within her power.* In this conviction she was encouraged by the opinion of one of the first medical men of the age*, and fortified with his assurances of

---

* The late Andrea Vaccà of Pisa.

success, she commenced the work, which employed three years in completing, was executed with the utmost zeal and attention, and has since its publication, been highly commended by all who are capable of distinguishing such a composition from the venal compilations of needy book-makers.

The present edition has been carefully revised; the trifling errors and more offensive vulgarisms, which had crept into the work (after it was out of the author's hands) have been expunged, and several useful observations have been added; so that there is every reason to hope that " A Grandmother's Advice to Young Mothers," may hereafter conduce more than ever to the health and happiness of those innocent and interesting creatures for whose benefit the work was undertaken.

CONTENTS.

INTRODUCTION.

                                                                           Page

CHAPTER I.—On Pregnancy and Child-birth 1

CHAP. II.—On Nursing 12

PART THE FIRST.

TREATMENT OF INFANTS FROM THEIR BIRTH TILL AFTER TWO MONTHS OLD, AND THE MALADIES TO WHICH THEY ARE LIABLE DURING THAT PERIOD.

CHAP. I.—Manner in which a new-born infant should be washed and dressed.—Wooden bathing vessel.—Cushion stuffed with chopped straw.—No pins in the clothes.—First shifts.. 32

CHAP. II.—Cleanliness.—Excoriations.—Washing the Mouth.—Flannel.—Night-dress.—Caps.—Time of washing.—Of dressing. 39

CHAP. III.—Modes of Cleanliness.—Of Sleeping.—Cradle.—Care of Sight—And of all the Senses. 44

CHAP. IV.—Rooms inhabited by Infants.—Manner of holding them.—Of giving them Fresh Air 50

CHAP. V.—Infants ought to have the Mother's Milk as soon as possible.—Medicine seldom necessary.—Want of Appetite.—Mucus in the Stomach.—Handling gently.—How the Head should be cleaned.............. 55

CHAP. VI.—Internal Pains.—Crying.—Costiveness.—Strangury.—Growing thin.—Distortions of Face. 62

xiv   CONTENTS.
                                                              Page
CHAP. VII.—Jaundice.—Red Gum.—Hiccough.—Looseness.—Gripes. 67

CHAP. VIII.—Cold in the Head.—Sore Eyes.—Coughs and Colds.—Accidental Sore Mouth.—Thrush 73

CHAP. IX.—Convulsions—their various Causes, and the manner of treating them...................... 81

CHAP. X.—Bringing up Children without Human Milk... 86

CHAP. XI.—Hints respecting Hired Nurses............ 94

PART THE SECOND.

MANAGEMENT OF CHILDREN FROM TWO MONTHS TO TWO YEARS OLD.

CHAP. I.—Manner of Making Children Hardy.—Clothing.—Shoes.—Exercise. 98

CHAP. II.—Learning to Walk.—Bathing. 104

CHAP. III.—Teething—often irregular in time and order.—Diarrhœa.—Dysentery 107

CHAP. IV.—Vomiting.—Pain before the Teeth appear.—Hard Substances unsuitable to the Gums.—Lancing the Gums.—Bleeding.—Blistering...................112

CHAP. V.—Advantages of Air and Exercise.—Bowels to be kept open.—How to treat Spasmodic Symptoms.—Eruptions 118

CHAP. VI.—Weaning, how to be effected with ease.—What Food proper for Children.—Necessary Cautions 124

CHAP. VII.—Variety of Food proper for children under two years old.—Sugar 130

PART THE THIRD.

TREATMENT OF CHILDREN AFTER TWO YEARS OLD.

CHAP. I.—Diet.—Regular hours of Eating.—Fruit.—Evacuations.—Bed-rooms..............................134

CHAP. II.—Pulse.— Feverishness. — Slight Diarrhœa.— DoubleTeeth.—Irregular Growth................142

CHAP. III.—The Heads of Children should be kept cool.—Running at the Nose not to be disregarded.—Short Hair.—Bad Habits.—Dangerous Tricks.—Damp Shoes 147

CHAP. IV.— Cleanliness. — Cold-bathing. — Cold Drink.—Slight Indispositions.—Precautions 154

CHAP. V.—Chopped Lips.—Chilblains.—Slight Burns.—Bruises.—Wounds 163

CHAP. VI.—Cautions respecting the Treatment of Girls at a Critical Time of Life 174

PART THE FOURTH.

OF DISEASES COMMON TO CHILDREN OF ALL AGES.

CHAP. I.—Division of Diseases.—Fevers. 180
CHAP. II.—Intermitting Fevers or Agues 185
CHAP. III.—Eruptive Fevers.......................188
CHAP. IV.—Small-pox.— Cow-pox....................191
CHAP. V.—Measles................................198
CHAP. VI.—Scarlet Fever.—Slighter Maladies of the same Nature 208
CHAP. VII.—Colds and Coughs......................216
CHAP. VIII.—Hooping-cough 222
CHAP. IX.—Sore Throats 229
CHAP. X.—The Croup 234
CHAP. XI.—The Mumps. 239
CHAP. XII.—Diarrhœa.—Dysentery.—Cholera Morbus 241
CHAP. XIII.—Hydrocephalus, or Water on the Brain ..253
CHAP. XIV.—Convulsions..........................258
CHAP. XV.—Worms 267
CHAP. XVI.—Scrofula 278

xvi　　　　　　CONTENTS.

                                                                                 Page

CHAP. XVII.—Rickets 291

CHAP. XVIII.—Cutaneous Diseases................297

PART THE FIFTH.

GENERAL OBSERVATIONS RESPECTING CHILDREN OF ALL AGES.

CHAP. I.—Food.—Purification of Water.—Children should not be pressed to eat.—Irregularity of Appetite.—Sweet things.—Children naturally Gluttons.—Do not require food in inflammatory Diseases. 305

CHAP. II.—Clothing.—Covering the Bosom and Arms.—Ornaments injurious to Health.—Beauty to be acquired.—Ligatures of all sorts bad........................313

CHAP. III.—Evacuations.—Exercise.—Amusements.—Warmth.—Change of Air.......................320

CHAP. IV.—Heat of Rooms.—Crookedness.—Round Shoulders.—Unwholesome Postures.—Sleep.—Beds.—Nocturnal Terrors. 329

CHAP. V.—Painted Toys.—Independence.—Praise.—Wonderful Children.—Indolence.—Deformed or Discontented Persons should not be about Children 338

CHAP. VI.—Sensibility.—Jealousy.—Punishments.—Courage.—Peevishness............................345

CHAP. VII.—Praise.—Forgiveness.—Religion.—Learning.—Accomplishments 355

CHAP. VIII.—Physicians.—Medicines.—Treatment of Children when Ill.—Conclusion.................. 362

APPENDIX.—List of Medicines, and some necessary Directions. 371

INTRODUCTION.

CHAPTER I.

ON PREGNANCY AND CHILD-BIRTH.

A PREGNANT woman, who desires to produce an offspring well constituted in body and mind, should pay the strictest attention to her own conduct, both physical and moral. She should carefully avoid any species of excess, and endeavour to keep her mind in the greatest tranquillity; she should contrive to have agreeable occupations, to enjoy the fresh air, and to take regular and moderate exercise; and she should also indulge the caprices of pregnancy, though not in too great a degree. A peculiar state of the stomach may enable it to digest a certain portion of apparently unwholesome food, but it is always imprudent, and sometimes dangerous, to yield entirely even to what appears an instinct of nature, when nature deviates from the common track.

Food taken more frequently, and in smaller quantities than at other times, would (in many cases) diminish that uneasiness of stomach which seems to belong to the first months of pregnancy, and which might often be rendered scarcely perceptible by proper attention to the state of the bowels. Women of a costive habit of body, generally, suffer more from what is called the breeding sickness than those of a contrary constitution; and such should therefore have recourse to the aid of medicine; which, it is scarcely necessary to say, should be of the mildest sort. Bleeding is also sometimes requisite, and many women are taught to believe it so much so, that if they have had occasion for it in the first, the same necessity will occur in every succeeding pregnancy; but this is a false, and may often prove an injurious opinion. Were more judicious arrangements made respecting diet and exercise, it is probable that all these artificial aids might generally be dispensed with. If a pregnant woman eats a great quantity of animal food, drinks fermented liquors in abundance, and leads a sedentary life, her situation will naturally produce an extraordinary fulness of the blood-vessels, and incur the necessity of bleeding and other medical aid: but to one who eats moderately of meat, vegetables, fruit, &c., drinks chiefly water, and takes exercise (especially on foot) every day, for her amusement, such assistance will probably be unnecessary.

Loose and light clothing is, also, of the greatest importance to the well-being of both the mother and child, and numerous instances are on record of the pernicious consequences of tight lacing during the time of pregnancy. And here I cannot help remarking, that this species of self-torture frequently (perhaps I may say always) fails of the desired effect; for when nature has determined that a woman shall retain in part that increase of bulk occasioned by pregnancy, which it is the object of tight stays to prevent, nothing will protect her from it. Indeed, were I to judge from my own observation, I should say that this unnatural practice was likely to occasion the defect (if such it may be called) which it was intended to prevent, as all those women whom I have known to be most eager in taking this precaution, have been disappointed in their hopes; while others, who have never thought on the subject, but followed the simple dictates of nature, and consulted only their own convenience, remain perfectly free from the dreaded augmentation after having brought forth ten or twelve children.

But I am sorry to say that, both during the time of gestation and parturition, many things are done every day which must be in the highest degree prejudicial. It is an evil of no small importance for women to be obliged to have recourse to the assistance of the other sex at the time of labour, and one by no means necessary; as I have the *best authority* for asserting that there are very few cases indeed in which a female midwife, who has had the regular instructions, and gone through the professional examinations, (and no others should be suffered to practise,) is not as capable of exercising the obstetric art as a professional man. In expressing my opinion on this subject, however, I wish to have it clearly understood, that I by no means recommend the employment of the common sort of female midwives; on the contrary, I believe their ignorance, and the temerity by which it is usually accompanied, to be the cause of many fatal accidents; and I am convinced that no ill-timed delicacy ought ever to induce a woman who can have better assistance to trust herself to the care of such persons. Until it becomes the general custom (perhaps I should say *the fashion*) to employ female midwives, I would advise those who can afford the expense, to have present, for their own comfort, the best female practitioner that is to be had, under the direction of a professional man, who should be in the house to apply to in case of necessity. For the consolation, however, of those who cannot take this precaution, let it be remembered, that in nineteen cases out of twenty, (perhaps a much greater proportion,) no assistance whatever is necessary to a woman in labour, and therefore no skill is required; but only good sense enough to leave nature to do her own work.

The presence of a person disagreeable to the

sufferer must always be more or less injurious; and, in fact, the first appearance of the accoucheur has sometimes had such an effect on the nerves at the commencement of labour, as entirely to drive away the pains; so that he has been obliged to retire until the contractions of the womb were established in such a degree as to be beyond the influence of the imagination.

In general, the whole business of labour is too much hurried. The slow and gradual operations of nature are not sufficiently respected: the females who are present urge the sufferer to "help herself," and the unnecessary and useless efforts she is thus induced to make, only tend to debilitate her and her offspring. If women did but know something more of the animal economy, they would patiently submit to a little longer suffering, rather than run the risks attendant on making too great exertions, or receiving too much assistance. But in this, as in a thousand other instances, people run into fatal errors by allowing art to usurp the place of nature.

When a labour is tedious, the woman requires nourishment; and this should be proportioned to that which she has been accustomed to take. One who is in the habit of drinking wine and strong liquors may without danger apply to their aid during the time of labour: remembering, however, that the quantities should be less than she has been used to take at other times. But if a woman, who has always lived abstemiously, should be plied with heavy nourishment and spirituous drink in this situation, the consequences might be extremely dangerous.

Another great source of evil, is the prejudice common amongst women, that they must be in great danger as long as the after-birth remains in the womb; and, for this reason, the expulsion is seldom left to nature, which in most cases would require no artificial aid to bring away either the child or its appendages. The common expression, " is she safe yet?" to demand whether the after-birth has been expelled, clearly shows the vulgar opinion on this subject; i. e. that the woman is in danger of dying while it is retained. It is unnecessary to point out what must be the situation of a woman impressed with this idea, as long as this substance remains within her, which, if left to nature, it would often do for several hours (or perhaps even days) without any injury, but the contrary. The instructed midwife, whether male or female, is well acquainted with the circumstances which render it necessary to extract the *placenta* by force; and where there are not these indications, it is best to trust to nature. At all events, the ignorant should refrain from interfering with or hurrying those who have studied their profession. But this is one of the many cases in which every old gossip thinks she has a right to give her opinion and advice. Constitutions differ so much that there can be no general rule to judge by. To one woman it may be natural to expel the after-birth in five minutes, to another in five hours after the birth of the child; and the premature extraction, even when not attended with danger, is usually followed by severe *after-pains* * and unnecessary loss of blood.

Another injurious custom, which produces similar effects with the last mentioned, is that of changing all the clothes too soon after delivery. Matters should be so contrived, that the linen necessary to be removed immediately, may be taken away without raising up or disturbing the body of the woman; and any further changes of clothing should be deferred for several hours, until she may have taken nourishment and repose.

In urging the necessity of avoiding fatigue, I only repeat what is continually recommended by medical writers; but, as this book is intended for those who do not peruse their works, I think it requisite to enforce the greatest attention to this subject. No one should be with a woman in labour but the necessary assistants, unless she herself should express a particular desire to the contrary: her wish, of course, should be indulged; and, as it

---

* For the relief of these pains, perhaps nothing is better than *penny-royal* water, warm, which may be taken frequently in the quantity of two or three ounces: not, however, when there is an excessive loss of blood.

is not likely to extend to many persons, it cannot produce the bad consequences resulting from a number of unnecessary spectators. After the pains of labour are over, the utmost tranquillity is necessary; and care should be taken that the visits of relations and intimates, too soon after delivery, do not occasion some dangerous alteration. Many women have been thrown into the most perilous situations merely by tedious and fatiguing attentions of this sort; and I have myself known instances of some who have narrowly escaped with their lives. In general, silence, solitude and darkness, for the first eight-and-forty hours, are advantageous, if not absolutely necessary: and the mind of a woman, who has happily borne a promising child, is not liable to become melancholy for want of society.

It is natural for a healthy woman to feel an extraordinary desire for frequent nourishment during the first two or three days after delivery; but she should be very cautious as to the quality of her food for the first week, that she may escape, or more easily pass through that inflammatory state commonly called the milk fever. I say nothing of the quantity, which is usually the more important consideration, because the quality, for the first few days, should be of a sort not likely to occasion an excess in eating; and after that time the desire for food is not so keen.

A woman of a good constitution, who suckles her child, will not require savoury dishes or fermented liquors to give her an appetite, nor will she be likely to have occasion for medicine during the time of her confinement. It may, however, sometimes happen that in consequence of remaining in bed, and even the strongest women should be cautious not to leave it too soon, (especially in cold weather,) some assistance to the bowels may be required during the first week or fortnight; and in this case it would be far better to employ a simple clyster, which acts only on the parts that want it, than derange the stomach by having recourse to purgative medicines. When the work of digestion goes on well, why do any thing that may disturb it? And if the lower bowels, from being accidentally over-heated, do not perform their functions properly, why not apply the remedy to the part which requires it? A clyster relieves the overloaded bowels without offending the stomach, a part of the human body the most important, and which requires to be treated with the greatest respect.

What I have said in regard to the little necessity for medicine, refers only to the state of those women who follow the dictates of nature in administering to their offspring the food that Providence has destined for them. Those who are either so unfortunate as not to be able, or so unnatural as not to be willing, to suckle their children, must be treated as persons in a state of induced malady; and accordingly have recourse to the aid of physicians and apothecaries.

I cannot leave this subject entirely, without saying a few words on the unnecessary pain to which women in labour are frequently exposed, when they are obliged to lie for hours on one side; a thing sufficiently disagreeable at any time, but particularly irksome when severe pain produces a desire to vary the posture. I cannot think that accoucheurs would enforce this law if their patients had courage to remonstrate; but as no one who has not borne children can be aware of the great difference between one position and another in this excruciating state, it cannot be expected that professional men will make any change in the established customs, unless induced by the representations of those whose sufferings they wish to alleviate.

The reasons assigned for this dreadful rule of making women lie on the left side during the time of delivery, are by no means unanswerable; and in other countries, where it does not exist, the accidents it is alleged to prevent, do not occur more frequently than in the British isles. It appears to me of great importance that all unnecessary inconveniences should be avoided, as productive of additional irritation, and therefore inclining to fever after the actual pains of child-birth are at an end;

and that the persons about a woman in labour should not consider the present moment alone, but always look to the consequences after delivery, especially when the mother is not destined to nourish her offspring according to the dictates of nature.

CHAPTER II.

ON NURSING.

Though it is not now the custom, as formerly, for every opulent mother to throw her infant on the bosom of a stranger, for that nourishment which nature commands her to administer from her own, yet it is still far too common for women of a certain rank, and their imitators, to submit to this barbarous refinement, which is often injurious to the health of both mothers and children; and which all who see it in a just point of view should use their utmost endeavours to abolish.

It is certain that there are women who, from a principle of conscience, should refrain from suckling; but the number of those unfortunate persons is comparatively so small, that if no others abstained from the performance of this first maternal duty, the exceptions would be scarcely observable. Women of a very scrophulous constitution, those who have strong symptoms of pulmonary consumption, and such as are liable to some sorts of uterine debility, should endeavour to remedy their own defects by procuring for their infants the milk of more healthy nurses. Some few, also, there may be, who, either by excessive debility of nerves or uncommon weakness of stomach, are rendered unfit for this office; but, generally speaking, every woman who is capable of bringing forth a robust, healthy child, is capable of supplying its appropriate nourishment.

Many women are discouraged from suckling their children, by apprehensions of the great confinement and excessive fatigue attendant on the duties of a nurse; and many others are induced to give it up, after the trial of a few days or weeks, on account of some temporary inconvenience or accidental malady. But none of these should prove sufficient obstacles to mothers really determined to follow the dictates of nature in this matter. No doubt the employment of nursing must be accompanied with a good deal of restraint during the first few months, but the inconveniences are not such as should ever deter a *rich* woman from making the attempt; and as to the *poor*, we know they are obliged to submit to necessity. None are so capable of executing this office with satisfaction, as those who have it in their power to hire the assistance of trusty and estimable persons to relieve them from a great part of the fatigue attendant on nursing; and, in truth, the services of such persons can never be too highly valued nor too well rewarded.

The greatest fatigue to which *poor* women are exposed in the time of suckling, is that occasioned by having their infants to sleep with them, especially during the period of dentition, or any other troublesome indisposition; but to a woman who can repose in tranquillity with no other disturbance than having the child brought to her two or three times in the night, and who is not obliged to clean or to watch it during the hours usually devoted to rest, the fatigue is comparatively trifling; especially as the infant (if well taken care of, and not of a sickly constitution) will often sleep six or seven hours together.

It is not indeed possible for a woman who is nursing to be long absent from her child during the first three or four months, but after that time it may be brought to take regular meals, (eight, nine, or ten times a day, at stated hours,) so that the mother need not be prevented from going out for exercise or amusement during the intervals. At three or four months old it might be advantageous to feed the child once a day*, the most suitable hour for which would be about noon; and when once this becomes a habit, the mother may leave the child for three hours together, as it will probably

---

* The properest food for a child in health, at this age, is very thin panada, made of good white bread and water which has been already boiled and left to grow cold, with loaf sugar sufficient to make it as sweet as the mother's milk. This should be given very slowly, from a little boat made of box-wood, and should not be hotter or colder than the natural food.

sleep for two hours after this meal. This will be quite sufficient until the preparation for weaning commences, as the child at six or seven months old will be able to eat a piece of bread out of its hand. I do not believe that a child who has plenty of milk would require any other food until old enough to show a desire for it; but it is always prudent to prepare it, by the habit of feeding, to take medicine easily in case of illness, or to be weaned prematurely, if pregnancy or any other accident should render the mother incapable of continuing to afford it nourishment from her bosom.

And here I must suggest that the danger of becoming pregnant is not nearly so great as is generally supposed. Very few women are liable to this accident during the first twelve months of giving milk; and there are some who might continue for three years without apprehension. A year is quite long enough for healthy children to suck; and at any time after five months they may be weaned with perfect safety, if no malady should intervene. It is only necessary in case of being taken from the breast early, that particular attention be paid to the quality and quantity of their food; but this subject will be treated more at large in its proper place.

A woman who is giving milk should eat oftener than at other times; and, in fact, one who is a good nurse will have a much greater appetite during the period of suckling than at any other. She should not, however, be too ready to increase her quantity of meat, but rather let her additional meal or meals be of broth and bread, oatmeal, rice, or barley-gruel; or milk, if it agrees with her. A strict diet, and the prohibition of various sorts of food, is quite unnecessary; in all probability, whatever has before agreed with the mother will not injure the child, though perhaps, in regard to a hired nurse, a little more caution might be necessary. There is nothing more erroneous than the very common practice of giving strong liquors, such as porter, ale, wine-whey, &c. to nurses: a woman who has been accustomed to these things may certainly continue the use of them, but she should carefully avoid increasing the quantity. If giving milk should occasion great thirst, (as is sometimes the case,) it should be assuaged with plain water, or milk and water, rice or barley-water, tea, or infusions of other herbs, &c.; but by no means with any thing of a spirituous nature. The advice here given is calculated for all ranks of society. Let the woman who is nursing, eat and drink whatever she has been accustomed to find agree with her stomach: but, let any additional food she may require be rather of a cooling than a heating nature, both for her own sake and that of her child. The powers of digestion among other persons being almost as various as their faces, it is impossible to prescribe exactly what sort of food nurses should make use of. A certain kind of nourishment being suitable to my stomach, is no reason that it should agree with another: there is, indeed, but one universal rule on this subject, and this should be extended to all persons, times, and situations:—*Moderation in every thing.*

It is in the constitution of many women to be able to nurse only a few months, before the periodical evacuation returns to its usual course; but this should not be a subject of alarm; and some of the best nurses I have seen, have been of this constitution. It is, in fact, neither advantageous to the child, according to the prejudices of some; nor injurious, according to the prejudices of others; but to the nurse it is rather debilitating, and therefore it would be requisite for her to have more repose than usual during those few days, and perhaps take food of a more nutritious quality. Should any retention afterwards occur, it will be right to watch whether the milk diminishes, and how it agrees with the child's stomach, for fear of pregnancy, as in that case it would be better to begin weaning immediately; though I do not believe that the milk becomes directly so very unwholesome as is generally supposed: but no woman can be strong enough to afford nourishment to both the child in her womb and that at her breast, without injuring herself. I must here again repeat, that women in general (whether they have the monthly evacuation or not) are by no means likely to become pregnant during the first twelve months of nursing. I lay a particular stress on this point, because I well know that hireling nurses, and those interested to protect them, insinuate every objection that can prevent women in the higher classes of society from bestowing the natural nourishment on their children; and that there are many ladies of rank who are deterred from fulfilling the first duty of a mother, not by the fear of being obliged to stay away from this ball or that masquerade, but by the dread of not doing justice to their offspring if they do not live exactly as the nurses whom they hire. Except in extraordinary cases, twelve months' milk is abundance for any child; and, to many, five or six would be sufficient; especially from the mother's bosom. Of course this must be understood of mothers who are free from the defects before specified.

It is not by any means necessary that a woman who is nursing should lead the life of a recluse; and were it not for the present absurdly late hours, there would be no reason (after the first five or six months) why a lady, who suckles a healthy child, should not enjoy an hour or two of the diversions she has been accustomed to, even in the crowded assemblies of the metropolis. Whatever amuses the mind and raises the spirits is beneficial during the period of giving milk; but all excesses are injurious at this time : and, in fact, at what time are they not so?

A woman who is suckling need not be alarmed by a fit of illness, unless it be of a very serious nature; and to such maladies nurses are not very subject. Those who have an interest in preventing women of a certain rank from nursing their children, fail not to take advantage of the first indisposition, however slight, to suggest the necessity of either weaning entirely or procuring a hireling to supply the mother's place: however, a mother, who is anxious to perform this her first duty, should not be influenced by their counsels, but immediately apply to some respectable physician, who will either tranquillize her mind in pursuing her design, or give her satisfactory reasons for relinquishing it. A woman may be very ill without any bad quality being communicated to her milk; and a good medical practitioner is the only person who can decide whether the nature of the malady is such as to produce any injurious alteration. Those who are not rich enough to have the advice of a really skilful physician, should observe with attention the state of the child: as long as it looks well and does not appear to suffer from indigestion, there is nothing to dread; but in cases of fever, as the milk is usually diminished by that circumstance, the mother should drink plentifully of diluting liquors, and (if necessary) the child should also be fed.

A woman should never suckle her child immediately after any violent agitation of mind. Children whose nurses are of an irritable temper, are very liable to derangements of the stomach and bowels; and these effects, when produced by the milk of a stranger, have sometimes proved extremely dangerous. A nurse should keep her mind as tranquil as possible; and, when disturbed by any accidental circumstance, should delay suckling her child as long as she can without inconvenience, and until after she has taken food. I have known a child in perfect health attacked suddenly by convulsions, in consequence of the mother having imprudently put it to her breast just after seeing a person fall down dead.

Many advantages attend on the habit of making children suck at stated times; and this (when there are no particular reasons to prevent it) may generally be brought about before the child is three months old. It occasions a regular flow of milk to the breasts, which conduces much to the cleanliness and comfort of the mother; it renders the process of digestion easier to the stomach of the child; and it also removes some of the difficulties attendant on weaning.

The chief point to be observed in a woman who

is nursing, is whether the stomach be in a proper state. One who is subject to indigestion or other signs of debility in that part, cannot prove a good nurse if they continue: but this is no reason for not making an attempt. Every mother, who has none of these positive disqualifications before mentioned, should endeavour to suckle her child; and, in many instances, the employment would prove advantageous to her own health; if, however, after a fair trial, the weakness of stomach appear to increase or even remain undiminished, it is a proof of some great defect (natural or acquired) in the woman's constitution, and, in all probability, the health of both mother and child would suffer by persisting in the attempt to nurse. Delicacy of nerves, weakness of bowels, bilious complaints, and many other diseases, are not to be considered as impediments of sufficient importance to prevent a woman from suckling her own child, though they might justly be considered as such in a hired nurse; and (as I have said before) a slight illness is no reason for weaning a child.

Among the lesser objections made to nursing, is the inconvenience of being constantly wet with the milk, the consequent sour smell, &c., &c. All this is generally much exaggerated, and by a little attention may be avoided. A pocket-handkerchief, folded in such a manner as to be several times doubled over the breasts, is easily changed when it becomes wet, and all possibility of the milk passing through the outward clothes may be prevented by a piece of oiled silk*, three or four inches square, (with the corners rounded off,) covered on both sides with linen, and sewed at the inside of the shift; by which means, even if the handkerchief should be wet through, the milk cannot penetrate the oiled silk; and by changing the handkerchief as often as is requisite, all the above-mentioned inconveniences are avoided. There is no occasion for the oiled silk in the night-shift, as a couple of pocket handkerchiefs, not folded, but gathered up, (as is done to put in the pocket,) will be sufficient to prevent the passage of the wet, if the mother take care to suckle her child the last thing before she goes to rest.

I am thus particular about trifles, because I wish to remove every objection, which may occur to the most scrupulous person, in a matter of so much importance as the first duty of a mother. As soon as the child can be brought to take regular meals, the milk will flow into the breasts at regular hours, (which by-the-by tends much to preserve the form of the bosom,) and all the inconveniences of suckling will be greatly diminished. A woman who cannot submit to a little trouble, which lasts but a

---

* This should be exposed to the air for some time before it is used, to take off the disagreeable smell.

short time, for the benefit of her child, does not deserve to have a child.

It is of great importance for a nurse to avoid all unnecessary fatigue, and there are few things which tire more than bending forward to suckle an infant on the lap: for this reason, until the child is old enough to sit while it is sucking, or the mother expert enough to raise it in her arms to the breast, it would be better for her to lie down when the child has occasion to suck; at least during the first five or six weeks, when women are so subject to weakness and pain in the back.

Many a mother has been deterred from continuing to suckle her child, by an inconvenience of the most painful sort, to which some persons are extremely liable, and from which others are completely exempt. I mean what are called *chopped* or *sore nipples*,—a complaint which many women require the greatest care to prevent. The best means of avoiding this, is to prepare for nursing during the last five or six weeks of pregnancy, by putting a little brandy on the nipples twice a day; taking care previously to apply a little butter, and with a soft rag to rub off any part of the skin which can be removed in this way: once will be sufficient for this, and the brandy will harden the soft skin afterwards. Just before the child is put to the breast, the brandy should be applied, and also as soon as the nipple is out of its mouth. There is no occasion to be very particular in wiping off the brandy, but merely to touch the part gently (with a bit of fine linen) before the child sucks; the infant cannot be injured by what adheres of the brandy, and the mother may, by rubbing the skin too hard. The nipples should be kept constantly covered with something soft and cool until all danger of soreness is past, which will be in about five or six weeks. The best substance that can be used for this purpose is the skin of a calf's kidney, cut into pieces about an inch and a half square; these should be kept in rose-water, and changed every time the child is put to breast, drying them well first, and warming them between the hands or with the breath, lest they should occasion any sensation of cold, which it is of the greatest importance to avoid. For the same reason, on taking the child from the breast, the mother should instantly cover the nipple with her hand, and be careful to draw her clothing over that side before she strips the other, for the impression of the air, after the heat of the child's mouth, may cause a chill. These are, in appearance, very trifling subjects to dwell upon, but they are of great importance to a woman who suckles, and such as none can explain but those who have learnt by experience.

Though a woman is afflicted with sore nipples, she should not for that reason be persuaded to give up nursing. She must only contrive to put the child as seldom as possible to the breasts, that they may have time to recover, and therefore she should give only one side at each meal; this is, in fact, quite sufficient during the first few weeks; only when there is no reason to the contrary, it is more convenient to make the child take half its quantity at each side, that the milk may be equally divided. Many ointments and washes are recommended for the cure of sore nipples, but I know of none so safe as honey of roses, which there is no occasion to wash off before the child is put to the breast.

The persons about women of fortune are always ready to catch at the first shadow of an obstacle to persuade them to relinquish the task of nursing, and the accident of the nipples becoming sore, has been the occasion of many disappointments. I once knew a lady who was on the point of yielding to the advice of an old nurse, who assured her it was impossible for her to continue to suckle on this account, when she happened to overhear one of the housemaids (who was making her bed) say to the other, " God help the poor! If my lady was a poor woman, she would be obliged to go on suckling the child." The lady, being one of those persons who consider nursing as a positive duty, was shocked to think that any thing short of absolute impossibility should prevent her from performing it, and determining to support as much pain as a poor woman could have done, succeeded perfectly in her attempt.

During the whole time of giving milk it is particularly necessary to avoid wearing any thing tight across the bosom, and also to shun the impression of very cold air; the last should be guarded against by a light covering, for any thing too warm over a part which must necessarily be so often stripped, might occasion exactly the bad consequences it is designed to prevent. Many women require some support under the breasts during the time of suckling, but this should be made with great caution; stiff stays, or any other article of clothing that can press on them, as well as damp or cold, may at any time during the period of nursing, occasion an obstruction in some of the milk vessels, and produce a painful and tedious malady, ending in an abscess. This, more frequently, occurs during the first few weeks, because the bosom is, at that time, more susceptible of all impressions; but a woman who is giving milk is never perfectly secure from it. The first symptom of the obstruction is a sensation of tightness, accompanied with pain, resembling a slight rheumatism in some part of the breast, where a hard lump is felt, and the pain increased on touching. In a few hours after (sometimes sooner, sometimes later) a fever commences, with violent shiverings: the best thing that can be done then, is to go immediately into a bed well heated, and to drink plentifully of such warm diluting liquors as are most likely to keep up a constant perspiration. At the same time local applications should not be neglected; but these must be managed with the greatest caution, to avoid any impression of cold while they are changing. A bag of hot bran, or a poultice of oatmeal laid upon the spot where the hardness is felt, so as to keep it in a continual sweat, will sometimes disperse it in four-and-twenty hours, especially if the child is strong and sucks often; and, to avoid all danger in uncovering the ailing breast, a piece of soft flannel (covered with linen) with a hole in it just large enough to let the child take the nipple conveniently, should be warmed and laid over it when the poultice is taken off; and care should be taken that this last be hot when it is put on again.

I remember once to have seen a person cured by taking in bed, during the shivering fit, a large glass of weak hot punch, which produced a violent sweat, that was kept up by drinking elder-flower tea more than four-and-twenty hours: at the same time a poultice of hot *polenta** was applied to the part affected, and changed every two hours. This woman had been giving milk about seven months, and was per-

* Polenta is thick porridge made of Indian corn and water, and is common food in the country where this circumstance occurred.

fectly well on the morning of the day on which the malady commenced, but having occasion to walk to some distance, and the weather being very cold, she put on for warmth a dress which she afterwards found too tight on her bosom; and as she was returning home suffered much, at the same time, from a penetrating wind. The pain and swelling of the breast was felt at three o'clock in the day, but the fever did not commence till about nine at night. The complaint went off entirely in three days, and one thing which contributed much to the cure was the child being very strong and sucking a great deal.

It frequently happens that a malady of this nature, after being neglected for some hours, baffles all the power of resolvent applications and turns to a painful tumour, which in the course of some weeks ends in suppuration. For this reason, if the common remedies produce no effect after the trial of a few hours, and the inflammation runs high, a professional man should be consulted without delay, as local bleeding and other medical assistance may still suffice to check the progress of the complaint.

All physicians agree that when a mother is able to suckle her children, there is nothing which contributes more to her own health as well as theirs; and it has been often remarked, that women are less exposed to death during the time of pregnancy and of nursing, than at any other period of their lives. It has, also, been frequently observed, that the latter occupation is particularly favourable to beauty, and this is by no means an illusion of the imagination; for the prosperous state of health which it produces, and the satisfaction attendant on fulfilling a great, and at the same time an agreeable duty, must clear the complexion and brighten the countenance. But it is an extraordinary fact in the history of mankind, that a duty which requires no written law; a duty which is ever the same in all countries and in all ages; a duty respecting which there can be no difference of conscience, no speculative doubts; a duty, in short, which is pointed out by the Creator of all beings,—should have been so often and so generally neglected; and that women the most scrupulously exact in their attention to all lesser obligations, should have considered themselves exonerated from the most important. But this is one of the many inconsistencies which abound amongst human creatures in a state of civilization, and which would almost justify a doubt of their being designed for such a state.

It appears to me that enough has now been said on this subject, to encourage and assist those women who really wish to suckle their children; and it is also to be hoped that the contents of the foregoing pages may be sufficient to determine such as waver, or have obstacles thrown in the way of their intentions. To convert those who spontaneously oppose the laws of nature, is far beyond my expectations.

In regard to *Weaning*, it is of equal importance to the mother and child that it should be done by slow degrees; and if the child is a twelvemonth old and in good health, it need not be a matter of great difficulty. One meal only should be taken away at a time, and for this some other sort of food should be substituted. The mother must consult her own convenience respecting the hour suitable for this privation; but, if not hurried by any particular circumstance, she ought to make no further change for a week after taking away the first meal of milk, and give about six weeks to the entire weaning, leaving an interval of four or five days after every diminution of the milk diet. Much inconvenience to the mother is avoided by this mode of weaning; and the child, becoming by degrees accustomed both to the change of diet and the privation of the amusement of sucking, escapes what old nurses (and even some medical writers) consider as a disease, under the name of the *weaning brash;* an indisposition entirely occasioned by imprudence.

When a woman has almost completed the weaning of her child she should diminish the quantity of her own nourishment, and abstain from drinking, more or less, according as she finds the state of her milk. If (when the child has quite left off sucking) she finds the milk continue in such abundance as to give pain, she should take some purgative * medicine; but it is very probable that in gradually weaning, the milk, without this assistance, may go away of itself, which is far preferable. To those women who are able to milk their breasts it is easy to obtain relief if oppressed by the quantity, and for those who cannot, there are artificial aids. Should there be much uneasiness from swelling, a little oil of sweet almonds, rubbed on gently two or three times a day, is the best application to make use of; and the breasts, as long as there is milk in them, should be covered with flannel or soft fine wool.

That part of weaning which belongs to the management of infants, will be treated of in its proper place.

* One of the best for this purpose is the sulphate of potass, (sal polychrest,) of which may be taken from two drams to half an ounce.

PART THE FIRST.

TREATMENT OF INFANTS FROM THEIR BIRTH TILL AFTER TWO MONTHS OLD, AND THE MALADIES TO WHICH THEY ARE LIABLE DURING THAT PERIOD.

CHAPTER I.

MANNER IN WHICH A NEW-BORN INFANT SHOULD BE WASHED AND DRESSED.—WOODEN BATHING-VESSEL.—CUSHION STUFFED WITH CHOPPED STRAW.—NO PINS IN THE CLOTHES.—FIRST SHIFTS.

THE physical and the moral education of man should both commence from the first moment of existence; and in fact they are so closely united, that it is impossible to neglect the one without committing error in the other.

The infant just expelled from the womb of its mother, is a being of such a delicate nature, that it requires to be handled with the utmost caution; for it is very possible that a slight injudicious pressure on some important part at this time, may occasion deformities in mind and body, which do not attain their full development till many years after, and are then ascribed to causes far different from the true. For this reason it were much to be wished that the women whose office it is to perform the earliest services to new-born infants, might always be well-instructed midwives; and that no one, who has not some knowledge of the organization of the tender being, should be allowed to wash or to dress it in its first state of natural debility.

Any one who has observed the different manner in which an ignorant nurse and a skilful midwife touch an infant just come into the world, must have been struck with the extraordinary contrast. The former, supposing it a thing of course that the child should squall, tosses and rolls it about without ceremony, as if it were only a bundle of rags; whilst the latter lifts it in the gentlest manner, avoids every sudden motion, and endeavours by all means to save it from uneasiness. I have myself seen a clever midwife wash and dress a robust infant for the first time, without once making it cry. The thing is therefore possible; but not indeed if it is to be immediately washed in cold water, as is practised in some places. This custom has been opposed by many eminent physicians, and I am convinced it can never be too much discouraged. The use of cold water, during the first weeks of existence, is very likely to occasion those pains in the bowels which are so common amongst young children, that old nurses consider them as necessarily belonging to their age; but which are probably amongst those maladies to be prevented by judicious treatment. A slight augmentation of cold in the atmosphere is capable of producing spasms and diarrhœa in adults of delicate constitutions, and there is every reason to suppose that infants are affected in the same manner: how much more, therefore, by the immediate contact of cold water!

It is painful to witness the severe discipline that children are usually submitted to as soon as they come into the world, preparatory to being exhibited for the admiration of relations and other visitors. In the first moments of their existence, they suffer through the vanity of those around them; and not unfrequently in so great a degree as to save them from ever suffering by their own: for children, when they happen to be born extremely delicate, are not always able to survive the fatigue of being washed and dressed by an unskilful hand.

The first wrapper of a new-born infant should be a piece of light flannel, lined with soft linen, in which it should be covered all over, except on the face; and if the person who receives it be not expert at passing this over the head conveniently, a little cap of the same materials should be prepared, so that no part but what is necessary for breathing, should be exposed to the air. In this state it should be allowed to remain, lying perfectly still (on its side) for two or three hours; but not unobserved during that time, as some accident might occur for which medical assistance would be requisite.

The washing of a new-born infant ought not to give it pain; and in fact, if performed in a convenient manner, would rather be likely to occasion agreeable than disagreeable sensations. The best method I have ever seen is that employed at Vienna, where they have for this purpose a wooden vessel made in the form of a long oval tub, of dimensions proportioned to the use for which it is designed. It is filled with tepid* water, (in which may be mixed a little brandy or soap if thought necessary,) and in this bath the infant is placed by the midwife, who supports it under the back of the head with one hand. After it has remained three or four minutes in the water, which should be in sufficient quantity to make it float, she rubs it tenderly all over with a soft sponge, and then dries it gently with a warm napkin. An attendant should be ready to cover the child the moment it is lifted out of the water, and care should be taken to put the napkin *first over* (rather than *under*) its body, as that will prevent it from feeling a painful sensation by the impression of the comparatively cold air. It is

---

* As warm as milk just drawn from the cow.

scarcely necessary to add that this first washing should take place in a warm room, with all doors and windows closed.

Besides the wooden vessel above mentioned, there is also prepared a large square cushion, which is used in dressing the child; and this is laid on a table, which is extremely convenient for the person employed in this office. It is filled with chopped straw in such a manner as to be pliable to the weight of the infant, and may be pressed into any form that is commodious. On this the child is laid when taken out of the bath, a warm napkin having been previously spread over it; and, after being well dried in a position which gives no fatigue, the child is thus dressed without having its arms pulled about unnecessarily, or being forced into the unnatural posture of sitting. The clothes of the child are made to fasten behind, and so shaped as to cover the breast and arms; a necessary precaution in cold climates, and an advantage in all. Indeed I have been convinced by repeated observation in various countries, that children who have their bosoms and arms covered for the first two years, are not subject to those severe coughs and inflammations of the lungs which are, during the time of teething, fatal to so many in the British Islands.

Another thing in the dress of infants at Vienna (as well as in many other places on the Continent) deserves also to be imitated; which is, that not one pin is employed in their clothing, every article that requires to be fastened having strings; and the person who ties them turns the child on its side as it lies on the straw cushion, so that it suffers no inconvenience. Some English nurses may, perhaps, say that it is impossible to dress a child entirely without pins: but what is done in one place may be done in another, and I recommend nothing of which I have not witnessed the advantage.

As long as it is necessary to have the child swathed, this is done with peculiar ease by laying it on its back on the straw cushion, holding up the feet with one hand (or making an attendant do so) and rolling the bandage round it with the other. The only pressure that should be made on the body of an infant, is that which is required for some time after the division of the umbilical cord; and which is often a beneficial part of the clothing, after it has ceased to be the necessary bandage of a wound. The swathe should be made of soft linen doubled, without seam or hem, and should have two strings at one end, long enough to go once round the body and to tie. It should be rather more than an inch and a half in breadth and two or three yards in length, according to the size of the child. When this is applied by a judicious hand, it is in many cases advantageous, especially where there has been any griping or looseness, both on account of warmth and of gentle pressure on the bowels; and might in some instances be continued with good effect for three months, or even longer if the weather be cold: for no diminution in a child's clothing should ever take place except in a warm season.

The first shifts should be made with broad, flat seams, and should never be large enough to fall into plaits; every thing that touches the skin of an infant should be soft and smooth; those therefore who cannot afford to have shifts of fine cambrick, should make use of very old linen for this purpose. Every thing the child wears should be made to tie with narrow tape or flat bobbin, and care should be taken to put the knots where they cannot occasion uneasiness.

To many readers this exactness may appear superfluous: for those who have not been accustomed to observe young children with a medical and philosophic eye, are by no means aware of the early development of their physical and moral sensibility, and therefore do not pay sufficient attention to the trifling circumstances which may hurt their feelings. An affectionate mother will not, however, despise these precautions, but consider every hint which may contribute to the welfare and comfort of her infant as well deserving her notice.

CHAPTER II.

CLEANLINESS. — EXCORIATIONS. — WASHING THE MOUTH. — FLANNEL. — NIGHT DRESS. — CAPS. — TIME OF WASHING. — OF DRESSING.

THERE is nothing of greater importance to the health of young children than cleanliness, though in some cases this (as I shall show hereafter) may be carried too far. If the first bath does not perfectly cleanse the skin of the new-born babe, it should be repeated in the same manner the next day; and after this second washing, it seldom happens that a third bath is necessary for the mere purpose of cleaning, though it may be required medicinally in case of gripes, eruptions, &c., &c. Afterwards it will be quite sufficient to wash the head and face, the throat, the hands, the arm-pits, and those parts which come in contact with the excrements; and this should be all done (on the straw cushion) with tepid water and a fine sponge: a soft warm towel should be used for drying. The head may be washed once a-day with tepid water and a little brandy; once a-day is also sufficient for all the other parts, except those liable to be touched by the evacuations. When the towels are wet with urine, the child's skin should be wiped dry before fresh linen is applied, and when there has been a discharge from the bowels, it should be washed clean with the sponge and tepid water.

If great care be not taken in washing the creases made by the flesh of very fat children, they are liable to have the skin of those parts become sore and inflamed: bathing them, frequently, with spring water or rose-water, is generally sufficient to prevent this inconvenience; but sometimes it is necessary to apply some sort of powder. For this purpose various substances are employed: in some places common hair-powder is used: in others the powder of decayed wood, and sometimes hair-powder mixed with a little sulphur: but I believe all that is necessary (in general), after washing and drying well, is to apply some farinaceous substance to the parts inclined to be sore. Great care should be taken that nothing irritating is used, and therefore the common hair-powder sold in shops is not perfectly safe. Starch well powdered and pressed through a fine sieve is, probably, the best thing that can be employed for this purpose. Fine rags dipped in rose-water and laid on the parts are sometimes beneficial, and to render them more so, they may first be smeared with a little clean suet or spermaceti ointment. If these applications are not found sufficient, the advice of a physician should be asked before any astringent substance is tried;

as these sort of excoriations may be produced by causes which require medical aid to discover and to cure.

When there is no disease in the mouth of an infant, it should never be cleaned with any thing but a soft linen rag dipped in *fresh spring water*. This should be repeated three or four times a-day during the first month, (afterwards once a day will be sufficient,) and when done with gentleness, usually gives pleasure to the child. I have often been distressed by the shrieking of infants a few days old, during the operation of having their mouths cleansed with sugar and other substances, which old nurses think proper to use for that purpose; and I am inclined to suspect that the manner in which these are applied is one cause of the sore mouth so frequently to be met with (in the first month) as a mere local complaint. When I have seen nothing employed but cold water, I have seldom observed a child to cry or ever be affected with this species of indisposition.

The clothing of young children should be light, warm, and loose; indeed it should be such at all ages; but we ought to be more particular in paying attention to the comfort of infants, in their first state of weakness, when we cannot judge how much they may suffer from oppression, cold, and pain, than at a more advanced age, when they become capable of expressing their sensations by words.

Fine flannel is certainly the most appropriate substance that can be employed in the covering of children, and care should be taken that their clothes be moderately loose without being so large as to incommode. The use of woollen clothing is advantageous to children of all ages, and is frequently beneficial in a medical point of view when applied next the skin; but by those who are in health it should always be worn over linen, except on the feet of very young children, which are, I believe, in the British Islands generally covered with flannel, and to good purpose. The long petticoats (when not too heavy) are of great use; they keep the lower extremities warm, save infants from the trouble of wearing shoes and stockings, and also prevent servants from teaching them to walk too soon.

A child who sleeps with its mother or nurse will not require flannel about the feet at night, but it should always have a night-dress to put over the shift worn by day. A waistcoat made to cover the chest and arms, and fasten behind, is the best form of additional clothing; and in cold weather this should be made of very soft flannel.

Whatever covering is put on the head should be light; and, generally speaking, the thinner a child's cap is the better: but this of course must be adapted to circumstances, and experience may show that one child requires to have the head kept warmer than another. No positive rule should be laid down, as there must always be some exceptions. Great care should be taken that the caps be not too tight; the chin-stay should be broad and soft, and left rather loose.

With respect to changing the linen on the body of a young infant, there are different opinions; but in this (as in almost every thing else) the middle path is the best, and consequently the shifts should not be left too long without changing nor be changed too frequently. Every second day (or perhaps every third) would be often enough; however, the least appearance of dirt or bad smell (which may easily arise from a drop of milk running down on the bosom) should be a reason for putting on clean linen; which should always be well aired, and warm (but not *hot*) during the first few weeks, and perhaps longer.

No alteration in an infant's clothing should be made when it is sleepy; and for this reason, whatever is to be put on before it is laid to rest, should be such as requires but a moment's arrangement, that its temper may not be irritated by delays when it is impatient for repose; indeed a child should always be undressed before it is oppressed by sleep, and the regular time for changing its shift, washing, and every other necessary annoyance, should be soon after it awakes in the morning.

CHAPTER III.

MODES OF CLEANLINESS.—OF SLEEPING.—CRADLE.
—CARE OF SIGHT, AND OF ALL THE SENSES.

THE comfort of young children should be attended to in every respect; and there are few things which (until they are inured to it by neglect) gives them more uneasiness than having their clothes wet with their urine. It is not sufficient to watch that this should never occur in the day-time, but it is, also, particularly necessary to guard against it in the night. The best means of doing so, is to have a piece of oil-cloth about two feet square, covered with a flannel case, to lay under the child in bed. The oil-cloth should be exposed to the air for some time before it is applied to this use, that the bad smell may go off; and it should never be allowed to touch the child without the flannel case, as the cold (and perhaps other qualities of this substance) might be hurtful. The flannel should always have a linen towel laid over it, but not a case of linen, as this last could not be removed without much disturbance, whereas the towel may be easily changed; and if the flannel should have got wet, the whole thing may be turned in a moment; however, if care be taken to arrange the towel conveniently, and to change it when necessary, the flannel will probably remain sufficiently dry; at the same time, it would always be expedient to have a second oil-cloth and flannel case prepared, lest the one should happen to be wet on both sides. This contrivance is also useful to the mother or nurse with whom the child sleeps, as by drawing the oil-cloth up between her and it, she may avoid the disagreeable sensation of being wet with the urine of the infant.

Children in perfect health, may soon be taught cleanliness, by putting a vessel under them on the lap when there is any sign of their having an evacuation; and when once accustomed to this they are not content to do without it. This practice may be begun at five or six weeks old, if there is no reason against it; but in case of a violent cough or lax, it must be discontinued, as a descent of the lower bowel is not an uncommon complaint in infants; and, therefore, when any malady occurs which may cause weakness in that part, it should not be left unsupported*. Children, who have acquired habits of cleanliness, and who have careful observing attendants, may be left without towels

---

* For the same reason the little chairs which are made for children of one or two years old, should always have the hole as small as possible.

(in a great measure) at four or five months old, and this is always an advantage.

It is a matter of dispute whether an infant should sleep at some distance from its nurse or on her arm, and several medical men have asserted that the latter is extremely unwholesome. No doubt the person who sleeps with a young child should never keep it so close to her mouth as absolutely to inhale her breath; but otherwise it is probably a matter of indifference, and it can scarcely be injurious to an infant to come in contact with the body from which it derives its proper nourishment. I have seen many fine children who have slept on their nurses' arms till eight or nine months old; but when the nurse happens to be a heavy sleeper, this may be attended with danger, and in such a case, the various circumstances must be considered and the most expedient plan adopted. It is scarcely necessary to say, that no person who suckles a child, should allow it to lie at the breast for hours at night, while she sleeps; the infant could scarcely acquire a worse habit, and it is attended with numerous inconveniences.

The use of the cradle has been objected to by many persons, and some have gone so far as to assert that it deranges the brain. There can be no doubt that violent motion of any sort is capable of injuring the brain, as well as other important parts of a new-born infant; but when a gentle movement is beneficial and composing, (especially in illness,) it has always appeared to me that the regular motion of being rocked in a cradle, is far preferable to being carried and jerked about in a woman's arms according to her caprice, especially in very cold or very hot weather: in the former, because of the probability of some part being exposed to the air which ought to be covered, and in the latter, because of the child being heated by the contact of animal warmth, when perhaps it ought to be kept particularly cool. The most reasonable objection which has been made to the use of a cradle is, that it gives children a bad habit, a want more than is necessary; but, as there are many cases in which the advantages greatly preponderate, it is, at any rate, one of those matters in which opinions may differ without occasioning any bad effect.

At the same time that I approve of the use of a cradle, I should by no means recommend putting an infant to sleep in it at night: on the contrary, I am convinced that the warmth of the nurse is extremely beneficial to the child; and we may observe amongst our domestic animals (from whom many a useful lesson might be taken by human mothers) that instinct always leads them to impart the heat of their own bodies to their offspring, in this first state of weakness.

Attention to circumstances apparently trifling

may often prevent both maladies and deformities. It is generally known, though not always sufficiently observed, that the manner in which the bed or cradle of an infant is situated may occasion a permanent squint. Young children should never have the light on one side; neither is it good to have it opposite the eyes. The best position is that in which the light may come from behind, but not in such a manner as to cause the infant to throw up its eyes: any thing that occasions a momentary distortion may be productive of bad consequences, and therefore, in playing with young children, we should always take care to be nearly in front of them, lest they should be induced to give any forced movement to their eyes. There should be no glaring colours opposite to an infant's bed, and it should not be suffered to fix its eyes long on a lighted candle, or on any thing that glitters. The irritation of strong lights and brilliant colours is very likely to produce those inflammations in the eyes which are ascribed to other causes, and often pass for the effects of cold: and parents, who are very anxious about every thing which concerns the welfare of their children, should pay great attention to the colour of the walls of those apartments particularly destined to their use. Green is generally considered to be the colour most beneficial to the sight, but there are many shades of gray and brown sufficiently inoffensive to be placed before the eyes of infants.

Servants are very fond of sitting opposite to blazing fires with children on their laps, as the flames divert and prevent them from being troublesome: but this practice should be absolutely prohibited, as the origin of many complaints, but especially those of the eyes.

It is indeed of the greatest consequence to protect all the senses of young infants from being offended by too strong excitements, particularly of a disagreeable nature. They should be guarded against all loud and harsh noises, rough handling, powerful smells, and nauseous or pungent tastes; but, above all things, the sense of sight should be treated with the greatest delicacy, as it is the most important and the most liable to injury.

CHAPTER IV.

ROOMS INHABITED BY INFANTS.—MANNER OF HOLDING THEM—OF GIVING THEM FRESH AIR.

The room inhabited by an infant should (if possible) be neither small nor low: it should have a good chimney, not liable to smoke; and should be kept particularly clean. No foul linen, dirty vessels, or remains of food should ever be left in it; nor should any persons sleep there, except those necessary to attend on the child. The candles burnt in a nursery should be particularly free from bad smells, and the night-light as small as possible. When the bed-room is washed, the child should be removed into another for that night; unless in the heat of summer, when, by having the floor washed with boiling water early in the morning and the windows left open for several hours, it will, probably, be quite dry before evening. There is nothing more necessary to guard against than damp, which has occasioned the deaths of many infants. When children are not accustomed to it, it gives them cold; and when they are so used to it as not to be affected in that manner, it often produces still worse consequences. The over-cleanliness of washing rooms in bad weather, where children are obliged to sleep, has often done irreparable injury.

The manner of holding a young child is a matter of no small importance, as the foundation of maladies depending on the internal structure may be laid within the first weeks of its existence; and some careless or awkward mode of handling it, at that time, may be the occasion of future disease or deformity. By being held always on the same arm, an infant may easily be made crooked; by always being put to sleep on the same side, a similar effect may be produced: but these are trifling in comparison of the harm which may be done by making a child sit up before its neck is strong enough to support the weight of its head. When infants are robust and well-proportioned, they may perhaps escape injury, notwithstanding the manner in which many nurses choose to hold them sitting up before they are able to keep their heads erect; but if a child happens to have the head a little too heavy, or the spine a little too weak, it is impossible to calculate the extent of evil which may be produced by a foolish attempt to force it too soon into the most unnatural and unwholesome posture to which the human frame is habituated. The best way to avoid this danger, is not to put an infant sitting up at all till after two months old, but always support it (either when on the lap or in the arms) in a reclining posture, with the hand or arm behind its neck, so as never to let the head hang forward or fall back.

These may appear to many unnecessary, and perhaps absurd precautions, since we have often seen children grow up very healthy and free from all the dreaded evils, who have been made to sit up, with their heads hanging like flowers too heavy for their stalks; but we have also seen many die of unknown maladies, and of convulsions, the causes of which were not apparent, and which may possibly have proceeded from some injury to the spinal marrow, unobserved, and irremediable if it had been observed. When we consider the number of infants who perish in the first two months of their existence, it is surely well worthy the attention of a mother to prevent even the most remote cause of harm to their delicate frames. There is the same reason for avoiding to make children sit up, as there is for not swathing them like Egyptian mummies, in the manner customary in so many parts of Europe: the greater number of those who have been dressed in this way are as straight and well made as those who have not; but the practice is better to be shunned, on account of the injuries which may, and sometimes do, happen in consequence of it. Children will by degrees acquire strength to hold up their heads, and some much sooner than others; but it is better not to run risks by anticipating the progress of nature when it may be retarded without danger.

Though infants should not be taken out till after they are a month old, as the open air can afford them no advantage or amusement, and may do them harm before that age; yet the atmosphere of their rooms should be constantly changed, and even in the coldest weather, if *not damp*, the windows ought to be left open for a quarter of an hour every day. The child should be taken into another room during that time, and not brought back to its own until the air has been warmed again by fire. Of course this is to be understood of a child in good health: in cases of illness, every thing must be conducted in a different manner. It is scarcely necessary to say, that in dry, warm weather, the windows of a nursery should be often opened during the day; the hours being adapted to the season and climate.

Infants should be brought by degrees to endure the cold air, as any sudden transition is injurious to them. Those born in winter require particular attention: they should not be taken out so soon as those born in summer; and it would be better to have the air of their rooms kept warm, than to load them with heavy clothing.

It should always be remembered that it is by no means safe to take young children into the open air too soon. Until a month old they can scarcely derive any advantage from going out; and even after that age, it should depend on the time of year and the country where they are born. The pleasure they begin to show on being taken out at five or six weeks old, proves that exercise in the free air is then good for them; and, therefore, if the weather be fine, they should enjoy it every day; but with their bodies sufficiently covered to prevent them from feeling cold, and their eyes carefully guarded against the impression of strong light. As soon as the child shows any fatigue or uneasiness, and especially if it appears to suffer from cold, it should be brought into the house; and in damp weather, children under two months old should not be taken out at all.

CHAPTER V.

INFANTS OUGHT TO HAVE THE MOTHER'S MILK AS SOON AS POSSIBLE.—MEDICINE SELDOM NECESSARY.—WANT OF APPETITE.—MUCUS IN THE STOMACH.—HANDLING GENTLY.—HOW THE HEAD SHOULD BE CLEANED.

It is a very common and hurtful practice to prevent the new-born babe from sucking until the mother's milk is come (as it is called); that is to say, until the woman is oppressed by the accumulation of this fluid, and the breasts consequently distended to a painful degree. In this state the child finds great difficulty in obtaining its nourishment, and if weak, is utterly incapable of drawing it: the vain efforts fatigue and put it out of humour, and the nipples of the mother become sore by the useless irritation of the child's gums. All this trouble would probably be avoided by putting the infant to the breast in a few hours after its birth; when it would procure a small quantity of milk at a time, the purgative quality of which would assist the evacuation of the *meconium*, and prevent the necessity for medicine; while the mother's breasts would fill by slow degrees, and escape that painful swelling which results from not allowing the child to suck as soon as it ought.

The custom of purging infants as soon as they are born, may often be attended with bad consequences. If the child is to have the advantage of being suckled by its mother, the first milk will probably be found sufficient to clear off the black substance contained in the bowels: and in all cases a certain time should be allowed, to let it appear whether nature be adequate to the performance of this office. Instead, therefore, of administering a dose of physic to a child in the first hour of its existence, it would be better, when there are no great symptoms of uneasiness, to wait many hours before this expedient is resorted to. It is not impossible that the retention of the *meconium* for a certain time after the birth, as well as the evacuation of it by slow degrees, might contribute to prevent those pains in the bowels so well known under the name of gripes; and that the length of time this ought to remain varies according to the individual circumstances. But in this, as in many other important matters, nature is not consulted; every constitution is to be cut down to the same measure, and all are to be indiscriminately purged in the same manner and with the same quantity of medicine.

When a child is not destined to have the benefit of its mother's milk, it is sometimes (but not always) necessary to give some assistance in clearing the bowels of their first contents: and substances not positively of a purgative nature might often be found sufficient to produce the desired effect. A little brown sugar or honey, mixed in a spoonful of warm water or thin gruel, would frequently answer the purpose as well as any thing else; but as these do not usually come out of an apothecary's shop, they are seldom supposed to be adequate to the purpose. If a medicinal substance is really found to be necessary, a little magnesia and rhubarb, or either of these alone, in a spoonful of warm fennel-water, with enough of white sugar to make it agreeable to the taste, will probably prove effectual. What might be still better is a tea-spoonful of the *syrup of Endive*, mentioned in the Appendix to this work. These are preferable to oil of sweet almonds, castor oil, or manna, which have been employed for the same purpose. Oily medicines, when they do not perfectly succeed in purging, are injurious; and manna deranges the stomach more than is necessary.

When circumstances render it expedient for an infant to have milk of three or four months old, one of the chief precautions to be taken at first, is not to let it suck much at a time. Notwithstanding the facility with which young children vomit, they are by no means secure from indigestions; a species of indisposition very likely to occasion convulsions, the danger of which every one knows.

If a new-born infant shows a desire for food (as sometimes will happen) before it is convenient to put it to the breast, a spoonful or two of warm fennel-water, with a little sugar, will probably satisfy it, and be the safest thing it can have.

When a healthy child will not suck in twenty-four hours after its birth, the cause must be examined into, as it is likely that there is some substance in the stomach which must be evacuated, either naturally or artificially, before the infant can acquire the appetite which it ought to have. This is one of the cases where it may be necessary to employ purgatives or emetics, respecting which the attendant physician should be consulted, as something more active than the common remedies may be wanting to produce the desired effect.

When it appears that a young infant has a great deal of *mucus* in the stomach, it should not be left an instant alone, as examples are not wanting of children who have been suffocated in their sleep by an accumulation of this substance, which they were unable to throw off while lying down. And for this reason, amongst others, an infant should never be laid on its back, but alternately on each side; and for the first few days it should never be left half an hour in its bed or cradle without being looked at.

By great attention in the manner of handling and dressing children during the first weeks of their existence, not shaking them about unnecessarily, not interrupting their sleep, nor suffering the cold air to strike on their stomachs and bowels; I am convinced that many of their early maladies might be prevented. But the women who are employed about them in the first period of their lives, take no care to avoid rough and abrupt movements in handling them; and, in particular, make no scruple of rousing them from sleep for the purpose of washing and dressing; not seeming to be at all aware that a sort of disturbance which would derange the nerves of a delicate adult, must have a still worse effect on the more tender frame of a young infant. Nor are they by any means sufficiently exact in protecting from cold the body of the child, which should not remain for a moment uncovered without being gently rubbed by a warm hand.

It is an imprudent act of cleanliness to remove all at once the scurf which sometimes gathers on the head and even spreads over the forehead of very young infants; and this is, probably, one of the reasons why we often see the children of persons in easy circumstances tormented, just after their birth, with that troublesome stuffing in the head which is in some places vulgarly called *the snuffles*. When the infant is somewhat inured to the external air, at two months old, or later, (according to the season of the year,) whatever scurf adheres so firmly to the head as not to come off in washing, may be safely and effectually removed, by rubbing a little butter on a small part of the head one day and cleaning it with a box comb the next, before it is washed: then a little more butter should be rubbed on another part of the head, which should be cleansed in the same manner the day after; and in thus removing the scurf by degrees, the head becomes clean in a very short time, without any danger of cold. In many places the lower class have a prejudice against removing the scurf from their children's heads at all, waiting till it comes off of itself; but this is also an error, and leads to many of the bad consequences of dirt, as they neglect to wash the head, which should be done every day as long as the scurf is suffered to remain. When the head is once perfectly clean, the best means of preserving it in that state is by a brush, which should at first be soft, and as the child advances in age should be changed from time to time for one harder. The seldomer a fine comb is applied to the head of an infant the better, and on no account should those of ivory, bone, or tortoiseshell be ever used; for, even when they do not wound the skin and produce a sore, (as frequently happens,) they are very likely to augment the production of that substance they are intended to remove. But I shall return to this subject again when I have to treat of children more advanced in age.

CHAPTER VI.

INTERNAL PAINS. — CRYING. — COSTIVENESS. — STRANGURY. — GROWING THIN. — DISTORTIONS OF FACE.

The first maladies of infants (which are in a great measure the effects of imprudence) may be rendered much lighter by immediate remedies; and many pains in the stomach and bowels relieved in the first moments by the mere application of heat and a slight pressure. Every old nurse knows by experience that it is often possible to tranquillize a young child in a violent fit of screaming, by only laying it on its belly across her knees, and while she gently moves it back and forward, patting it softly on the back with her hand. This, in the first moments of pain, will often be found sufficient to produce a discharge of the wind which occasioned its uneasiness, and prevent farther bad effects; but if, through laziness, or a notion that young children ought to cry, this is neglected until the duration of pain has occasioned either convulsions or inflammation, no advantage can be expected from it, and recourse must be had to medical treatment.

The crying of an infant should never be disregarded: it is the sign of some pain, or some want which ought to be attended to. The cry of hunger is that easiest to be understood by the person who suckles the child, and when there is no reason to suppose that its uneasiness proceeds from that cause, it should not be put to the breast, but other expedients should be tried to tranquillize it: such as rubbing the stomach and bowels with a warm hand, placing the infant gently in different postures, stripping it to examine if any part of its clothing may have hurt it, and giving it a little motion in its cradle or on some one's knees; taking great care, however, that no abrupt or violent movement be employed. When the inquietude does not proceed from disease, these expedients will generally be found sufficient to restore its tranquillity. In such cases, however, the evacuations of infants should always be observed; and if there is any thing extraordinary or irregular in them, the appropriate remedies should be applied.

New-born infants are sometimes affected with an obstinate *costiveness*, which, if not attended to in time, is likely to produce fever and convulsions. When a child who has not evacuated the *meconium* appears uneasy, it should have some laxative medicine; and if that does not produce the desired effect, a clyster should be administered. Brown sugar and warm water, with the addition of a little good oil or barley-water, with a little honey, may answer this last purpose as well as any thing else. Should this treatment not prove sufficient to remove the child's uneasiness, it would be expedient to try a tepid bath, before any stronger remedies are resorted to: but if that fails, a physician should be immediately consulted. For no very active medicine should ever be given to an infant without the advice of a professional man, to whom all that has been already done for its relief should be accurately detailed.

New-born infants are also subject to a *retention of urine*, for which the tepid bath is likely to be the best remedy; and, if the child has not yet been put to the breast, a spoonful or two of fennel-water may also be of use. When this retention, or a difficulty in passing the urine, occur in a few weeks after the birth, it is sometimes less easy to remove; but in this case too the bath should be tried, or warm fomentations (with camomile, elder flowers, &c.) over the lower part of the belly, and the bowels should be cleansed by means of a clyster: when that is done, a tea-spoonful of syrup of white poppies*, with two or three drops of spirit of hartshorn, mixed in a large spoonful of warm water, may be given to the child. But if these remedies are not found suffi-

---

* This is a medicine which should never be got from any but a respectable apothecary, as it is not always prepared as it should be; and when it is not, may produce dangerous effects, instances of which I have known.

cient, medical assistance should be sought without further delay.

It sometimes happens that a child born with the appearance of being very fat, falls away extremely in a few days after; but when there is no symptom of disease, when the appetite, sleep, and evacuations are all natural and regular, there is no cause for uneasiness about the infant's health, as will soon be evident by the manner in which it thrives after some weeks. A young mother should, therefore, be on her guard not to let herself be persuaded (as has sometimes happened) that her milk disagrees with her child; nor should one who has a hired nurse be induced to form an unfavourable opinion of her on this account: and, if no mark of indisposition appears in the infant, no disadvantage can result from the delay of a month or five weeks; and in that time the real state of the case will appear.

Mothers have no reason to be alarmed at the distortions of face, or irregular breathing of newborn infants, as there are none free from those effects of the extreme sensibility of their nerves; and if not accompanied with any symptom of disease, they are of no importance. When, however, a very young child is observed to smile often in its sleep, it should be watched; and if it should awake suddenly, crying and drawing up its legs, these are signs of some pain in the bowels, for which relief should be sought. This pain, however, may be so slight, that rubbing the belly gently with a warm hand, turning the child on its face across one's knees, or merely changing its position, may be sufficient to remove or send away the wind which has disturbed its repose.

CHAPTER VII.

JAUNDICE.—RED GUM.—HICCOUGH.— LOOSENESS.—GRIPES.

MANY children have the *jaundice* very soon after their birth; but this malady, when occasioned by no organic defect, is of little consequence, and either passes away of itself or yields to the use of some mild purgative. Should it continue obstinate after the administration of gentle remedies, a physician should be consulted.

The *red gum* is a slight disease extremely common amongst new-born infants, and often continues for several weeks: its general character is so well known, that it is scarcely necessary to say it appears in small red pimples, which come in blotches, chiefly on the face and arms. But it sometimes happens (especially in hot weather) that it assumes an appearance which alarms those who have never seen it before in that shape, and which, therefore, I think it right to mention more particularly. The eruption is very abundant on all parts; and some of the spots grow large and suppurate, running into each other, and forming an irregular sort of pustule, that appears to penetrate below the skin, and threatens to leave a mark, which, however, it does not. The best remedy for this malady is a tepid bath, composed either of milk and water or of water in which some bran has been boiled. In this the child may remain about ten minutes: and here I must again urge the extreme caution requisite in the use of warm baths, which, when employed by awkward or careless persons, may be the occasion of more mischief than advantage. The room in which the bathing-vessel is placed should be moderately heated; the cloths for drying the infant of a convenient warmth; and while one person lifts it out of the water, another should be ready to cover it instantly, so that it may be in no danger of suffering from the comparative cold of the surrounding atmosphere.

A child should not be put into the bath either immediately after sucking, or when it appears to be very hungry. As soon as it is well dried and covered, it should be put to the breast; when it will probably suck eagerly, and then sleep quietly for some time.

The bath diminishes the irritation and uneasiness produced by the eruption, cleanses the pores of the skin, and promotes the perspiration requisite to carry off the disease. If (as generally happens) the malady is combined with derangement of the stomach and bowels, in consequence of acidities, it will be right to give a few grains of rhubarb and magnesia (two or three of each) mixed in a little fennel-water, with a sufficient quantity of sugar to make the child swallow it without disgust; for even at that early age, whatever is taken unwillingly is less beneficial than it might be. This should be repeated if it does not purge in a few hours, and the quantity increased if necessary; as it is only by experience we can learn what dose is required for different constitutions, and it is always right to begin with small quantities, when not under the direction of a medical man.

If, after the warm bath has been used, and the evacuation produced by the medicine been sufficient, the child should still continue uneasy and restless, a small tea spoonful of syrup of white poppies may be given at night. This treatment will generally be found sufficient to abate the disease; but should it not, the purgative medicine may be repeated in a day or two; and a repetition of the bath may also be expedient, if the eruption has not been diminished by the first application of it.

Any other sort of eruption than the above-mentioned, appearing on an infant under two months old, would render the immediate advice of a physician necessary; especially if the child has a hired nurse, as very different treatment might be required, which nothing but a medical examination into the particular circumstances of the case could determine.

Many infants vomit frequently; but if it be with

great ease, and the milk thrown up curdled, it is of no consequence, especially in the first two months: it is, however, better that children should not vomit; and I have good reason to think that those who are suckled by their mothers are less liable to this inconvenience than those who have hired nurses.

The *hiccough* in young infants may generally be stopped by a little powdered sugar, or a few drops of cold water. If their breasts are well covered, they will not be liable to it, as it is frequently occasioned by the impression of the cold air on that part.

Most people are aware of the necessity of attending to the state of the bowels in young children; but many of those intrusted with the care of them do not know that, in nineteen cases out of twenty, the way to cure a *looseness* is by the administration of a purgative medicine. Indigestion, acidities, and superabundance of bile may be causes of the complaint, and till the substance which offends is carried off, the malady cannot be removed. Nurses are apt to believe that children who take no other food than their milk cannot suffer from indigestion; but this is a great mistake, as nothing is more likely to occasion that complaint than milk in too great a quantity, or of a quality that does not accord with the stomach of the child. In case of too great a discharge from the bowels, let the cause be what it will, there are no safer medicines than those I have already mentioned; the quantities being increased according to the age of the infant and other circumstances.

It is a common saying amongst old nurses, that "the strongest children are those who have *gripes* till three months old, for they suck the more and thrive the better." This is a dangerous prejudice, and frequently prevents maladies from being sufficiently attended to. *Any appearances of pain or uneasiness in an infant should be immediately examined into, and means sought to remove them.* The evacuations should be observed; and when they have a sour smell, a little magnesia should be given now and then, mixed in fennel or weak mint-water, with half a grain of rhubarb. Slimy, frothy stools, should be treated in the same manner, only increasing the quantity of rhubarb and diminishing that of magnesia. When a child has a great deal of wind without any wrong appearance in the evacuations, the fennel or mint-water may be given alone, or two drops of spirit of hartshorn in a spoonful of warm water and sugar. The stomach and bowels may be rubbed now and then with brandy or camphorated spirits, which can be sufficiently heated by putting the bottle which contains them into a bason of warm water: in applying this, however, great care must be taken lest a drop of it should fall on any part where the skin is particularly tender; for any thing that makes a child cry is likely to increase this complaint. But the chief thing to be attended to, both for the prevention and cure of gripes, is the manner of putting on and off the child's clothes; as I am fully convinced that the principal part of these sort of maladies is occasioned by the cold air striking on the stomach and bowels, through carelessness in washing and dressing infants.

In regard to the assertion so often made, that there are no stronger, finer children than "those who are constantly griped during three months," it is easily explained. Infants who are able to support continual pain, and the inattentions by which it is probably occasioned for so long a time, without some dangerous disease, must have very strong constitutions and a great propensity to thrive, which enables them to resist all the dangers that surround them: whereas children of delicate frames are thrown into convulsions by similar causes, and either sink under the malady or are saved by the skill of the physician, who in such cases must have some authority.

When a child, not suckled by its mother, is constantly troubled with gripes, the nurse's state of health should be enquired into, her milk examined, and her diet altered or medicated according to circumstances.

CHAPTER VIII.

COLD IN THE HEAD.—SORE EYES.—COLDS AND COUGHS.—ACCIDENTAL SORE MOUTH.—THRUSH.

Young children are often afflicted, even in the first month, with a troublesome *cold in the head*, which hinders them from breathing through the nose, and renders sucking difficult and painful to them. For this complaint (which is usually the effect of great negligence or over-cleanliness) it might be useful to bathe the feet in warm water with salt in it, for about ten minutes; using the same precautions in drying which are recommended after the entire bath, and then wrapping them up in warm flannel. The best time for doing this is before the child goes to sleep, on account of the feet being well covered; but if that should not be convenient, it will be easy at all times to keep the feet of an infant sufficiently warm. The top of the head ought perhaps to be covered a little more than usual, if the weather be cold, especially at night; and the old nurse's practice, of rubbing grease on the bridge of the nose and between the eye-brows, should not be forgotten.

If, in consequence of a cold in the head, a young child should have sore eyes, the mother's milk will generally be found the best application. She should milk her breast on the eyes, so as to let the liquid run into the corners, every time the lids are fastened together, or the eyes filled with glutinous matter. If this remedy and a dark room are not sufficient to cure the malady in a few days, it will require the advice of a physician: and more particularly if the child has a hired nurse.

Colds and *coughs*, in the first stage of infancy, generally proceed from carelessness or ignorance in the persons who are entrusted with the care of children: either by exposing them to currents of wind, putting on their clothes not sufficiently aired, leaving the bosom uncovered in cold weather, or dressing them so awkwardly as to keep them longer naked than is necessary. It would be difficult to specify half the causes, or detail half the instances of inattention which occasion the maladies of infants; but I am thoroughly convinced that much of pain and misery, afterwards, might be traced to these sources.

When it appears that a young child has caught cold, the greatest care should be taken to keep the air about it of an equal and moderate temperature; for which reason it should not be carried from one room to another, through passages and staircases. If there be cough or difficulty of breathing, the feet should be bathed, as before directed for a stoppage of the nose, and if there is reason to suspect any soreness in the throat, (which may be discovered by the sound of the voice,) a piece of fine flannel should be put round the neck, and the chest also covered with the same from the throat down to below the pit of the stomach; these two strips of flannel being sewed together in the form of a T. But if this should occur in the autumn or winter season, to a child of six or seven weeks old, and especially if the cough be severe, it would be prudent at once to put on a flannel waistcoat next the skin, which might perhaps prove the most effectual remedy. It should be made of the thinnest, softest materials; should fasten behind and cross over at least an inch and a half. It should not be left off as soon as the malady is cured, but be continued till the warm weather, and then cut away by a little strip at a time, so as to accustom the child by degrees to do without it. Infants who wear flannel next the skin should have many changes of it, and great care should be taken to wash it well, or it will grow hard and lose much of its warmth.

In case of a hard cough, equal parts of syrup of squills and mucilage of gum arabic may be mixed together, and given in the quantity of a tea-spoonful three or four times a-day; and if this should make the child vomit, it will do no harm: indeed, if the cough be accompanied with a wheezing sound, and there is the appearance of much *mucus* in the chest, the properest remedies are those which produce vomiting. When this is required, half a grain (or more as may be found necessary) of ipecacuanha powder may be given in a tea-spoonful of simple syrup, or of sugar and warm water, just before the child sucks, and repeated according to the effect it produces. This quantity is for a child of five or six weeks old; to one of as many months a whole grain may be given at first, and increased if that quantity should not answer the purpose, which however it generally does, if the medicine be good, and the child put to the breast immediately after taking it. It is of much importance that the feet of an infant who has a cough be kept warm, and therefore great care must be taken to have them constantly covered.

In giving any medicine to a very young child, attention should be paid to let it swallow very slowly, for fear of exciting a cough; and when there is any powder to be taken, the person who gives it should stir the liquid with a finger the whole time the infant is swallowing, that the powder may go down by degrees, and not remain in the bottom of the spoon to stick in its throat at the last. After the child has vomited sufficiently to relieve the difficulty of breathing, and the other symptoms of the chest being affected, a little syrup of white poppies may be given at night in the same manner as directed in treating of the red gum.

This method of cure will generally remove or much diminish an infant's cold in a few days, but if it does not, I know of nothing else which should be done without medical advice; and would recommend consulting a physician immediately, lest bleeding or blistering might be necessary or the apparent cold be only the symptom of some other malady. I shall return to the subject of colds when I come to treat of the diseases of children of more advanced age.

If for any reason it should be necessary to feed a new-born babe, great care must be taken that the food be not too hot. Wooden boats or ivory spoons are to be preferred to silver, because they do not retain so much heat, and have not such sharp edges; in every thing that is to be done for children by servants, the causes of offence should be removed as far as possible; and though a tender mother or experienced nurse might be so careful in the manner of using the boat or spoon as to render the materials they are composed of a matter of indifference, it is by no means the same with regard to all persons employed about infants. Any thing a little too hot, or any sharp edge touching too roughly the mouth of a very young child, may occasion sores which sometimes become very troublesome and continue a long time. If such a malady should appear, the best remedy is borax finely powdered, and mixed with the best honey that can be got, in the quantity of one tea-spoonful of the former to about three of the latter: a very little of this gently applied with the finger to the spot which is sore, four or five times a-day, will generally effect a cure very soon, when the complaint proceeds from such causes as those above mentioned. If, after a few days' trial, this remedy is found of no use, it will be right to consult a physician without delay, lest the malady should be of some other nature and require different treatment.

There is a disease called *the thrush*, (*aphtha*,) which in its mild state appears very like the above-mentioned accidental indisposition, but is usually accompanied with some derangement of stomach or bowels. It begins with small white blisters on the tongue and inside of the mouth; and if attended to immediately, is sometimes very easy to cure; but if neglected, may soon extend the whole length of the stomach and bowels, and become a very dangerous disease. While the blisters are white, and the child has no fever, nothing more will be necessary than to apply frequently the borax and honey as before directed. Should there appear any uneasiness in the throat, or in breathing, a little ipecacuanha may be given to procure slight vomiting; and in case of sour-smelling stools, or too many of them, a sufficient quantity of rhubarb and magnesia* to purge gently; for this is a malady in which none but very mild remedies should be given, except by the order of a physician who has examined the particular circumstances of the case. Should the treatment here directed produce no good effect, and the spots change their colour, it would be proper to apply for medical advice, as this is a disease which may very soon end fatally; and should it be an epidemic malady, (as it often is,) the professional man will be best able to determine what remedies are most likely to prove beneficial in that particular season.

The best way to guard against this disease, is to take care that the child does not get milk heated by too full living, over exercise, &c. As soon as it is perceived, the mother or nurse should drink plentifully of rice water, or other diluting liquors, and all her food should be of a more cooling nature than before, at the same time that she should not make too great a change in her diet. If the child has a hired nurse, the state of her health and quality of her milk should be particularly examined, lest there be something in it unsuitable to the constitution of the infant. It is, however, to be observed, that the mild sort of thrush is not unfrequently produced by teething, and when a child's mouth, in sucking, feels very hot to the breast, it

* The quantities of medicines, proportioned to different ages, will be found in the Appendix.

would always be right to look whether there are any blisters in it. Nothing is better to prevent this kind of thrush than washing the mouths of infants with cold water, several times a-day, in the manner already advised.

CHAPTER IX.

CONVULSIONS—THEIR VARIOUS CAUSES, AND THE MANNER OF TREATING THEM.

More children are destroyed during the first two months by *convulsions* than by any other malady. They are produced, at all ages, by a variety of causes, but the younger the infant, the more slight may be the occasion of the disease, and the more difficult to discover. When caused by any organic defect, they generally end fatally in a short time, which may be considered as a fortunate circumstance; for any mal-conformation sufficient to produce such effects, must ever prevent the well-being in mind or body of the individual so born. But many accidental causes occasion convulsions, which are easily cured by proper treatment.

It is sometimes difficult to discover the immediate cause of a fit of convulsions in a very young infant; but as the remedies in the first instance are the same, let the malady proceed from what it may, this is not a matter of very great importance. The first remedy to be tried, in all attacks of convulsions, is the tepid bath, in which the whole body of the child should be immersed up to the neck: but if a sufficient quantity of water for this purpose cannot be immediately procured, and there is at hand as much only as will serve to bathe the feet and legs, it is better to make use of that without delay; as warm water applied to the extremities will sometimes answer the purpose of checking the convulsive movements.

As soon as the fit of convulsions is over, means must be used to prevent a return, and for this purpose it is necessary to examine as far as possible into the cause which may have excited them. This will frequently be found in some derangement of the stomach or bowels, for which a purgative medicine is the best remedy. Should the child be naturally of a costive habit, it will be better to begin by giving a clyster with oil, honey, or brown sugar; and care must be taken to keep the bowels sufficiently free afterwards by some mild purgative medicine. For this the syrup of endive, directed in the Appendix, will be found well adapted, as well as in most cases when it is necessary to purge young children.

When there is reason to suppose that convulsions have been occasioned by indigestion, acidities, bile, &c., the purgative medicine should be given immediately, without waiting to administer a clyster, as the danger of the malady returning can be prevented only by carrying out of the stomach, as quickly as possible, the acrimonious and offensive substances which may have produced it. When the child has been sufficiently purged, and the stomach and bowels appear to be thoroughly cleansed, a tea-spoonful of syrup of white poppies may be given with good effect. It is to be observed, however, that this medicine does not agree equally well with all stomachs, and will sometimes make infants vomit. When this is found to be the case, it will be better to give two or three drops of Hoffmann's anodyne liquor in a spoonful of fennel water instead of it.

If a child be much troubled with wind, as usually happens after a complaint in the bowels, and especially when convulsions have been suspected to have arisen from that cause, a few drops of tincture of rhubarb, in a spoonful of mint or fennel water, may be given once a-day till the complaint be removed. Rhubarb, in all shapes, is by far the best medicine which can be given to young children; and by increasing or diminishing the quantity, and varying the mode of preparation, it can be made purgative or tonic. The only objection to it is the very disagreeable taste, and there are ways of disguising this which should never be neglected; for the less uneasiness of body and mind to which we subject children the better.

But with respect to convulsions, the causes above mentioned, though the most frequent in the first two months, yet are by no means all which are to be dreaded. Infants have been seen to recover immediately from violent convulsions on being undressed, when it has been discovered that pins have run into some part of their delicate bodies, or some articles of their clothing been too tight. But if the advice given in this work be attended to, it will be impossible for these causes to exist.

Another very probable cause of convulsions is the red gum, or any other eruption, being driven from the surface of the skin by the effects of cold; but the greatest care should be taken to avoid this cause: should it occur, the warm bath is the proper remedy, and two or three drops of spirits of hartshorn may be given in a little warm water and sugar.

I shall return to this subject again in another part of this work.

Though worms have been met with in children under two months old, yet it has been so rarely that I do not think it comes within the scope of my plan to consider this as one of their diseases; and any circumstance so extraordinary should certainly be a reason for consulting a physician immediately.

Infants under two months old, though not free from the danger of epidemic and contagious diseases, yet are less liable to them than those more advanced, and therefore I do not consider this as the proper place to treat of such maladies, but shall proceed to mention an important subject which belongs to this part of my work *.

* To many persons it may appear, that in saying so much about the cure of diseases, the author transgresses the bounds she had prescribed to herself; but on examination it will be found that this is not the case. She would always recommend those whose circumstances enable them to procure the assistance of a *really skilful* physician, to profit by his experience even in trifling maladies; but as this book is designed for mothers in every rank of society, many of whom live at a distance from medical aid, and others only on extraordinary occasions can afford the expense attendant on having *good* advice, it is but just to point out to such persons the means of curing slight indispositions, and of retarding (perhaps removing) danger in severe maladies; to mark the period when the aid of a physician must, if possible, be obtained, and to prevent the incalculable evils which continually occur in consequence of following the advice of ignorant pretenders.

CHAPTER X.

BRINGING UP CHILDREN WITHOUT HUMAN MILK.

When a mother cannot suckle, and no proper nurse is to be found, a healthy child may be safely brought up without the breast: and if great attention be paid to the mode of feeding, may become as strong as if it had been nourished with its natural food.

Those who have the means of providing an ass, would do well to give the child three or four meals in the day of the milk of that animal; this should be drawn from the udder at the moment it is wanted, and given of the natural heat, which, if the weather be very cold, may be retained by putting the vessel into which it has been milked, in a basin of warm water. The froth should be taken off the milk before it is given to the child, but it should not be let to stand, as even a quarter of an hour's contact with the air might produce a considerable alteration in the quality of the milk. Very thin barley, rice, or grit gruel, or panada made of good white bread and pure water, should form the intermediate meals, and be varied according to circumstances. In some cases, a little weak chicken-broth may also be given once a-day, especially if there be much acidity in the stomach. For those who cannot be provided with asses' milk, that of a cow, with two third parts of warm water, and as much white sugar as will give it the sweetness of human milk, may be substituted; this should be given twice a-day at least, fresh from the cow, and if it be not very rich, need not have quite so much as two thirds water.

One thing to be particularly observed in bringing up children in this manner is, that it is always better in the beginning to give rather too poor than too rich diet; if the food be not sufficiently nourishing, the infant will shew a craving desire for more in quantity, and the necessary alterations may be made accordingly; but if the food should happen to be too rich, it may produce indigestion, which is particularly dangerous for children who are not brought up exactly according to the dictates of Nature.

It should be remembered, that every thing given to a new-born infant ought to be made as sweet as its natural food, and of the same warmth.

It is very advantageous that children who are brought up by hand should suck their food, and for this purpose the simplest (and therefore best) contrivance is a bit of sponge or cotton put into the neck of a phial bottle, with a sufficient part left out of it to bear proportion to the nipple of a woman's breast; over this should be tied a piece of soft leather, full of small holes, and this should be again fastened round the rim of the bottle. One great advantage of a glass vessel is, that the quantity taken by the child, at each meal, can be accurately measured, and the food can be seen, so that the child may not continue to suck when there is no more. Besides, there is nothing so easily kept clean, or in which the want of cleanliness is so soon discovered; and indeed a young child should always be fed from something either open or transparent, as great care should be taken to prevent it from swallowing too fast. The sponge should be taken out of the bottle and washed well every time the child has sucked, as also the leather covering; and if cotton be used, it should be changed every time: what remains of the food should be immediately thrown away, and the bottle carefully washed. There have been many contrivances for making children suck artificially, but I know of none more safe and convenient than the simple method here advised. Vessels not made of transparent substances are liable to conceal dirt, and if they have long spouts, can hardly fail of being less clean than they ought to be. A glass vessel, in the form of a small Indian rubber bottle, with a little rim round the top, is certainly the best thing from which to make an infant suck its food.

The evacuations of a child who is brought up by hand should be particularly observed, and alterations made in its food according to their appearances. In general infants require little medicine, but their nourishment may be rendered medicinal in various ways. If a child who has not the breast be costive, grit gruel may be found preferable to barley or rice, and *brown* sugar may be used to sweeten its food instead of *white:* should this not answer the purpose, a little good honey may be substituted for sugar, which will often be found to succeed. Honey should not however be used too frequently, as it is likely to cause an acid in the stomach. Broth made of very young veal, with a little salt in it, will, in some cases, remove costiveness; and for children who are constitutionally subject to acidities, may be preferable to any thing else. At all events, it may be given for a change, when food of this sort is often necessary.

A child brought up by hand, not being in its natural state, may possibly have more occasion for medicine than one fed from a woman's breast: when the bowels therefore cannot be kept in a proper state by varying the food, a little syrup of roses or of rhubarb, or a small quantity of magnesia, must be given now and then, but only when absolutely necessary.

Children who have not the breast, are apt to have much less evacuation from the bladder than those who are suckled; and this is a thing which should be particularly guarded against, as it may be the means of augmenting a predisposition to gravelly complaints, if any such should exist, as it frequently does in young infants. For this reason, great care should be taken that the food of children brought up by hand be sufficiently liquid, and if the urine should seem to be in too small a quantity, the fennel-water (so often recommended before) may be frequently given. It is not likely that a child fed in the manner I have directed, will have too small a secretion of urine, care must therefore be taken to distinguish between that and the spasmodic retention before mentioned, for which the warm bath is a necessary remedy.

In many cases, it would be right to give a child brought up by hand, a spoonful of the *gravy* of roasted meat every day; not the *gravy* that is on the dish, but that which runs out of meat (sufficiently roasted) when it is cut, and every appearance of fat should be taken off, by laying bits of clean white paper on the top, until no speck of grease remains. When a child does not appear to thrive, when there is much acid in the stomach, or when there may be any suspicion of a scrofulous taint in the blood, this is an excellent remedy, if it be found to agree with the infant's stomach.

When a child brought up by hand is subject to a looseness, the food should be composed chiefly of good white bread (or biscuit) made into panada, with either water or milk, and sweetened with very white sugar; or rice gruel with a little cinnamon; or chicken-broth with a bit of mace boiled in it; and for drink, toast and water with lemon peel: grits and barley are better avoided. If the looseness be sufficient to be considered as a disease, the child must then be treated as directed for diarrhœa; but what I allude to here is that state of bowels which may be occasioned by the food not being exactly suitable to the stomach of the infant.

Another thing of great importance and seldom regarded, is to give the child food, during the first two months, as often as it ought to suck if it were brought up naturally; and when the food is as light and thin as it should be, the child will require to have it as often. The custom being generally to give thick victuals to infants brought up by hand, they do not require to be fed so frequently; but this is a bad practice, and until the child be three or four months old, the nearer the food approaches to the liquid state of human milk the better.

When the child is subject to an habitual looseness, or does not appear to be sufficiently nourished by its food, there are many things which may be tried, such as salop, sago, arrow-root, &c.; but all these should be made very thin, and given in small quantities at a time. For a healthy child, who thrives well, they are unnecessary. One thing, however, is to be observed here, that though chronic diseases do not appear at this early age, yet, when there is any suspicion of scrofula in the blood, it would be right to feed the child with nourishment of a more tonic nature than is generally necessary; and therefore some portion of animal food might be given from the first; beginning with weak broth, and making it stronger according as the stomach of the child appears able to bear it. Bread is, also, in this case to be preferred to unfermented grain, and with milk and broth, should constitute the chief part of the nourishment of those children in whose families any thing of scrofula has been observed. This malady will be treated of in its proper place; and it is earnestly recommended to mothers, to pay particular attention to what is said on that subject, as perhaps it is the only disease which may be safely and successfully combated from the first moment of a child's existence. When it is possible to procure a good nurse for an infant of this constitution, it is far preferable to bringing up by hand; and a robust woman who has been accustomed to live rather full, would be the best to entrust it to, if her milk on trial should be found to agree. However, when the mother of the child has good health, and her blood is free from suspicion of that particular malady, she would, undoubtedly, be the best nurse it could have; and besides her milk, the child might be accustomed to a spoonful of gravy or good broth every day, the quantity of which might be increased by degrees.

CHAPTER XI.

HINTS RESPECTING HIRED NURSES.

As bringing up by hand is not suitable to every constitution, there are cases in which a mother, unable to nurse her child, may be obliged to give it to be suckled by a stranger; and it is scarcely necessary to say, that the greatest caution should be employed in the selection of a proper person for that office. All books which profess to treat of the management of children, contain ample instructions on the manner of choosing a nurse, and full descriptions of the various physical and moral qualities required: from my own experience I can add nothing to what has been said, repeatedly, on this subject, and must only refer to those who have been accustomed to examine and to recommend such persons.

No hired nurse should ever be allowed to have any medicinal substance at her command, nor any servant appointed to attend upon her: the former to guard against a direct injury to the child's health, by the incautious administration of drugs; and the latter to prevent an indirect one, by giving habits of indolence to a person whose milk will be rendered more wholesome by the exercise of making her bed, sweeping her room, &c. It is by no means necessary that a woman who suckles (especially during the first months, when infants pass so many hours in sleep) should be perfectly idle, as nurses in great families are usually permitted to be: and, in fact, the lazy, gossiping habits which such persons generally acquire, are extremely disadvantageous to them, both in a physical and moral point of view.

It is an unfortunate thing to have a necessity for hired nurses, and a difficult matter to treat them properly; but when they fulfil their engagements, and act with fidelity and obedience towards those who have been obliged to confide in them, their good conduct should be acknowledged and recompensed with more generosity than is usual. Nurses are often spoiled by absurd indulgence during the time of suckling, and thrown off with neglect when it is over: and I have, sometimes, suspected a degree of concealed jealousy to be the true motive of this unjust treatment.

Amongst the many disadvantages attendant on the employment of hired nurses, is the great desire they generally have of making the children they suckle excessively fat; for which purpose they not only urge them to take as much milk as they can possibly swallow, but also frequently resort to means still more hurtful, such as giving them malt liquor, and other things capable of bloating them into a prodigious size. These over-fed children are subject to frequent indigestions, and often have their unnatural abundance of flesh carried off, all at once, by some severe bowel complaint, which is ascribed to teething, and, therefore, does not affect the credit of the nurse, who boasts "What a fine child she had reared until the sickness of his teeth had pulled him down so much:" at the same time that it is extremely probable, the child might not have had any such malady, if it had been naturally and moderately fed. In all epidemic and contagious diseases, these *crammed* children are in the greatest danger; and there is nothing which a mother, who is under the necessity of having her child suckled by a hireling, should more carefully prevent than the overloading its stomach with milk or any other sort of food; a circumstance of much greater importance than others to which more attention is usually paid.

I have often been induced to suspect that many of the maladies of children, during the time of teething, proceed from being suckled by women who drink too much of strong liquors; and in more than one instance I have been convinced of the justice of this opinion. Those mothers, therefore, who have the misfortune to be obliged to employ hired nurses, should pay the greatest attention to this subject;

and not let any pretence of weakness or fatigue persuade them to allow any spirituous or large quantities of malt liquors or wine, to be taken by the nurse. If a nurse be disturbed in the night, and feel herself tired in consequence next day, it is much better to get some other person to attend on the child for two or three hours, and suffer her to repose during that time, than to permit her to drink more wine or strong beer than usual, by way of acquiring strength. Sleep is always likely to increase the quantity and improve the quality of the milk, but strong liquors can only injure both.

I must not omit to mention, that it is very difficult to have children weaned gradually who have hired nurses; partly, because it is almost impossible to prevail on them to suckle at regular times, and partly, on account of the prejudices and superstitions common to that class from which the mother's substitute is usually selected. Children, therefore, who are not suckled by their mothers, are more exposed to that artificial malady attendant on weaning in the manner generally practised, and more likely to want the assistance of medicine at that time.

PART THE SECOND.

MANAGEMENT OF CHILDREN FROM TWO MONTHS TO TWO YEARS OLD.

CHAPTER I.

MANNER OF MAKING CHILDREN HARDY.—CLOTHING.—SHOES.—EXERCISE.

When a child is born strong enough to arrive at the age of two months, uninjured by any of those complaints which have been already mentioned, it may be considered to have escaped a considerable part of the dangers which surround a human being on first entering the world. If the season be mild and the child healthy, it should be accustomed by degrees to stay longer in the open air and to have more exercise; and should it not begin to cut teeth until the usual time, it will have three or four months to thrive and grow robust before any natural cause of indisposition is likely to occur. This space should be occupied in fortifying the constitution, and for that purpose, the utmost attention should be paid to the child's clothing, sleep, amusement, *and comfort in every respect.*

The only true way of making children hardy (and this may be begun very early) is by letting them be a great deal in the open air, covering them sufficiently when it is cold, to enable them to enjoy it: but they should never be kept out longer than appears to give them pleasure; for it is impossible that either the air or exercise can be of service to an infant who is shivering, shrinking, and looking blue, in the arms of its attendant; and this, unfortunately, often happens to those whose parents are not sufficiently aware of the necessity of warm clothing, and who are not very particular respecting the persons to whom they entrust their children. The servant who carries the child stops to gossip with some acquaintance in the cold; perhaps exactly where there is a current of wind, and the poor babe (if no worse consequence result) at least suffers during that time all the painful sensations which cold occasions to a delicate frame, and which are so likely to augment its weakness.

It is a very mistaken opinion, which many persons entertain, that cold air and cold water must always be strengthening, as they frequently produce exactly the contrary effect. I have long been convinced by observation and experience, that children who are brought up according to the usual method intended to make them hardy, are by no means likely to be the most robust; and that many a child has been weakened by the cold water and the cold air intended to make it strong. The instances given to evince the good effect of these excesses, are no proofs of their advantages, but only show that a child, naturally strong enough to resist that sort of treatment, is born with a very excellent constitution; for otherwise it would, probably, have fallen a sacrifice (like so many others) before the shrine of prejudice. Mediocrity appears to be the happiest lot of man, and whenever, either physically or morally, there is any attempt to pass that boundary, the balance is lost and evil exerts its influence.

I have already said all that is necessary respecting the first clothing of infants; and though their habiliments must be altered as they grow older, yet one general rule should predominate from first to last; they should always be light and loose, but warm or cool according to the season, and particular feelings and constitution of the child. At five or six months old, the clothes should be shortened, and shoes put on. The first shoes ought to be made of soft woollen cloth, with a thin leather sole, to accustom the child to the imprisonment of its feet with as little pain as possible. These, after a few weeks, may be exchanged for light leather; and thus, by degrees, the tender feet may be accustomed to thicker and harder covering, by the time the child begins to have occasion for a stronger protection to them. It is by no means a matter of indifference how the shoes of very young children are made: if too tight, they occasion corns, which I have seen in more than one instance on feet under a year old; if too loose, they impede the progress of the wearers when they begin to walk, and render them liable to fall; but the first shoes should rather be too large than too small.

When it can be contrived to shorten the clothes in summer, it will certainly be the best time; but as this is not always convenient, if necessary to make the change in cold weather, it would be better to put on half-boots instead of shoes, that the ankles may not suffer from cold. These are more suitable than stockings; which, for many reasons, would be rather an incumbrance at that early age.

Among the many requisites to be sought after in the persons to whom young children are entrusted, one, which though apparently trifling should not be forgotten, is the power of holding them equally on the right and on the left arm. It is necessary that the child's position should be changed when it is carried out, both for its present comfort and to prevent any danger of its growing crooked; and it is also necessary that the servant who carries a heavy child, should be able to make use of either arm for this purpose, that she may avoid the fatigue which might tempt her to sit down with it in cold weather, or give it to a stranger to hold.

Some physicians, to ensure a great deal of air and exercise for children, have recommended the use of little carriages; and when these are made with very good springs and a soft cushion to sit on, and drawn about on gravel walks or smooth roads, there is no objection to them; especially when a child is eight or nine months old. But if made without springs, and used on a rough road, the dangerous consequences may be much greater than at first appear. A sudden jolt may occasion a trifling hurt in one of the hips or adjacent parts, of which no one is aware at first, as the infant's crying is ascribed to some other of the many causes liable to produce that effect; and when at length the child begins to walk, is first discovered an incurable lameness or daily increasing deformity, for which no one can account, and for which there is no remedy. There is no place where one meets with more deformed people than in Dresden: and as the air of that country is wholesome, and the Saxons a strong, healthy race, I have felt inclined to ascribe this to the common custom of putting very young infants into little carriages without springs, in which they are dragged over excessively rough pavement. This mode of exercise, being extremely accordant with the laziness of servants, should be especially attended to, and not permitted but in certain cases, and with the necessary modifications. I am the more particular in mentioning this subject, as I have seen these little carriages strongly recommended (without any precautions) by some of the best medical writers, who probably had not been led, by any circumstance, to consider the inconveniences and dangers attendant on the indiscriminate use of them. Until a child is six or seven months old, the safest mode of giving it exercise is to have it carried in the arms; or, if in a carriage, on the lap of some person who will be careful to protect it from violent jolts. We should guard against all the possible injuries, from unknown or uncertain causes, through which children may be destroyed by acute disease, or rendered miserable by chronic maladies or deformities.

CHAPTER II.

LEARNING TO WALK.—BATHING.

In regard to walking, an accomplishment which nurses pique themselves on teaching at a very early age, it would be far better to prohibit all premature instructions, and prevent as much as possible all the usual aids. If a healthy child of five or six months old, is laid down with its face towards the ground * for a few minutes, three or four times every day, it will soon learn to rise up on its hands and feet, and move a few steps backwards and forwards; after a short time, it learns to go on all-fours; (which heavy children will sometimes continue for several months;) then rises on two legs, by the help of chairs, or any other support convenient to it, and so walks about for some time longer; then tries to stand quite alone; and at length discovers its power of moving in this manner, from one place to another, without assistance. Children who learn to walk in this way, are firmer on their limbs, less liable to crooked legs, and far more secure from falling, than those who have been handed about by their attendants: however, I must confess, that they do not in gene-

* A smooth dry meadow would probably be the best place.

ral walk so soon: for a child permitted to learn to walk of itself will scarcely go alone before twelve or thirteen months old. I do not consider this as a matter of serious importance, though I approve of the practice, and should recommend it to those who can make it convenient: when, however, the other method is adopted, I cannot help urging the expediency of banishing from nurseries (except on very extraordinary occasions) those common aids to the laziness of servants, leading-strings and go-carts; things quite unnecessary for strong, and often injurious to weak children.

Many people think it right to put children into the cold bath as early as at two or three months old, and are in such a violent hurry to make them strong, that they run the risk of putting an end to them entirely. Until children have all their teeth, (which is seldom before the end of two years,) I am convinced that it would be better to defer this practice, unless particular circumstances should occasion it to be ordered by a physician. In regard to merely washing the skin, a healthy child will not want to have the water warmed in summer; at the same time, it is better not to search for the very coldest that can be found for this purpose; and in winter it may be as well always to have it a little warmed. The slightest appearance of indisposition should indicate the use of tepid water; and on many occasions, (as has been already shown, and will be still further hereafter,) an entire bath of tepid water is not only the simplest, but the best remedy that can be used. Sometimes a bath of much warmer temperature may be required; but in such cases, it will be ordered by a professional man. As a medicine, cold bathing, especially in the sea, is frequently necessary; and to healthy children, (after the time of dentition is over,) it is a matter of indifference, and if agreeable to them, is as good a way of washing the skin as any other: but as a constant habit, I should think it better to be avoided. Why add to the necessities of persons in health? I shall say no more on this subject here, as there will be occasion to return to it again.

As soon as children begin to go into the open air and to meet strangers, they become more liable to epidemic and contagious diseases, as well as to those maladies from which extreme attention may in a great measure preserve them; but there is a subject which belongs peculiarly to the period of existence which this part of my work is confined to, and which, as it occasions more or less inconvenience and indisposition to every child, requires to be treated at full length. The reader will easily guess the subject I allude to is *teething*.

CHAPTER III.

TEETHING.—OFTEN IRREGULAR IN TIME AND ORDER.—DIARRHŒA.—DYSENTERY.

THE time of *teething* is so very irregular, that some children begin to show symptoms of its approach so early as the age of two months*. The surest mark of teething, at that age, is the great quantity of clear water which runs from the mouth; heat of the mouth, restlessness, looseness, &c., &c., may proceed from other causes; but this particular symptom always gives reason to expect an early dentition.

The time of teething is, to many children, a season of imminent danger, in which great care and some skill might save the lives of many who fall victims to the various diseases attendant on it. Every slight indisposition during the whole time of dentition, should be watched with particular attention: it should be observed, whether the maladies which appear are to be ascribed to that or to some other cause; and complaints should not be disregarded, because they are supposed to be the inevitable consequences of teething. Coughs, which

---

* Those who have teeth before that age, as well as those born with them, are extraordinary instances; and what are treated of here are only common facts.

are the effect of having caught cold, are often supposed to be occasioned by the teeth, and the proper remedies for a cold neglected, until the cough becomes so bad as to occasion inflammation of the lungs, which, joined with the irritation and fever produced by teething, attains such violence as to end fatally. A child's cough should never be neglected, but especially during the time of dentition; and whether it proceeds from a cold or any other cause, some remedy should be sought.

It is a general opinion, that when the teeth are cut late, there is more danger than when they begin to appear at the usual time, which is about the age of seven months. When the cause of this delay is either disease or debility, it is natural to suppose that teething will be difficult; but when the late appearance of the teeth is not attended with any morbid symptom, that circumstance alone should occasion no alarm. The same opinion attaches to any uncommon appearance in the order of cutting the teeth; but a mother need not be frightened, though she may perceive irregularities, both in the time and the manner of teething. I have seen children cut their first teeth at various times, between four and twelve months old, with perfect safety; and others in great danger, who had but just reached the usual period. I have also, several times, seen the teeth come out in the most irregular manner, (such as one tooth in the under jaw, and then two or three in the upper, or an upper tooth come out first, and then the two under, &c.,) without any great difficulty: but it must be confessed, that in general, this sort of irregularity is attended with more indisposition, than when, at the natural time of seven or eight months, the two under front teeth appear first, then the two upper, and so on, in the order which every woman who has had children under her care knows.

The *diarrhœa*, so common during the time of teething, when it is neither too violent nor of too long duration, is not a bad symptom, and often prevents fever and convulsions. While it is a *mere looseness*, unattended by pain, fever, or loss of appetite, it is rather salutary than otherwise, and requires no medicine. A little chicken broth, with a bit of mace or nutmeg boiled in it, may be given once or twice a-day, according to the age or circumstances of the child; and should it be already weaned, rice-water, sweetened with fine loaf-sugar, is the best thing it can drink. Should there be the least appearance of fever with the lax, it will be better to omit the broth, and give rice-gruel or panada instead of it. No astringent medicine should be administered without the orders of a physician, as the worst consequences may result from injudiciously checking a discharge from the bowels. Should the diarrhœa be attended with fever, a slight emetic of three or four grains of ipecacuanha may be given, and afterwards a grain of rhubarb every day for a week or a fortnight; to which, in case of the evacuations having a sour smell, a few grains of magnesia may be joined, until it be removed.

Should there appear symptoms of *dysentery*, or blood and mucus in the stools of children, as sometimes happens during teething, it would be expedient to give a tea-spoonful or two of oil of sweet almonds, and a clyster* of rice-water, with a little gum arabic dissolved in it. Gum arabic may, also, be dissolved in the child's drink, which should be barley or rice-water, sweetened with fine white sugar. After the child has been sufficiently purged, syrup of poppies may be given in the manner directed for other complaints; and also a small clyster, composed of about half an ounce of tepid water,

---

* In regard to clysters, several things are to be observed. One is the mode of administering them, in which great care should be taken not to hurt the child; and for this reason the bag and pipe may perhaps be the safest instrument to employ for infants; but with either that or the syringe, the pipe should be directed parallel to the back-bone, and the liquor injected very slowly. Another thing to be observed is, that some children have an extreme aversion to this remedy; and it is very difficult to administer it with any good effect when they scream and cry. They may be held so as to prevent hurting the bowels, but they cannot be prevented from shrieking; so that, unless positively ordered by a judicious physician, a clyster should never be given to a child by force, as there are but few cases in which this is absolutely necessary.

with six or seven drops of laudanum, which, if retained in the bowels, will not fail to check the irritation and forcing. If these remedies are not found sufficient to cure the malady, a physician should be consulted without delay, as this is sometimes a dangerous inflammatory disease, and great medical knowledge is requisite to treat it properly.

CHAPTER IV.

VOMITING.—PAIN BEFORE THE TEETH APPEAR.—
HARD SUBSTANCES UNSUITABLE TO THE GUMS.—
LANCING THE GUMS.—BLEEDING.—BLISTERING.

AMONGST the variety of complaints to which children are liable during the period of dentition, none is more difficult to cure than the *purging and vomiting* by which so many are carried off. The diarrhœa alone (however difficult it may sometimes be to treat) is of less consequence, as there is always aid to be expected from medicine, and also from food adapted to the circumstances of the case; but the vomiting (which is sometimes convulsive) often baffles all attempts to check it, as the remedies are immediately rejected by the stomach. The application of warm flannels to the stomach and bowels, and a warm bath (as before directed) for the feet, should first be tried; then an entire bath of tepid water, and afterwards volatile liniment* with laudanum, (in the proportion of a dram of the latter to half an ounce of the former,) may be

* See Appendix, spirit of hartshorn.

rubbed on the stomach. I have known the effervescent saline draught produce very good effects; and recollect particularly one case in which it succeeded after many other remedies, besides those just mentioned, had been tried in vain. The child was about fifteen months old, and had been two months weaned; the vomiting had been unceasing for two days, and was stopped at last by this medicine, prepared in the following manner:—a dram of carbonate of soda was dissolved in an ounce of water, to which was added rather more than half an ounce of syrup of white poppies: of this mixture, a very small tea-spoonful[*], with half a tea-spoonful of fresh lemon-juice, was given during the fermentation, which immediately checked the vomiting; and in a short time, the child was able to retain on its stomach a purgative medicine, which was thought necessary: the vomiting returned once or twice in the course of two or three days, and the saline draught continued to produce the same effect as at first.

In a cold climate, or a cold season, one of the first remedies to recur to in diarrhœa, dysentery, or vomiting, is warmer clothing, both for the feet and the body. A piece of flannel over the stomach

---

[*] Twice this quantity may be given to a child of three years old, and four times as much to one of seven, in case of severe vomiting.

and bowels, and worsted shoes, socks, or half-stockings, for a child who has never before worn any thing of that sort, may sometimes prove more efficacious in removing those maladies than any internal remedy; and the materials of this additional clothing may be thicker or thinner, according to the season of the year. One thing necessary to be observed in the use of flannel, is to have it perfectly dry; as it attracts the humidity of the atmosphere so much, that in situations where linen does not become damp, flannel does: indeed, when this last is employed for medical purposes, it should always be applied warm.

Slight inflammations of the eyes, during the time of teething, are very common, but of little importance. I have often observed a red spot on the white of the eye, at the side where the tooth was coming out, and at first supposed this was the effect of cold; but repeated observation convinced me that it was only an attendant on the pain and inflammation belonging to the tooth, and required no remedy. However, a little tepid milk and water, or rose-water, to bathe the eye, can do no harm.

The great pain of the teeth takes place twenty or thirty days before they cut through the gums, and all that can be done is to relieve the indispositions they occasion. The nurse of a child who shows symptoms of inflammation during the time of teething, should live on more cooling diet than before; should diminish her quantity of meat and wine or beer, and drink a good deal of diluting liquors; but one who suckles a child in whom symptoms of debility appear at that time, would perhaps have occasion for more tonic food, and to take bark or some such medicine; but this last is a case much less common than the other, and one in which the advice of a physician would be necessary.

Sometimes rubbing the gums of children gives them great relief; at other times they cannot bear to have them touched. The hard substances which are given them to put in their mouths do more harm than good: a bit of liquorice-stick or of dry iris-root, a small wax candle sewed up in linen and dipped in sugar or honey and water, are things far preferable to ivory or coral; but, perhaps, one of the best of all is a little cake made on purpose, of flour and sugar, with a sufficiency of egg to make it tough (not hard), and formed into a convenient shape for the child to put into its mouth; and in case of necessity, there are medicinal substances which can be conveyed by this means.

It has been recommended to lance the gums, as a mode of making the teeth come out more easily; but some good physicians have disapproved of the practice, and I have seen it tried more than once without any advantage. When half a tooth is out, and a sharp corner of it, still under the gum, irritates the child's nerves, (as is frequently the case,) lancing that part may be of great use: in other cases I should rather think it injurious, as I have seen troublesome ulcers ensue from the wound. However, as some persons of great eminence have approved of this remedy, no doubt there are circumstances in which it must be beneficial; and therefore, if ordered by a respectable physician, should be employed with confidence: but I would recommend that the operation be performed by a skilful practitioner.

Aphthæ in the mouth are not uncommon during the time of teething: but this is generally a slight malady; and a little honey of roses rubbed on the spots, two or three times a day, will usually be found a sufficient remedy: if, however, it does not answer the purpose, the complaint may be treated as has already been directed for the *thrush*.

Amongst many other spasmodic symptoms to which children are liable during the time of dentition, is a *retention of urine*, for which the warm bath is the proper remedy. If the bowels are confined, it would be right to give a clyster (a slight infusion of single camomile flowers would be suitable); and after that has produced the desired effect, a tea-spoonful of syrup of poppies on going to rest at night.

An extraordinary quantity of blood going to the head, which shows itself by excessive sleepiness, redness of the face, and heavy breathing, is one of the most dangerous complaints that a child can have. For this it would be necessary to bleed immediately; and a leech applied behind each ear might answer the purpose: but if it be possible to have the advice of a physician instantly, it would be better, as bleeding with the lancet might be necessary. No delay, however, should be made in seeking some remedy, as children have died during the time of teething with symptoms of apoplexy, which the timely application of leeches, and the employment of sinapized baths, or fomentations to the feet, might have prevented.

Sometimes blisters behind the ears are very beneficial. They serve to draw off the inflammation from the gums, and are also very useful for swellings of the glands under the jaws, which sometimes occur during the time of dentition; especially if a running behind the ears has been imprudently checked.

CHAPTER V.

ADVANTAGES OF AIR AND EXERCISE.—BOWELS TO BE KEPT OPEN.—HOW TO TREAT SPASMODIC SYMPTOMS.—ERUPTIONS.

When children have a great discharge of clear water from the mouth, they generally have less fever, and fewer dangerous symptoms in teething. Nothing promotes this discharge so much as air and exercise; and I have often seen children who, while shut up in a room, were uneasy and peevish, with the mouth hot and dry, on being carried into the open air in a fine day, begin to run at the mouth abundantly, and immediately grow lively and good-humoured.

Great attention should be paid to the state of the bowels during teething; and children whose constitution it is to have them confined, may possibly require some opening medicine from time to time. Rhubarb and magnesia, or any of the various preparations of rhubarb, are the safest to employ for this purpose; but when there is extraordinary difficulty in purging a child, (or any other uncommon symptom,) a physician should be consulted, who may direct what medicine, and what quantity of that medicine, should be administered. The bowels of children who are not of a particularly costive habit, may often be kept in a proper state without the assistance of medicine, by changes in their food. To such as are already weaned, stewed fruit, honey on bread, barley or grit gruel, with brown sugar, good mealy potatoes, and broths in which aperient vegetables have been boiled, will sometimes have a sufficient effect; but if medicine be required, very small quantities should be tried at first, for there is nothing more injurious than to purge children unnecessarily.

The *slight spasmodic symptoms* which usually attend teething, though of no great importance, should not be disregarded, as they are only a lesser degree of that irritation which sometimes produces the most violent convulsions. When children start out of their sleep with an appearance of terror, or in tears, grind their teeth, or breathe irregularly, the cause should be enquired into. If it proceeds from indigestion, or any thing wrong in the stomach or bowels, a slight purge will generally remove it; but if, after the first passages have been cleared, the same symptoms should continue, it is evident that they are occasioned by the teeth, or some unknown cause irritating the nerves. As a remedy for this, from three to six drops of spirit of hartshorn may be given in two or three spoonfuls of barley or rice water, and a tea-spoonful of syrup of white poppies, more or less full, according to the child's age.

Rashes and eruptions of various kinds are very common during the time of teething; but if not driven back by cold or the application of medicinal substances, are seldom of any great importance. Sometimes the fever throws out a rash which disappears in a few days without any bad effect, if it has not been checked prematurely by any imprudence, or accidental cause: in case, however, this should have occurred, the immediate use of the tepid bath is the best means of recalling it to the surface of the skin, and preventing all bad consequences.

Eruptions on the head occasioned by teething require only to be washed very clean, and well dried: sometimes a very slight purgative may be necessary for a child that is very fat and robust, but if these eruptions are removed by external remedies, children are liable to be carried off by convulsions or hydrocephalus; whereas, if let alone, they will go away as soon as the teething is over. A very common complaint is a moisture behind the ears, which is sometimes accompanied with much inflammation, and disfigures children greatly for a time. All outward applications should be avoided, except such as are necessary to keep the parts clean or relieve itching. Milk and water, rose-water, or a decoction of marshmallows, or elderflowers, may be used with safety; but nothing of an astringent nature should be employed. Sometimes children are affected with troublesome and disfiguring eruptions during the whole time of dentition; and when they are ascertained to proceed from this cause, it requires only a little patience to see them removed. It is sometimes very easy to drive them from the surface of the skin; but the injudicious cure of a cutaneous malady is very likely to end in convulsions, hydrocephalus, asthma, inflammation of the lungs, or acute fever; diseases rather more to be feared than any temporary ugliness. In a short time all the disfiguring complaints which occur in consequence of teething disappear; and no children grow up clearer or handsomer than those who have had eruptions while cutting their teeth.

A very slight eruption driven from the surface of the skin is capable of producing violent effects. I recollect an instance of a child who, after cutting his four front teeth without any symptom of indisposition, had a red spot (about the size of half a crown) come out on his forehead, which, for some time before the appearance of each of the next three or four teeth, became inflamed and covered with moisture. The child's beauty was much spoilt by this eruption; and the family physician being consulted, ordered an ointment which perfectly cured it in a few days: but the next teeth were preceded by violent convulsions, which returned from time to time during the whole period of dentition, frequently occasioning serious alarm to the medical attendants, and rendering the child (who had been a fine strong boy) weak and sickly for many years after. Another instance I saw of a child, who, a few weeks after a distinct but severe small-pox, was attacked by an eruption all over, of small suppurating pustules, accompanied with great uneasiness and itching, which soon dried off, and were succeeded by fresh ones. The person to whom the child's mother applied for medical advice, being of opinion that the eruption was only a temporary malady attendant on teething, as the child was otherwise in perfect health, prevailed on her to make use of no remedy either internal or external for a few days, intending to order the tepid bath if the complaint continued; but at the end of another week the eruption began to diminish, and in a few days cleared off perfectly, without any medicine. I mention this to show that these sort of eruptions do not require so much medicine as is generally supposed, but I by no means intend to advise that they should be neglected; on the contrary, it is always necessary to ascertain the nature of an eruption, particularly if it continue long, as there are various contagious maladies of this sort, which may be communicated to a child, especially by a hired nurse, and which should not be allowed to take their course without medical assistance. But these would require the advice of an experienced physician, both to distinguish and to cure.

In another part of this work I shall have occasion to return to the subject of eruptions: what I have said here is sufficient to put mothers on their guard respecting the treatment of those which are occasioned by dentition.

Convulsions I shall also treat of fully in another place; for though a convulsion be a common malady during the time of teething, I do not consider it so much a complaint belonging to that period, as an accidental disease, and frequently the consequence of mismanagement. A well-formed child, who has been taken proper care of from its birth, and had sufficient air and exercise, will not be liable to convulsions in consequence of dentition.

CHAPTER VI.

WEANING, HOW TO BE EFFECTED WITH EASE.—WHAT FOOD PROPER FOR CHILDREN.—NECESSARY CAUTIONS.

ONE more subject remains to be mentioned here, as peculiarly belonging to this age, viz. WEANING; a thing of the greatest importance, and by which children in general suffer a great deal of unnecessary illness.

The time of weaning is of little consequence, if the child be in good health; and in cases of indisposition, some require to be weaned sooner, some later. It has been recommended by physicians, that children suspected of a predisposition to rickets should not be allowed to suck long; but those who are free from any tendency to this malady, and suffer from feverish complaints or from coughs during the time of teething, should (if possible) have the breast a few months longer than would otherwise be requisite. In general, from nine months to about a year old, is the proper time for weaning: but, except in case of illness, there is no necessity for being extremely exact on this point. When, however, children suffer much in teething, great care should be paid to select an interval of health for the weaning, and their diet should be particularly watched until the dangers of dentition are quite over.

I have already mentioned how very advantageous it is to both mothers and children to effect the weaning gradually. Of all the children I have known to be weaned in this manner, I have never seen one affected by that indisposition, which I have so often heard talked of by old nurses, (and even read of in medical books,) under the name of the *weaning brash*.

When a child is weaned at five or six months old, the directions given for bringing up by hand * are the most applicable to the circumstances; but, if between the ages of nine and thirteen, the case is quite different. It is natural that children should then know how to eat, and therefore, it is no longer necessary for them to suck their food. The best thing to give them, (at any age,) in the commencement of weaning, is panada, made with good bread and good water, and white sugar enough to make it as sweet as the milk they have been used to; and if a child has been subject to wind, a little lemon peel, cinnamon, or ginger, may be infused in it: the panada should be very smooth, and given at

* See Part I. chap. 10.

first once, and then twice a day. As soon as the child is to have three meals of its new food, one should be of bread and weak broth; but the chief food of children, till quite weaned, should be bread and water.

When children have entirely left off sucking, cow's milk fresh from the udder (not skimmed milk) may be given to them, and their food may be varied with broth, rice, barley, grits, &c. Eggs are good nourishment for children: the *yolk* may be given as soon as they are weaned, and when the stomach is accustomed to more solid food, the *white*, which is harder to digest, may also be allowed. A child just weaned, should, for a week or two, be nourished chiefly with liquids. Barley or rice water, or milk and water, are the best things it can drink between meals, and at night; but the giving children drink at night would be better avoided entirely: if that is not possible, the habit must be broken off gradually and by slow degrees; as also that of drinking between meals, which all children require for some time after weaning.

When children are first weaned, they should be fed five or six times a-day; but when they begin to take solid food, this may be diminished to four, and perhaps at last to three hours; this, however, like all other secondary matters, requires no positive rule, and must depend on circumstances. Bread and milk for breakfast, made in the beginning of the consistence of thick cream, but mixed with a little hot water, is the best thing to give them for the first week: the bread should be grated fine, the hot water should be poured on it, and then the milk. When milk is given without water (which it may in a short time) it should be warmed, not boiled, and if it could be had hot from the cow it would be best. A child who is just weaned may have two meals of milk in the day, and one of bread and broth; the others may be of gruel, made of either rice, barley, or grits; or the yolk of an egg hot from the hen, either raw or very little boiled. After some time the bread and milk may be given without the bread being grated, the egg may be boiled in the common way, the rice, &c., may be given in substance, and many other things may be tried; such as good mealy potatoes, oatmeal porridge, stewed fruits, puddings, &c. The effect of every new kind of nourishment on the stomach and bowels should be carefully watched, and any thing that seems to occasion a looseness, or passes through undigested, should be prohibited for the present. Butter and fat should be positively prohibited during the first two years; and the less children ever eat of any greasy substance the better. However, as all children are fond of bread and butter, I do not suppose it can be injurious to them; but the butter should be good and fresh and given in moderation. Buttered toast (in the way it is usually made) should never be given to children, and indeed, till after two years old it would be better to keep butter from them altogether: after that time it may perhaps be beneficial, which *fat broths* and *cooked grease* never can be. *Good* buttermilk is an excellent drink for children; and so is what is called in Ireland *two-milk whey*, when it is well made.

A variation of diet should take place according to the state of a child's bowels, which are not always regular, even in perfect health. For example, if a child happens to be costive for a day or two, oatmeal or grit-gruel, with brown sugar, may be given for breakfast and supper, and mealy potatoes with broth at dinner; or a meal of stewed prunes, or bread and honey. On the contrary, if a child be inclined to a looseness, rice, with very fine sugar, boiled in milk, may be given; also the yolk of an egg boiled rather hard, bread toasted very brown, &c. I mention only a few of the substances which may be useful for these two different tendencies to indisposition; but there are many others which may be employed to vary a child's food. Sago, arrow root, salep, &c., may be given to delicate children; but for those who are strong and healthy they are unnecessary, and in truth good bread ought to form the chief part of the food of children under two years old. They should not, however, be allowed to have a piece continually in the hand; but should have it at regular times with their meals, while they eat four or five times a-day, and between breakfast and dinner, when that number is reduced to four or three.

It is a great error to give children large quantities of food by way of strengthening them; and still greater to let them drink wine and strong liquors, which should be reserved for medicinal purposes. I have never seen more evident marks of acquired debility than in children who were crammed with nourishing things, and drank wine or beer, several times in the day. Even the simplest and wholesomest food, when given in too great abundance, may become hurtful; as in the instance of a child of two years old, whom I remember to have seen suffering under a high fever, occasioned by an indigestion of very good bread. This child had lately recovered from a worm fever, and with her returning health had acquired that increase of appetite so frequent in such cases: her mother having observed this, was very careful to have her meals of a moderate quantity, but never thought of using any precautions respecting stale bread, of which the servant, who took care of the child, one day suffered her to eat so much, that it produced the effect above mentioned.

Nothing is better for children than cow's milk, when it agrees; but there are constitutions and circumstances to which it is unsuitable, and if persisted in, may become very injurious.

CHAPTER VII.

VARIETY OF PROPER FOOD FOR CHILDREN UNDER TWO YEARS OLD.—SUGAR.

Until a child has completed two years, it is better not to give it meat, unless there are substantial reasons for doing so. Bread, milk, broth, and eggs, should form the principal part of the nourishment of children, from the time of weaning till two years old. I know some people have a strong prejudice against eggs (about as well founded as that against sugar); and many will not permit their children to eat a new-laid egg boiled or poached, who will, nevertheless, feed them on puddings, in which eggs (often very stale ones) are boiled up with milk and bread, or flour, so as to render them far more difficult of digestion than in their simple state. It may be that there are stomachs with which eggs disagree, and for those it is probable that puddings are also unsuitable; but this is seldom the case amongst individuals in health: one of the true causes of objecting to give eggs to children, is a false notion, which many persons entertain, that this sort of food renders them liable to *break out*. I have seen a great number fed in the manner I recommend, not one of whom has been subject to eruptive complaints, which at least proves that eruptions are not the inevitable consequences of such diet.

I do not think children ought to be allowed raw fruit or watery vegetables, until they begin to eat meat; because these are things which they do not digest easily, and which, for that reason, are liable to occasion weakness of stomach, and produce worms and other maladies. Their food can, certainly, be sufficiently varied with bread, biscuits, potatoes, eggs, puddings, broth, milk, oatmeal and grits, rice, stewed and preserved fruit, and jellies of various sorts; to which, if necessary, may be added sago, salep, arrow-root, and tapioca.

Children who may be suspected of a predisposition to *diseases of debility**, should have animal food sooner than others. They ought to have broth at a very early age (three or four months old) and gravy before they are weaned: it should, also, be tried whether meat will agree with them at thirteen or fourteen months old; and if they are found to be capable of digesting it perfectly, (which may easily be discovered by examining their evacuations,) a very small quantity should be given, at first once a week, then twice a week, and so on by slow degrees, until they eat it every day. They

* Scrofula, rickets, &c.

may, also, have a little good wine, mixed with water, given in the same manner; but it must be particularly observed whether this sort of diet occasion fever, as in that case it would augment the debility it is designed to prevent. It has put me to pain when I have heard an old nurse lament over the pale face of a child during the time of dinner, but console herself with the reflection that " he would have a fine colour when he had drunk his wine." When wine produces this effect it can hardly be beneficial; and, indeed, unless ordered by a physician, it should never be given, without water, to young children.

The common food of the country they inhabit will generally agree with children in health; and those who live where it is customary to feed on potatoes and milk, oatmeal porridge, polenta, or other sorts of farinaceous substances, may safely eat of them in moderation; but I have no doubt that it is good to vary the food from time to time, always, however, watching the effect it produces, and having regard to the particular constitution of the individual.

Nothing is so positively wholesome as sugar; and there is no liquid which may be more safely allowed to children, when it is necessary that they should drink out of meal times, than sugar and water. If permitted to follow their natural propensities, they will frequently prefer it in illness to any other diluting liquor; and in this they should be indulged, as in many other instinctive propensities. Not only children, but adults, when their natural tastes are not corrupted by affectation or intemperance, are fond of sugar; and there have been of late years the most undeniable proofs of the salubrity of a substance, which is so often prohibited through caprice or mistaken care. There is nothing so useful in the weaning of children, as it induces them to support the change of diet with more patience, and also furnishes them with a substance which renders all the food it is mixed with more nourishing and strengthening to the stomach. As I shall have occasion to return to this subject in treating of worms, I shall say no more on it at present, except to recommend mothers to sweeten the food and drink of children who are just weaned, as much as they like.

There does not appear to be any other topic to treat of peculiarly connected with that part of a child's existence comprised between the ages of two months and two years, and I shall, therefore, here conclude the Second Part of this work.

PART THE THIRD.

TREATMENT OF CHILDREN AFTER TWO YEARS OLD.

CHAPTER I.

DIET.—REGULAR HOURS OF EATING.—FRUIT.—EVACUATIONS.—BED ROOMS.

The time of teething being over, there is no necessity for any further division in treating of the physical education of children, as there is no extraordinary change to mark. The second, or more properly speaking, *second part* of the *first* dentition, although it affects some delicate frames with symptoms of disease, yet, in general, makes so little impression on the health, that it cannot be distinguished as an important era in existence.

When the dangers and indispositions attendant on cutting the first set of teeth are past, there is no longer the same necessity for excessive strictness with regard to the diet of children in perfect health; though it should always be remembered, that errors in the quality, or excess in the quantity of their food, is likely to produce indigestion and fever; and these, if often repeated, may lead to that debility of stomach, which occasions worms and other chronic diseases. As they advance in years and strength, it is advantageous to leave them much at liberty on this subject: the difference between children of ten or eleven years old, who are allowed to eat of what they please, and those of the same age who are under a variety of restraints, is very remarkable; the former being usually moderate, and the latter almost always gluttons. It is good for children to be accustomed early to those things which they will be likely to partake of when they grow up, to prevent unwholesome excesses in after years: for this reason (and no other) they should be allowed a small portion of fermented liquor; but, in truth, the less the better, unless when it is ordered as a medicine.

Children, who are in such a state of health as to require a very strict diet, should not be present when other persons are eating, unless they are of an age and character to be convinced of the justice and expediency of the prohibitions imposed on them.

As soon as the maladies attendant on teething are over, those who have the care of a child should endeavour to discover if it has any peculiarities of constitution, whether any particular sort of food disagrees with its stomach, what is difficult of digestion to it, and what is absolutely indigestible. That which is digested with difficulty, or only in part, occasions uneasiness and more or less fever, which passes off in a few hours; that which is indigestible, besides these symptoms, produces an inclination to vomit, pains in the stomach and bowels, and frequently a diarrhœa, in which the undigested food passes off unaltered. One child may be able to digest a substance which would be difficult or impossible to another; and it is by no means the softest things which are always the easiest of digestion. Cheese and hard eggs are generally considered to be indigestible substances, and yet some children digest them as easily as bread; fish is very suitable to many stomachs, but difficult of digestion to a great number. Honey agrees perfectly with some children, whilst to others it is a cause of acidities and diarrhœa; many dislike it extremely, and neither that nor any other kind of food should be forced on a child against its will: a thing being called *wholesome* is no reason for obliging a child to swallow what is disagreeable. I lay a stress on this point, because I have seen children of four or five years old, suffer great disgust and vexation in being forced to eat spinage, turnips, barley, and other such articles of common food, without which they might very well have passed their whole lives, and which were probably unsuitable to their stomachs at that age.

It is scarcely necessary to say, that regular hours for food, exercise, and sleep, are of great importance to young and delicate children. The times of children's meals should be carefully attended to, and adapted to circumstances: some require to eat the moment they awake in the morning, whilst others find pleasure in taking exercise and air before breakfast; and the wishes of children on this subject should always be indulged. They should dine at two or three o'clock, and have a piece of bread between breakfast and dinner, if they be hungry; and to such as are ordered wine for a medicine there is no better time for giving it. It would be a great advantage, if the foreign custom of beginning dinner with some sort of broth or pottage*, could be introduced amongst children in the British Islands, as it would prevent them from overloading their stomachs with meat, and would be far preferable to the expedient employed for this purpose at some schools, of having a heavy pud-

---

* Barley, oatmeal, grits, or rice, boiled in broth, or mutton broth with turnips and bread in it, are those which most resemble the soups commonly used on the Continent. Broth with one-third milk, and the yolk of an egg in it, is very good for children, and a thing likely to please the generality of them.

ding served up first. Children should not be urged to drink during meals if they do not like it*; many healthy persons feel no inclination for liquids till they are satiated with solid food, and what appears to be a natural instinct should not be opposed. Sometimes children wish for drink immediately on sitting down to dinner, before they begin to eat; and though this is not good as a regular habit, yet they should be indulged in moderation; for it may be the consequence of having eaten without drinking some time before, or some other accidental circumstance may have occasioned thirst.

It is scarcely necessary to point out the great danger resulting from giving children unripe fruit. Ripe fruit in moderation will always be beneficial to children in health, and is of great use in many

---

* Nor should they be prevented from drinking at other times, if they shew a great desire for it; an accidental fit of thirst will be removed by a few glasses of water (the only thing which should be allowed); but when a child is habitually thirsty, there must be some cause for it, which should be inquired into and remedied, not by prohibiting liquids but by curing the indisposition which occasions the want of them. Some constitutions require more drink than others, and persons who insist on subjecting all to one rule, are liable to fall into pernicious errors. I have known a child of ten years old suffering under such a fever of thirst as to drink the water, with brimstone in it, which was left for a lap-dog, when all other liquids had been purposely removed out of her reach.

diseases. It is better that children should eat fruit with bread than by itself; for it has been frequently observed that apples and pears which have passed through a child undigested when eaten alone, have not done so when bread was eaten with them.

Sometimes children have a dislike to meat; and when that is the case, it is the last thing that should be forced upon them: indeed, it is not improbable that many children would be better nourished by eggs, milk, fruit, and farinaceous food, than by meat; but all this must depend on circumstances. Perhaps we should all be healthier and longer lived if we had never learnt to devour the flesh of animals; but it would be a hazardous thing to attempt to bring up the offspring of a creature become carnivorous by habit, without that sort of nourishment.

It is of great importance to pay attention to the evacuations from the bowels of children in health, that any diseased alteration may be immediately discovered; and it is also necessary to observe that they afford sufficient time to such matters. Strong children, when engaged in play (unless watched, and prevented from doing so) will often retain the contents of the bowels so long, that the inclination to discharge them passes by; and sometimes, an ephemeral fever is excited by the overloaded state of the intestines. Other inconveniences are also to be dreaded; and one of the greatest reasons for guarding against an accumulation of the excrements is, that sometimes the effort necessary to clear the bowels is so great that it may possibly occasion a rupture. Children should be taught to attempt an evacuation at a regular hour (after their first meal in the morning); and those who have the care of them should observe with what effect, that they may be reminded (if necessary) at some other time in the day, or at least not suffered to pass two days without a discharge from the bowels, as this may be remedied by some alteration in their diet. The quality of their evacuations should also be examined, and whatever sort of food is found to pass through undigested, should be prohibited for a time, until some change in the state of the stomach, or some augmentation of strength from the addition of years, may give them the power of digesting it. Any person accustomed to observe the evacuations of a child in health, will readily learn to perceive in them the appearance of maladies, of which many are to be ascertained by this means; such as worms, indigestion, dysentery, &c., &c. The examination of the urine is not so necessary in health; but in case of illness it is important, as there are many diseases of children in which the alteration, and especially the diminution, is a very decisive symptom.

The air that children breathe during the night is of the greatest importance; and for this reason, the rooms in which they sleep should be kept still more clean than those they inhabit by day: they should not be crowded with furniture, nor should any animals be allowed to inhabit them: dogs, cats, and birds should, therefore, be banished from that part of the house; and those who have no other place to keep them in, should not have such things at all.

It is good to accustom children to sleep either with or without a light, which can easily be contrived by leaving them in the dark for some hours after they go to bed: those who are used always to have a candle in the room, are liable to suffer very much when by accident the night-light happens to go out.

CHAPTER II.

PULSE.—FEVERISHNESS.—SLIGHT DIARRHŒA.—DOUBLE TEETH.—IRREGULAR GROWTH.

No very accurate information is to be obtained from the pulses of young children, even in acute diseases; and much more is to be learnt by the countenance and colour, the eyes, the tongue, the manner of breathing, and the smell of the breath. Any thing extraordinary in the aspect of a child demands immediate attention; and the habitual blackness under the eyes, to which so many are subject, should not be disregarded, as it is a symptom of that debility which occasions so many maladies.

In lively children, the presence of slight fever is often imperceptible while they are awake; but the quick, heavy breathing in sleep, is a sign of it; and when this is observed, the attendant should watch the result. Very young children, and all those of great nervous sensibility, are extremely liable to fever: a slight degree of pain, or the least difficulty of digestion, may occasion it; but this soon passes off, if they be allowed to repose; and if it be not accompanied by pain in the head, nor of frequent recurrence, is of no importance. When, however, this slight fever is perceived to return often, the cause should be ascertained; and if not evident to those about the child, a good physician should be consulted, lest it might prove the commencement of some dangerous chronic malady.

Children are sometimes very restless, especially in hot weather, from a sort of feverishness, which, though not absolutely a disease in itself, is capable of producing one by disturbing the repose necessary to health. For this inquietude, I have found two or three grains of purified nitre dissolved in a little water and sugar, at bed-time, very efficacious; and it is a thing that children take willingly. Sometimes the tepid bath is also necessary; and I have generally found that using it three or four nights in succession, before going to rest, was sufficient. A child who requires the bath in this way, should have but a very light supper at an early hour; and above all things, should not be pressed to eat if he shows no appetite. This trifling indisposition appears in children under five years old.

Some children of three or four years old are subject to a slight attack of diarrhœa, in certain changes of weather, or if they have been out in wind a little colder than usual: for this three or four grains of rhubarb, with a tea-spoonful of syrup of white poppies, and a table-spoonful of mint-water, given after the child is put to bed, is an excellent remedy. If the complaint should be such as to require a purgative medicine, this will do no injury; and when the looseness is merely occasioned by the irritation of temporary cold, it will generally be found an effectual cure.

The double teeth which appear between six and eight years old, occasion various degrees of indisposition, and sometimes excite symptoms resembling the commencement of chronic diseases. Some children only grow pale and thin for a short time, but others become languid, peevish, and heavy: and those who are affected in this manner require great attention, as it is very possible that maladies which have hitherto lain dormant, may be developed at this period. According as inflammatory symptoms, or those of debility appear, must be the mode of treating them. Some will require a cooling diet, and perhaps mild purgatives, whilst others will have occasion for infusion of bark or preparations of iron, strengthening food, and warm sea baths. Bathing the feet once or twice a week in warm water with mustard and vinegar, would be of use in either species of indisposition, the head being the part chiefly affected; and whether a child be heated or debilitated, whatever draws the blood to the extremities will be advantageous.

The best means of preventing all these indispositions will be to give children as much air, exercise, and amusement as possible; to take care that their sleep be not interrupted, that their minds be not disturbed, that they have nourishing food in moderate quantities, and that they avoid every thing which may produce or augment fever. When these teeth, four in number, are all cut, children who have suffered by them soon recover from any appearance of illness. There are many children who pass through this period of their lives without any sign of interrupted health.

The growth of children is often very irregular; sometimes proceeding with extraordinary rapidity for a few months, and then appearing to stop for a similar length of time. The former state is, frequently, accompanied with debility; and often occasions pains like rheumatism in the limbs: there is also, in some instances, a slight irregular fever, which requires that great attention should be paid to prevent and remove whatever may promote it. The pains only require chafing with a warm hand; but great care should be taken that a child in this state be not fatigued nor fretted. Children are apt to have a great appetite while their rapid growth continues, which diminishes, extremely, as soon as that ceases: neither the one nor the other should occasion any uneasiness to those about the children, nor do they require any particular treatment.

Children should always have their clothes perfectly well aired; and if (as sometimes happens to those of three or four years old) they shiver at putting them on cold, in a winter's morning, they should have them a little warmed. It is bad to give a painful impression of this sort the first thing in the day; and when a child shudders at the feel of cold linen, it is either a sign that he is not well, or not yet strong enough to bear it. A robust, healthy child will feel no unpleasant sensation, but rather the contrary, from cold thus applied to the skin; and it is far better for a delicate child to have its clothes made warm before they are put on, than to be dressed close to a fire, as is so frequently done. Indeed, except in particular cases of illness, children should never seek warmth by approaching a fire: the natural way for them to obtain it, is by running and jumping about; and mothers should watch that they are never prevented from doing so, by gossiping servants, who would much rather make them sit by the fire. Perhaps I shall be thought to encourage tenderness in children too much, when I say that those who are very young and delicate ought to have their beds a little warmed, in the depth of winter: but I am convinced by experience, that keeping them warm, in their first years, is the way to make them hardy afterwards.

CHAPTER III.

THE HEADS OF CHILDREN SHOULD BE KEPT COOL. —RUNNING AT THE NOSE NOT TO BE DISREGARDED.—SHORT HAIR.—BAD HABITS.—DANGEROUS TRICKS.—DAMP SHOES.

For many reasons, children should not be put to sleep together, nor with old people: each child should have a little bed to itself; and this should be (generally speaking) without curtains, for the purpose of keeping the head cool, a thing of more importance than is generally supposed. On this account also, their night-caps should be very thin: no children are so liable to cold in the head and running at the nose, as those who are accustomed to have their heads kept warm; and, therefore, perhaps, if they were to leave off night-caps in summer, and not put them on (except in case of a cold) in winter, it would be no disadvantage. However, this, like every thing else of the same sort, must depend upon the particular circumstances and constitutions; but certainly the cooler the heads of children can be kept, by day and night, the better. They should not, however, go out bareheaded, as both the heat of summer and the cold of winter are very likely to occasion running at the nose; which, straw hats, or the lightest beaver, are sufficient to prevent.

A running at the nose should not be neglected until it become habitual; as, besides being very troublesome and disfiguring to a child, it may, at length, lead to very disagreeable maladies in the nose, from the continual augmented secretion in that organ. Bathing the feet in warm water is one of the best remedies for a recent cold in the head*, and will often remove the complaint in a day or two; but if it continue for any length of time, a good physician or a surgeon should be consulted, who may be able to know whether this be a natural defect or an acquired infirmity: which it is of importance to distinguish, the latter increasing, and the former generally diminishing, as the child advances in years and strength.

The hair of children should be short till after eight or nine years old; as the cooler the head can be kept, the less danger there is of many maladies belonging to that part, especially water on the brain. When the production of the four double teeth, above mentioned, is attended with much inflammation, (as sometimes happens,) it is not improbable that this may occasion the development of that fatal disease;

* Persons who live on the sea-shore will find the sea-water very useful for this purpose.

and whatever diminishes the heat of the head is likely to be advantageous. Besides, there is reason to suppose that children who have a great quantity of hair are those most liable to eruptions on the head, and certainly in them these eruptions are the most difficult to cure. The trouble, also, required for keeping long hair sufficiently clean, and the length of time necessary for this purpose, is often a cause of much ill-humour, and many cross words, which would be better avoided between children and their attendants.

Mothers, whose vanity may be alarmed, lest constantly cutting the hair for so many years, should make that of their daughters coarse, may be assured that they have no cause for this apprehension, if the hair be constantly brushed: I have never seen softer, finer hair, than on girls who have had it short (like that of school-boys) until they were in their tenth year. In another part of this work, I have already expressed a disapprobation of fine combs*, which should never be used except on some extraordinary occasion. When there is any inclination to *break out* in the head, fine combs are very likely to promote it; and there is no doubt, that the heads of children, which are never touched by them, are much cleaner than those which are scratched and scraped every day. If any dirt ap-

---

* Sometimes called small-tooth combs.

pear on a child's head, which a brush will not take away, that particular part should be rubbed with a towel and soap and water; but, in general, the brush will be found quite sufficient to keep it perfectly clean. The more the head is combed, the more it will require to be combed; as any one will find who tries the experiment. However, it must be allowed, that there may be exceptions to this as to every other rule.

Children easily acquire bad habits; many of them of little importance, but disagreeable in appearance, and difficult to overcome. A temporary weakness of the eyes, or the itching occasioned by a trifling abscess on the eye-lid, (to which some children are subject,) frequently give rise to continual winking; and if a child who has acquired this habit, be not watched, and induced to correct it speedily, it may soon become an incurable defect. Squinting, when not occasioned by hydrocephalus, can scarcely be acquired by a child who has tolerably observing attendants. Looking into a broken or bad looking-glass, or through ill glazed windows, or any thing else which causes a distortion of the eyes, if frequently repeated, may produce this deformity; but these are things which must be evident to the persons about children, (if they are not unpardonably careless,) and should be immediately remedied.

Amongst many silly tricks played with children, is that of lifting them up by the head, so as to hang all the weight of the body on the neck; a thing which, certainly, no one aware of the excessive danger would ever practise. It is one of those follies which may lead to *instant death*, and can never produce any sort of pleasure or advantage; though there have been mothers absurd enough to suppose that it would add to the beauty of their daughters, by lengthening their necks. Children should be early instructed in the peril of this trick, and desired never to suffer any one to lift them up by the head. Tickling children is another foolish practice, attended with danger; which they should be cautioned not to allow, and not to practise upon one another.

All children, but particularly females or those who are very delicate, should be taught to change their shoes whenever they have got wet; and as far as it is possible, to guard against the feet getting wet at all by having strong walking shoes. However, while in exercise, it is of comparatively small importance; but sitting still, with the feet artificially cold from wet shoes and stockings, is hurtful to most people, and likely to occasion head-aches, sore-throats, coughs, colics, &c. The continued application of cold to the lower extremities, is particularly unwholesome for those who are subject to have too much blood in the head; and, as this is frequently the case with children, it is evident how very bad it must be for them to keep on wet shoes and stockings when they are not in exercise. I lay a particular stress on this subject, as an author of high reputation* has recommended that the shoes of children be made so as to let in water, by way of rendering them hardy: had he advised that they should go without any, he might have been right; for if shoes and stockings were never used, we should, probably, suffer no more from cold in the feet than in the face; and in fact, I have frequently cured maladies of peasant's children, in places where they are not accustomed to wear shoes, without any precautions respecting the feet, though I should (in similar cases) have advised worsted socks or stockings for those who had ever been used to cover them. But persons who have had early habits of clothing the feet, often find these parts most susceptible of cold; and this occurs even amongst adults of strong constitutions.

The way to make children robust is to guard them against the attacks of disease; and this is not to be done by braving dangers, but by shunning them. Healthy children should not, however, be kept in the house for fear of a shower of rain: if they get wet, there is little danger of their catching cold when they have well-aired clothes to change immediately; but if they must wait shivering in their

* Locke.

wet things, while clean ones are to be dried, even the strongest will be liable to dangerous maladies; the best method to avoid which, would be to strip the children, and put them into bed till dry clothes could be got ready.

CHAPTER IV.

CLEANLINESS.—COLD BATHING.—COLD DRINK.—
SLIGHT INDISPOSITIONS.—PRECAUTIONS.

CHILDREN who are well taken care of will acquire habits of cleanliness before they are aware of their advantages; and those about them should, as they advance in age, impress them with the necessity of continuing those habits without the assistance of others. They should be taught to wash* themselves as soon as they can do it conveniently; and they will be less inclined to become dirty through laziness, than if accustomed too long to depend on the aid of servants: besides, that which children do for themselves being done more to their satisfaction than what others do for them, they will be less inclined to dislike and neglect.

Cold bathing during the summer months, (that is to say in a river, lake, or the open sea,) is very agreeable, and of the greatest benefit to many children; but not to all: and it should be particu-

* Children should be cautioned against using the towel of any one who has an eruptive complaint, as herpetic maladies are sometimes contagious.

larly observed whether it agrees, as children for whom it is not suitable have sometimes no dislike to the water, but find pleasure in doing the same as their companions. But I have known more than one instance of severe maladies, occasioned by persisting in the use of the cold bath when it did not agree: it is evident that the water is unfit for a child who looks pale on coming out of it, and is sleepy and tired afterwards. When this is the case, bathing should be immediately discontinued, as it can only produce bad effects: however, it is to be observed that some individuals are affected thus by sea-bathing, who feel no inconvenience from fresh water; and, on the contrary, others who suffer from fresh-water bathing, find the sea of the greatest advantage. When the cold bath perfectly agrees, there is a glow over the face and the whole body on coming out of the water, and the child appears more lively and animated than usual. With regard to putting children into the water by force, it is more likely to injure than benefit: however, there may be extraordinary cases, in which this, like other desperate remedies, must be tried; and therefore, if prescribed by a really good physician, his orders should be obeyed. Baths, either cold or hot, should be used before meals, and children should always be well dried after them.

It would be right to teach children, as early as possible, that it is dangerous to drink any thing cold when they are heated by exercise: it is not difficult to impress them with a sense of this peril; and particularly necessary to do so, as they are naturally inclined to like cold liquid, and ought to be habituated to it, from the time they leave off drinking at night, and between meals after weaning. And here I must enforce, that nothing is more unwholesome for delicate children than to drink warm diluting liquors, when not suffering under some malady for which these are necessary. A warm beverage relaxes the stomach, increases perspiration, and promotes debility, and is therefore required in acute diseases, when we must weaken in order to cure. Except in such cases, children should have as little as possible of warm liquors; I do not mean to say that, in cold climates or cold seasons, they should not have their milk or gruel (or whatever else may be given to them) for breakfast warm, as those things, being eaten with bread, partake more of the nature of solid than liquid food; but if, for instance, a child is thirsty, after a plentiful meal of hot milk and bread, or potatoes or porridge, a glass of good cold water is much wholesomer than hot tea, or indeed any thing else.

The slightest appearance of indisposition in a child of any age should excite the watchfulness of the attendants, even though there may be no occasion for administering medicines. Maladies may also be often checked, by timely remedies of the simplest sort. Head-ache, with foul tongue, usually requires a purgative; inclination to vomit, an emetic; but when there is merely great heat of the skin, a high quick pulse, and excessive thirst, bed, quietness, and warm drink, will frequently be found sufficient.

If a healthy child be suddenly attacked with vomiting and purging, it is clear that there is something which ought to be carried off, and such remedies should be employed as promote this object. Warm water will often be found sufficient, (for little children sugar should be added,) and a few grains of ipecacuanha may also be given, if thought necessary. For purging, it will always be found safe to give weak chicken-broth, rice-water, or some other diluting liquor, in abundance, and perhaps a slight infusion of rhubarb; and in all indispositions of this sort a low diet will be the best. Meat, and every thing heating or difficult of digestion, should be prohibited. If the complaint should take a decided form, the proper directions for treating it will be found in the chapter on diarrhœa, &c.; and in case any violent or strange symptoms should appear, a physician should be immediately called, lest the malady might be occasioned by some poisonous substance, which would require a particular mode of treatment.

When any extraordinary symptoms appear in a

child whose general health is good, they need not terrify the parents, though they should be attended to, and the causes (if possible) discovered and removed; but a solitary and accidental sign of illness is not to be considered as a proof of disease. The caprices of Nature are numerous, and often occasion unnecessary fears.

A small quantity of blood appearing accidentally and without pain, sickness, or diarrhœa, in the evacuations from the bowels of a strong child, need not be a subject of alarm: it is a sign of being overheated; and the same cause, especially by too much exercise, has sometimes occasioned a little blood to be mixed in the urine, giving it a blackish colour and sediment, which has a frightful appearance. Repose, a cooling diet, and nitre, are the proper remedies in both cases. These symptoms are of no importance in a strong child, who has no other mark of indisposition, if not of *frequent recurrence;* but as they are not very common, (especially the black urine,) it is necessary to consult a medical man if they return often.

A child who wakens with a hoarse cough and sore throat, in cold weather, may be saved from a bad illness, by remaining in bed till after breakfast. The child should not, however, be obliged to lie down all that time, but should have the body and arms well covered with some convenient clothing, and be allowed to sit up and occupy itself with toys or books, according to the age and circumstances. After eating, the skin is less susceptible of cold, and, besides, the rooms will have had time to get warm. When this has been found necessary in the morning, it is prudent to bathe the feet at night with warm water and salt, and give some warm drink as advised for colds*. In bathing the feet for a recent cold or any slight indisposition, it is always better to mix salt in the water; and persons who live on the sea-shore may use sea-water for this purpose.

In cases of severe illness, when, either on account of violent pain in the head or great weakness, it is very troublesome to a child to be raised for the purpose of having the feet bathed, a person who is not very awkward may easily place a deep wash-hand basin under the bed-clothes; and by making the patient lie on the back, and raise the knees, (which is not a disagreeable posture to a sick child,) the bath may be used with good effect. I have often seen this method tried with success. Some one should hold the basin, and (for fear of accidents) there should be laid under it a large well-aired cloth, folded several times, which may serve to dry the feet afterwards; there should also be something put over the child's knees, to prevent the vapour of

---

* See Chapter VII. of the Fourth Part.

the warm water from damping the bed-coverings. It is scarcely necessary to say that this would not answer for a very unruly child or one in a violent delirium.

In case of leeches being applied to the breast of a child, (as is often necessary for asthma, inflammation of the lungs, &c.,) it is of great importance to guard against taking cold by exposing the part to the air for any length of time : to avoid this danger, a piece of flannel (which may have strings to fasten behind) should be laid over the breast, after having as many holes made in it as there are leeches to apply.

When a child shows symptoms of indisposition without apparent cause, it is always prudent to enquire what malady is in the neighbourhood, lest they should prove the forerunners of any contagious or epidemic disease, which might be rendered less pernicious by particular attention; and this is one of the advantages of having a family physician, especially in a great city.

If in any illness a child should evince a disgust to sweet drink, and express a wish for sour things, it is a sign the malady is bilious; and the instinct which points out acidulated drink ought to be indulged. A patient in this state, who requires food, will probably find what is called in Tuscany a *cordial* very palatable : this is made by mixing the yolk of an egg in a large cup of broth, and then adding a small tea-spoonful of lemon-juice, which may be poured on a piece of toasted bread.

The hiccough is an accidental inconvenience, rather than malady, to which all children are liable; and it is a common practice to startle or frighten, by way of curing it: this would be better avoided, and a little cold water or a bit of sugar will frequently answer the purpose of checking it: if these are not found sufficient, a few drops of lemon-juice or vinegar will seldom fail. When, however, acids do not remove it, and that it returns frequently, a physician should be consulted, as there might be something wrong in the stomach, which would require the aid of medicine to remove. Of course, it will be understood that I do not mean to speak of the convulsive symptom that appears in dangerous maladies; but the common hiccough, to which old and young persons are liable when in health.

If a child complains of acute pain in any part, of which the cause is doubtful or unknown, the advice of a physician is probably necessary, and should be sought without delay; as the continuance of suffering might produce dangerous diseases, which the timely employment of proper remedies could prevent.

Persons in restricted circumstances are often deterred from calling in a professional man by economical motives, reflecting that if an illness be of long duration, the expense may become considerable: but this is a great error; for in many cases, if medical assistance be obtained on the first attack of a malady, it may be extremely shortened, so as to give occasion for much fewer visits from the doctor than if he is not called in until it has lasted some days.

CHAPTER V.

CHOPPED LIPS.—CHILBLAINS.—SLIGHT BURNS.—BRUISES.—WOUNDS.

CHILDREN who are allowed to be as much in the open air as they ought, though they may find no other disadvantage from cold, yet are liable, in frosty and windy weather, to suffer from chopped lips, roughness of skin, and chilblains; but with proper precautions, these trifling inconveniences (for they seldom amount to any thing more) may be entirely avoided or greatly diminished. The first and chief care should be, to keep the children at a distance from fires, especially when they are just come out of the cold air, and are likely to return into it immediately; the next is to keep up the circulation by rubbing the skin sufficiently; and the third, to be very attentive in having it quickly and perfectly dried after washing.

The best way of preventing that very disagreeable swelling and cracking of the lips to which some children (as well as adults) are subject, is to wash them the first thing in the morning with very cold water and a coarse towel, and to rub them hard in drying. Children should be taught as soon as possible to do this for themselves, as they will bear harder rubbing from their own hands than from others; and if not counteracted by approaching the fire, this will be found a sure method of avoiding the above-mentioned inconvenience. For those who are liable to have the skin of the face become rough in cold windy weather, it is better, during the winter season, to wash it only on going to bed at night, with warm water in which some bran has been boiled, and to refrain from wetting any part in the morning, except the eyes, lips, and ears, which should always be washed with cold water.

It is easier to prevent than to cure chilblains: those children who are accustomed to warm themselves by the fire in frosty weather, will rarely escape them; but suffering the extremities to continue long cold is almost as likely to occasion this troublesome complaint. Children should be taught to warm them by jumping about and clapping their hands; and when they are too young to do this, their feet and hands should be rubbed for them, and shoes and gloves, well warmed, be put on to preserve the heat excited by friction.

When there is any reason to expect a child to have chilblains, worsted socks or stockings should be employed on the first appearance of autumnal frost, and gloves of the same with leather over them. The feet and hands should be rubbed night and morning with either camphorated spirits, brandy, vinegar, or brine; and at night, when the child goes to bed, the feet should be wrapped up in a piece of hot flannel.

Chilblains on the feet require the greatest attention, as they often prevent children from taking exercise, or at least render them unwilling to move: this should be obviated as much as possible (if the malady cannot be entirely prevented) by shoes of soft leather, lined with flannel or fur, and made in such a manner as not to press upon the swelling.

I have seen the smoke of *burnt bran* employed with the greatest advantage for children; and I recommend it with the more confidence, because I first learnt the use of it from an excellent physician. A little dry bran is thrown on a chafing-dish of live coals, over which the hands or feet must be held near enough to receive the thick smoke: a few minutes will suffice for this operation, which relieves the itching and diminishes the swelling. It should be frequently repeated in the day; and by employing it just before the child goes to bed, the effects will be more permanent. Another good remedy when chilblains burn and itch violently, is *very hot water*, which affords instant relief on plunging the parts affected into it; but this requires caution, and should be employed only when the child is in a warm room, and not likely to be exposed to cold for several hours after; nor would it answer for very young children.

If chilblains are so bad as to break, they must at first be dressed with emollient ointment, like other sores; and for this purpose, the common spermaceti ointment is as good as any thing else: afterwards, that is to say, when the inflammation is diminished, they should be covered with lint dipped in the vegeto-mineral water; and loose gloves should be worn constantly, partly to keep the air from the wound, and partly on account of the poisonous quality of this remedy.

If, notwithstanding every precaution and attention, chilblains should come to a great height, it is necessary to consult a medical professor, lest they may happen to be combined with some other disease which requires internal remedies.

When children begin to run alone, and to enjoy that degree of liberty which is necessary for their moral and physical welfare, they become liable to many accidents, for which the persons about them should be prepared; and though constant attention and much care will generally (though not always) prevent great hurts, yet small ones are scarcely to be avoided. Slight burns and bruises, which might become serious complaints if neglected, are frequently cured easily, by simple but immediate remedies; and the former especially, if quickly attended to, may be prevented from becoming troublesome sores.

For slight burns, the *immediate* application of spirits, ink, vinegar, forge-water, or very cold spring-water, will be useful; and I have many times seen large burns, when the skin was not broken, perfectly cured in a very short time by a cataplasm of soap and brandy. The soap should be scraped fine, and laid very thick on a piece of linen; the brandy poured on it, and then applied to the burn, which should be covered with linen dipped in brandy, while the soap is preparing: all this should be done very quickly, otherwise the remedy will be of no use. The cataplasm should not be removed for five or six hours, and should be kept constantly wet with brandy during that time. If this remedy is *instantly* employed, it will prevent any blister from rising. Another excellent application for superficial burns is *cotton*, which should be spread thick over the injured part, and fastened in such a manner that it may not be removed for many hours.

A burn, when any part of the skin has been broken, must be treated quite differently; and the simplest and readiest application is ceruse* mixed with salad oil, to the consistence of an ointment, by which I have repeatedly seen superficial burns cured without the assistance of any other remedy.

* It must be observed that *ceruse* is a most poisonous substance, and therefore should not be left in the way of children; as curiosity might tempt them to taste the powder, and its sweetness induce them to swallow it. For the same reason, in case of using it for burns on the fingers, they should be carefully covered, to prevent all possibility of being put in the mouth.

The materials for this ointment should always be at hand, to prepare it as quickly as possible: in the mean time the wound must be protected from the air by laying something hollow (a bowl or saucer) over the part, so as not to let any thing touch the hurt, and then covering it with a cloth. The ointment should be spread on strips of linen, and laid on the wound, so as to cover it perfectly; and then it should be bandaged over. The bits of linen, covered with ointment, may be changed once or twice a day; oftener, if the part feels hot and uneasy; and the ceruse which sticks to the skin should not be rubbed off till the wound is quite healed. This will generally prevent the suppuration of a slight burn : but if such should take place, the wound may be dressed with spermaceti ointment. These remedies are proposed as the most convenient to have recourse to without delay : there are many others equally efficacious; but I do not wish to load this work with more prescriptions than are absolutely necessary.

The foregoing advice refers only to slight, superficial burns: when more severe have taken place, medical assistance must be sought as quickly as possible; and in the mean time, the best thing that can be done is to keep the part that has been burnt in cold water till the arrival of the physician.

Superficial burns may extend over so large a portion of the skin as to occasion fever; which must be treated, like other indispositions of that sort, with confinement to bed and diluting liquors; also silence, darkness, &c., according to the intensity of it: but when a burn is severe enough to produce this effect, a professional man should be immediately consulted, as the complication of fever might totally alter the simple nature of the wound, and render a different method of treating it necessary.

It is right to observe, that when a burn has once occasioned a blister, especially on the lower extremities, it cannot be expected to heal rapidly, but will probably take three weeks before it is cured. For burns (or any other sort of wounds) on the legs or feet, it is necessary to keep the limb as much as possible in repose, and on a level with the body; so that a child who has had a hurt of this nature ought to lie on a bed or sofa great part of the day, at least during the first week*.

For slight contusions, when the skin is not broken, camphorated spirit, opodeldoc, vinegar, or salt and water are very good applications; but if there is a scratch as well as a bruise, nitre and water, or the vegeto-mineral water, would be better, as they do not smart so much. For those bruises to which

* Any considerable inflammation of the hands or fingers, would require to have the arm supported by a handkerchief suspended from the neck.

children are so liable about the forehead and eyebrows, and which sometimes look frightful, there is nothing better than to fold a piece of soft linen so many times as to make it about a quarter of an inch thick, and proportioned to the size of the bruise: this should be dipped in very cold water, laid on the part which is beginning to swell, and bandaged so as to press on it firmly, without, however, making the child very uneasy: it should be kept on for several hours, and must be unbandaged now and then to dip the folded linen in cold water; but should be immediately put on again, as the cold and the pressure are equally efficacious.

If a child has had a blow on the head without vomiting after it, this is a proof that no important injury has been suffered; but even when the stomach is affected by a hurt of this sort, it is no positive reason for being very much alarmed, though it is a proof that the blow has been severe. It would always, however, be prudent to use the sinapized bath for the feet of a child who had received a hurt in the head, and also to lower the diet for a few days. These precautions, employed without necessity, can do no harm; whereas the neglect of them, when they ought to be used, may be the cause of serious injury. It is almost unnecessary to say, that in any case which requires surgical assistance the least delay is dangerous;

and especially in regard to hurts on the head, for which immediate bleeding may be of the utmost importance.

In many countries it is the custom for children, till two or three years old, to wear leather caps, stuffed cushions, and guards of various sorts, round the forehead, to prevent the danger of that sort of blows above alluded to: but I believe them to be very bad things, on account of the unnatural degree of heat they must excite in the part; and would rather advise to run the risk of the possible mischief consequent to a fall, than that likely to result from keeping the head too hot.

With regard to scratches or slight wounds of the skin, the object should be to protect them from the impression of air and cold; and for this purpose, I have seen employed, with the greatest advantage, (by order of one of the first surgeons in Europe[*],) the skin which adheres to the shell of a raw egg, which should be put on without drying it: this sticks fast to the part wounded, and should be let to remain until it comes off of itself. If this should happen before the part be healed, the egg-skin ought to be renewed; and in case a suppuration takes place under it, a hole must be cut in the egg-skin, at the lower edge of the wound, and the matter pressed out; but it should not be taken off.

---

[*] The late celebrated Andrea Vacca, of Pisa.

As there is generally a contusion with these sort of wounds, some folds of linen dipped in vegeto-mineral water, should be laid over the part that is bruised, and kept wet while any inflammation appears. It is almost needless to say that the egg ought to be fresh.

A slight cut with any sharp instrument should have the edges brought close together, and a bit of diachylon, or common black plaster, laid over to keep them so. A wound which has been made in such a manner as to give reason to fear gravel or sand might have got into it, should be first washed with warm wine and water, and then covered with any one of the above-mentioned substances, to protect it from the air. Nature requires but little assistance in the cure of slight wounds; but when there is any considerable hurt, it is much better at once to consult a professional man.

Mothers should be very cautious how they blame servants who have the care of children, for the trifling accidents which may happen to them, lest it might lead to dangerous consequences, by inducing them to conceal falls and hurts, of which the bad effects might have been prevented by immediately relating all the circumstances with truth and accuracy to a good surgeon. No one who undertakes the care of a child would be so cruel and silly as to injure it intentionally, but an accident may happen to the most careful person; and any one who is found too careless to be relied on for the common degree of attention, should be instantly dismissed.

CHAPTER VI.

CAUTIONS RESPECTING THE TREATMENT OF YOUNG FEMALES AT A CRITICAL TIME OF LIFE.

The passage from childhood to maturity in females, is often attended with symptoms of serious malady, the natural consequence of mismanagement; but I will venture to affirm, that girls whose physical education has been, from the beginning, such as is recommended in this book, (and the moral not calculated to counteract it,) will not be likely to suffer any of the customary indispositions. Constant and diversified occupations, exercise and amusement, early rising, good nourishment, sufficient sleep, and tranquillity of mind, will, in all probability, bring the most delicate female through that critical period of her existence, with little inconvenience, and no illness.

If, however, it should happen that, from any hereditary defect or other accidental cause, a girl should be affected with symptoms of languor, debility, difficulty of breathing, &c., at the approach of that time of life, the aid of medicine may perhaps be required, although the regular attendance of a physician be unnecessary; and what are vulgarly called *courses of steel, forcing medicines,* &c., &c., are pernicious. The very idea of being the patient of a medical practitioner, and liable to take remedies continually, is sometimes enough to create disease in a person whose nerves are already agitated by the vicinity of an important revolution in the frame: and, therefore, it should be one of the first objects of those who are about a girl in this situation, to prevent her from supposing herself in bad health, and keep her mind as cheerful as possible; at the same time, the advice of a skilful physician may be obtained without parade.

The best medicinal substances in these cases are, probably, rhubarb and iron; but if a journey to some chalybeate spring (the resort of gaiety) should be convenient, that, without doubt, would prove the best remedy, as the change of scene, the exercise, and the diversions usual in such places, augment the salutary effects of the iron contained in the water.

Mothers, in the middle and lower ranks of society, should be very cautious not to keep their daughters too much confined to needle-work at this period of their lives, but rather employ them in the more active business of the household, and let them have as much air and exercise as possible: without, however, indulging idleness, which is one of the greatest enemies to health of body and of mind. To preserve the physical and moral welfare, it is necessary that all should be employed in occupations suitable to their respective situations in society: errors in the nature of employments for young girls are so very hurtful, that I cannot refrain from hinting, that such as only tend to nourish vanity, and fill the heads of females in the inferior ranks of life with silly and ambitious notions, are often injurious to their health at the critical period of which I am now treating.

We should be careful on all occasions not to impede the progress of nature by untimely remedies; but remain simple observers of what may occur, and be ready to administer relief in case any morbid symptoms should appear. When the periodical evacuation peculiar to females has once taken place, it is not to be expected that it should, immediately, continue in a regular course: this seldom happens; on the contrary it is not uncommon for many months to elapse without a return; and if a young girl, in this state, shows no other signs of indisposition, that alone is not to be considered as a disease, and attacked with medicine, as it is too frequently. When there are any slight complaints, they must be treated as on other occasions: head-aches, with baths for the feet; sickness of the stomach, with bitter infusions*; fever, with a low diet and diluting liquors; and debility, with some preparation of iron. But when a young female in this state has no symptom of illness, nothing should be done; for the mere delay of the monthly evacuation, even though it may continue three, six, twelve months, or more, should not be considered as a disease.

I am extremely anxious to impress on my readers the necessity of not counteracting nature in this particular operation, as I have reason to believe that fatal consequences have, sometimes, been the result of the injudicious administration of medicines on such occasions. Mothers would do well, however, to be more than commonly attentive to their daughters in these circumstances, and to prevent whatever may interrupt the circulation of the blood, or retard the establishment of the constitution; and above all things, those who are about young persons, at this period of their lives, are earnestly intreated to remember, that *uneasiness of mind is likely to occasion far more injury than drugs can ever remedy.* The moral feelings are often too

---

* I know nothing better for this purpose than the double chamomile, (commonly sold in apothecaries' shops,) of which a strong infusion should be taken cold, in the quantity of three ounces, about an hour before breakfast every morning.

little considered, and the physical too much; for mothers who make no scruple of wounding a daughter's sensibility, or mortifying her pride, will yet be very ready to cram her with pills and draughts, if she happens to look pale or complain of a head-ache.

No doubt there are uncommon cases which require medical assistance: convulsions of various sorts, as well as other alarming complaints, have attacked females at this time of life; but I only treat of the general course of things, and would strongly recommend that when any extraordinary symptoms appear, *the best physicians should be consulted;* and all quack remedies and prescriptions of ignorant persons carefully avoided.

When young girls have arrived at this period of existence, they should be informed that the human frame, during those few days, is more sensible to hurtful impressions than at other times; and, therefore, they ought particularly to refrain from any sort of food which they find difficult of digestion, and avoid wetting their feet, or exposing themselves much to cold. These precautions are quite sufficient; for it is, in reality, unwholesome as well as inconvenient to insist on a change of diet, and a number of whimsical laws and restrictions to which some persons submit, and which I have never known to conduce to the benefit of those who practise them. The less alteration that is made from their usual habits, by healthy females, the better they will find themselves as they advance in years; and those who are in a state of disease, should have their regimen directed by a medical man.

PART THE FOURTH.

OF DISEASES COMMON TO CHILDREN OF ALL AGES.

CHAPTER I.

DIVISION OF DISEASES.—FEVERS.

The only division of diseases necessary for such a work as this, is Acute and Chronic. Acute diseases may be defined—those which commence almost suddenly, are produced by some immediate cause, accompanied with high fever, and end in a short time. Chronic diseases are those which come on slowly, and are of long duration; they are often the consequences of acute maladies, and are generally more difficult to cure.

When a healthy child complains of fatigue without an adequate cause, there is reason to suspect the approach of fever; and if this first symptom be followed by head-ache, disgust to food, restlessness, unusual heat of the skin, and a quick pulse, continuing for a certain time, the actual presence of that malady may be inferred. Sometimes there is an alternate sense of cold and heat; but at other times, the cold is not perceptible. Great care should be taken to avoid every thing which may augment the symptoms; the child should be encouraged to lie in bed, and to drink plentifully of diluting liquors*. Should there be an inclination to vomit, it should be promoted; and if there has been no evacuation from the bowels for four and twenty hours, a clyster, or some mild purgative, may be given: this treatment will generally be found sufficient for ephemeral fevers †, and slight epidemic maladies of the eruptive kind.

If there be strong reason to suppose the malady occasioned by indigestion, and that it is accompanied by pains in the stomach and bowels, with a foul tongue, it would be necessary to give a purgative medicine immediately ‡. Calomel will probably be found the most efficacious; and if it should have no effect in five or six hours, it ought either to be repeated, or assisted by the administration of a clyster. If, however, there be a doubt re-

---

* Weak tea, water-gruel, barley or rice water, light lemonade, apple-tea, infusions of balm, sage, &c., currant jelly and water, syrup of raspberry, vinegar and water, &c.: and if the child prefer sugar and water, there is nothing better.

† Which last about twenty-four hours.

‡ Vide Appendix.

specting the cause of the malady, and no pains of the sort above mentioned, it will be better to use no other remedy than confinement to bed, and abundance of warm drink. Should there arise a difficulty of breathing, extraordinary sleepiness, or acute pain in any part, a physician should be immediately applied to, as bleeding might be necessary without delay; and it always requires medical skill to determine when that remedy should be employed for children.

In general, one of the most alarming symptoms that can appear in a child, is that state of stupidity and sleepiness which shows the brain to be affected; although, in eruptive fevers, it frequently occurs, even when they do not turn out dangerous. It would always be right to call in a physician when such a symptom appears; and in the mean time, the feet should be bathed or fomented (whichever is least disagreeable to the patient) with warm water and mustard and vinegar: no medical man will find fault with the application of this remedy; and in some cases of stupor or suffocation it may retard the danger till his arrival.

Fever, in young children, is to be discovered more by redness of the face, burning heat of the skin, thirst, and restlessness, than by the alteration of the pulse; if, however, that be also quick and full, it is certainly a corroborating symptom. Whenever there is any considerable degree of fever, children should be confined to bed; (by persuasion, not force;) but it is not, however, necessary to keep them very warm: on the contrary, no additional covering should be given, nor should any thing ever be done to force a sweat; though all precautions should be taken to avoid checking any which may naturally arise. Confined air sometimes impedes perspiration; and I have observed that opening a window in an adjoining apartment, so as to change the air of the sick person's room, often relieves oppression, and promotes the excretion from the pores: but this would of course require the greatest caution, and must depend on the season, and also on the situation of the patient's apartment, bed, &c.; as too much cold, or a current of air approaching too near, might produce dangerous effects. The child, if able to eat, should have only the lightest and most cooling food, such as stewed fruits, barley or rice gruel, &c., &c., and even these very sparingly.

When a child is suffering under a simple fever, the less medicine that is given the better; but if there be great uneasiness and impatience of the heat, a few grains of purified nitre in a little barley or rice water, on going to rest at night, may be of use.

Should a severe cough, pain in the chest, or difficulty of breathing come on suddenly, great benefit may be derived from a sinapism, made by wetting coarse mustard with vinegar enough to form it into a soft paste, which should be put into a very thin rag, (or rather gauze,) and applied to the chest, so as to touch as much of the skin as is usually covered with a blister, (about the size of a crown-piece, but larger or smaller, according to the age of the child,) and this should be kept on until it gives sharp pain and makes the skin very red, which will generally happen in half or three quarters of an hour: it should then be taken off, and the part covered with a bit of soft linen, over which a piece of flannel may be laid. Sinapisms on the feet require a much longer time than on any other part; but the complaints of the patient soon give notice when they ought to be removed. It is necessary to observe some caution in the use of sinapisms, as they sometimes produce the desired effect in a few minutes, and should not be left on afterwards; and although there is no danger of little children being too patient, it would be necessary to observe that those who are of an age to have resolution, do not endure the pain too long.

CHAPTER II.

INTERMITTING FEVERS OR AGUES.

INTERMITTING fevers, or agues, (as they are usually called,) are less common amongst children than adults; and when they do occur, the cause, and consequently the method of cure, is more doubtful.

The ague begins like other fevers, with a sensation of fatigue and uneasiness, which is followed by a painful feeling of cold, attended with convulsive shiverings more or less violent: these are succeeded by burning heat; the face, which was before pale and livid, becomes very red: the head aches, and there is great thirst; and this terminates with a profuse sweat. These three stages of *shivering*, *burning heat*, and *sweat*, form what is called *a fit of the ague*, which is of uncertain duration; but (generally speaking) the longer it lasts the heavier is the disease likely to prove. In one species of this malady, there is no fever on the second day; but on the third, it returns again, and so continues for a longer or a shorter space of time; and it is this periodical form which marks the nature of the disease, of which this species is called the *tertian*.

Sometimes the ague returns for a few hours

regularly every day, and this is the *quotidian;* at other times there are two days free from fever between the fits, and the malady is then called the *quartan.* The *double tertian* is that which returns every day, but one day severe and the next day slight : the third day's fever being the same as the first, and the fourth the same as the second. There is also a *double quartan*, as well as many other kinds of ague not necessary to be specified here ; but any disease of this nature appearing in a child, would require the advice of a physician.

The object during a fit of the ague is to shorten the cold stage as much as possible, the length of the others appearing to depend greatly on that : this may be assisted by putting the child into a bed well warmed, and applying hot bricks, or bottles filled with hot water and wrapped up in flannel, to the soles of the feet. Hot drink might also be useful ; but if it be given during the cold stage, the child is apt to vomit, which renders it unwilling to drink afterwards ; however, in the hot stage, when there is great thirst, infusions of aromatic herbs, and light lemonade, may be given plentifully ; and when the sweat comes on, the child must be kept as quiet as possible *.

* Many remedies have been proposed to shorten a fit of the ague ; but I do not specify any of them, as I do not think they ought to be given to a child without the order of a physician.

In regard to the medical treatment, I shall only say, that if a child who has been subject to worm complaints is attacked by an ague, there can be no harm in giving a dose of calomel on the day after the fit has taken place; and if the fever be shorter or slighter on the next day, another dose may be given in a few days afterwards, always selecting the day on which the child is free from the ague. If the disease should be entirely stopped by this means, the cure is to be completed by giving those tonic remedies advised for worms*. To prescribe the bark, and other medicines usually necessary for the cure of ague, it would be requisite to see the patient; and, therefore, the presence of a physician is indispensable: even when the malady is so slight as not to occasion much sickness, if a purge does not immediately remove it, medical advice should be sought, as some well-adapted remedy would probably be necessary to prevent the distemper from increasing or turning into something worse.

* See that subject, Part IV. Chap. XV.

CHAPTER III.

ERUPTIVE FEVERS.

ERUPTIVE fevers are those to which children are most liable; and whenever they are attacked by the symptoms of fever already described, particularly if there be vomiting, accompanied with severe headache, stupor, or delirium, pains in the back and loins, weakness of the eyes, and soreness of the throat, the approach of an eruptive disease may be suspected; and more especially if any epidemic malady of that sort be in the neighbourhood. Means should be taken to relieve the violence of these symptoms; and for this purpose the child should be kept quiet in bed, and have such acidulated liquors as may be most agreeable to it: the feet may be bathed or fomented; and bits of linen, dipped in vinegar and water, may be applied to the forehead and temples, changing them frequently. Those who have means of obtaining the advice of a good physician, for a child in this state, would do well to seek for it without delay: and those who have not, should be very cautious not to do too much. An eruptive disease must take its course;

and the chief thing is to avoid whatever may counteract the efforts of nature. In young and delicate children, convulsions are very common, but not dangerous; and all the symptoms preceding these sort of maladies are sometimes very severe, without being followed by any alarming consequences. I have more than once seen violent fever, accompanied with head-ache, stupefaction, delirium, and total loss of strength, vanish on the appearance of twenty or thirty pimples, dispersed over the surface of the body.

Nothing should be done to disturb or vex a child attacked by a fever; as fatigue of body or uneasiness of mind may change a slight into a dangerous malady. The child should be treated with the greatest gentleness, kept as silent as possible, and if the eyes are affected, in a dark room. Eruptive fevers generally continue from four-and-twenty hours to four days, before the spots appear; and (except in the small-pox) during that time the child should be persuaded to lie in bed: when it is necessary to change the linen or make the bed, the greatest care should be taken that the cold air may not strike on the skin, and every thing that touches it should be warm.

If an eruption should suddenly disappear, (which by the by, is generally the consequence of neglect or imprudence,) and bad symptoms follow, such as stupor, delirium, difficulty of breathing, violent pain in the head or elsewhere, sinapisms should be applied to the feet, and a physician immediately called. Sage and mint or balm tea, may be given for drink; and, for medicine, a few drops of spirit of hartshorn in a glass of warm gruel; but no wine, nor any thing of a cordial nature, unless ordered by a professional man. I am particular in mentioning this, because it is a common prejudice to suppose strong liquors proper for driving out eruptions; and there are many quack remedies for this purpose, which are extremely dangerous in their effects, and have sometimes occasioned diseases to end fatally which might otherwise have been cured. There is no case in which good medical advice is more necessary than in this.

There is a great variety of eruptive fevers which have no particular names, and I have seen many of which I could find no description in medical books; but as the chief symptoms are usually the same, there is no occasion for a different manner of treating them. Any which are accompanied with a low pulse, and other marks of debility, would require the immediate attendance of a physician, as it sometimes happens that dangerous epidemic diseases appear under this form.

CHAPTER IV.

SMALL-POX.—COW-POX.

It is with some hesitation that I mention a malady which ought long since to have been banished from all civilized countries; but having lately been both an ear and eye witness to its continued existence, it appears to me that my work would be incomplete were I to omit treating of one of the most dangerous diseases to which children can be exposed.

The SMALL-POX is epidemic and contagious in the highest degree. It is a malady of the most dreadful sort, as it not only menaces with death, like other violent diseases, but with a diminution of the senses and various sorts of deformity; from which even inoculation has not always secured the patient. However, although it has often taken a most malignant form, and committed ravages like the plague, yet it is sometimes mild, and (unless mismanaged) productive of no alarming consequences.

The malady commences with slight heaviness and inquietude, for some days, before the appearance of the fever, which shows itself with the general symptoms already described, but in a violent degree; and the alternations of cold and heat are strongly marked: the eyes are red, the throat sore, and besides severe head-ache, the patient suffers also from pains in the back and loins, and sometimes in all the limbs. The stomach is painful when touched, the nerves are very much affected, and young children are liable to be attacked by convulsions. But all these symptoms diminish as soon as the eruption begins to appear; which it usually does on the third or fourth day, in the form of spots resembling flea-bites, first about the mouth, then on the chin, the forehead, and the rest of the face; in the course of three or four days they spread over the whole body and limbs, and sometimes the face and eyelids are greatly swelled. About the fifth or the sixth day, the suppuration of the pustules* commences, but is not completed till the eighth or the ninth; when the spots, having become yellow and full of thick matter, begin to dry up, and fall off by degrees; so that the disease generally terminates about the fifteenth or sixteenth day. If the eruption be in great quantity, there is a return of fever during the suppuration, and the swelling of the face is removed to the hands and feet; but if there

---

* It is particularly necessary to observe the appearance and the duration of the *pustules* in the small-pox, as nothing else can fix the character of the disease with certainty; for other epidemic eruptive maladies have often a perfect resemblance to it in all the preceding symptoms.

are only a few pustules, these circumstances do not occur.

This is (as nearly as can be detailed in a few words) the usual progress of the mild, distinct small-pox; but even in that, there are varieties and deviations from the common course, which should not surprise those who witness them. According to the violence of the fever will generally be the eruption; and yet the most severe febrile symptoms have been known to precede the appearance of a dozen spots.

Persons who have the means of obtaining good medical assistance, would naturally seek it on the first appearance of so dreadful a malady as small-pox; but children, whose parents cannot afford the expense of a physician, may get through the mild species very well without one, (as there is perhaps no malady which requires less medicine,) if there be nothing done to interrupt the progress of nature.

Nothing is so dangerous as close, shut-up rooms, additional bed-coverings, and spirituous liquors; which are usually recommended by the ignorant, to prevent the eruption from disappearing, and are the sure means of changing a mild into a malignant small-pox.

A dose of calomel may be given with advantage on the first or second day of the fever, if there has been no evacuation from the bowels within twenty-four hours; and afterwards, if necessary, clysters must be employed for keeping them in a proper state. Head-ache should be treated as before directed, vomiting encouraged by drinking plentifully of water (or sugar and water) warm: should there be a looseness, it ought not to be checked; but the child should have a great deal of rice-water and toast and water to drink. Except when calomel is taken, acidulated drink may be given during the whole course of the disease; and when the heat of the skin is very great, the child may be indulged with having it cold. The windows of the patient's room should be left open as much as possible, in dry weather; with prudent attention, however, to the season, the climate, and other circumstances.

In the small-pox, cold air and cold drink are much more beneficial than in any other malady; there is, also, less occasion for confinement to bed, and the bed-clothes may be diminished if the patient complains of their weight or heat. **If a** child, in the fever of the small-pox, wishes **to go to** an open window, or out into the air, he should be indulged; and, in fact, when there is such a desire, it is a good sign, and a proof of the absence of some of the worst symptoms. Should a child in this state demand food, stewed fruit, bread, barley, or rice, may be given; but they should not be pressed upon the patient.

In regard to the bad sort of small-pox, I shall attempt no description nor advice, as it must require the attendance of a professional man; but will only say that, if the eruption should appear on the first or second day of the fever, with a small quick pulse, stupor and debility, the disease threatens to be dangerous; and a good physician should be sought without delay.

After the small-pox is over, some purgative medicine would be necessary: if the malady has been very light, one moderate dose is sufficient; but if there has been an abundant eruption, and much swelling of the face and extremities, two, or perhaps three, would not be amiss. Calomel and rhubarb are the most proper medicines for this purpose.

Symptoms of weakness and languor in a child, who has lately had the small-pox, should not be neglected, as all violent eruptive fevers are likely to develope maladies of debility.

It is very extraordinary that this fatal distemper **should** not have been eradicated in almost thirty years, which have elapsed since the happy discovery of the Cow-Pox, a safe and secure means of preventing it: and nothing is a greater proof of the obstinacy of prejudice, than there being still individuals who refuse this easy method of preserving their children from a malady so uncertain and so dreadful as the small-pox. This much, however, must be said in their favour, that vaccination has frequently been performed in such a careless manner as to produce a *false* cow-pox, which is no security against the small-pox: but the difference between the *false* and the *true* is now so well known that such errors are very unlikely to occur; and they may always be avoided by employing a professional man of experience and reputation: although there is no doubt that any young surgeon of good sense, who has attentively observed the progress of the vaccine half-a-dozen times, may be as deserving of confidence in this respect as a man of twenty years' practice.

There are several strong reasons for preferring the vaccine to the small-pox inoculation; but one alone would be sufficient; which is, that the former is *never* attended with the pain and danger which not unfrequently follows the latter, even under the most promising circumstances. I have had a great many and equal opportunities of seeing both practised; and having witnessed several instances of the inoculated small-pox producing very dangerous as well as painful symptoms, *impossible to occur in the cow-pox*, I would strenuously recommend all parents to bestow on their children, as early as possible, the inestimable benefit of vaccination. I have seen this successfully performed on individuals of various ages, (from one month to twenty years old,) and should prefer the age of five or six weeks, as children so young do not interrupt the progress of the pustules by rubbing or scratching, which it is difficult to prevent when they are much older.

Some instances of the small-pox after vaccination have occurred, but probably not more frequently than after the old-fashioned inoculation. The fact is, that this disease does sometimes (though very rarely, like other eruptive fevers) attack the same person twice, of which I have known some undoubted examples; but it appears positive that, when the small-pox returns a second time, or comes after the cow-pox, it never is attended with any fatal consequences.

I do not offer any description of the cow-pox, as it is an artificial malady, and belongs entirely to the medical practitioner.

CHAPTER V.

THE MEASLES.

The measles is an epidemic and contagious malady, to which children are very liable; and which seldom returns a second time. In general, the younger they are, the lighter is the disorder; and when not attended with any complication, and the patient of a good form and constitution, there is little to dread. But to very delicate children, or the offspring of consumptive parents, it is often a source of danger; and even in its mildest form, it is always a malady which requires great care.

The first appearance of this disease is that of a cold, especially in the head; with sneezing, running at the nose, weakness and watering of the eyes, and sometimes a cough. This continues for several days, and is frequently accompanied with great peevishness, restlessness, and melancholy. If the measles be known to be in the neighbourhood when a child is in this state, it should be a reason for giving the lightest and most cooling nourishment; and more care should be taken to prevent the child from going out, or being fatigued, than is usually necessary for a cold in the head.

The leading symptom which distinguishes the measles from small pox and scarlet fever, even in the very beginning, is the apparent cold in the head; which is a never-failing attendant on this malady. The fever commences like other fevers, but the disease sometimes takes various forms, attended with symptoms which require the immediate aid of a physician.

The eruption usually begins to appear on the third or fourth day, in the form of spots resembling flea-bites, about the roots of the hair and other parts of the face; which, during the fifth, sixth, and seventh days, spread over the entire surface of the body, in large blotches which are rough to the touch, being raised a little above the skin; the fever, &c., not always diminishing (as in most eruptive maladies) after the spots begin to come out. Besides the usual symptoms of a cold, there is often at the beginning of measles, an inclination to vomit, (which should be encouraged,) and also to bleeding at the nose: these symptoms generally afford relief: and I have observed, that when the nose bleeds much, the eyes are not so liable to suffer from weakness afterwards.

As soon as the spots begin to appear, the child should be confined to bed, as warmth and repose assist the eruption; and, even when the malady is slight, the room should be darkened, as the eyes are always affected in the measles. This, with the addition of plenty of diluting liquors to drink, will, in many cases, be found sufficient, without the use of any medicine. Infusions of herbs, barley, rice, or water-gruel sweetened with honey or sugar, light lemonade, &c., should be given, as may be most agreeable to the child's taste. If there be a wish for food, barley, rice, stewed fruit, or jellies of fruit, and bread, may be allowed; but no animal food, nor any kind of fermented liquor.

When the cough comes on, a large piece of flannel over the chest will, sometimes, by keeping up a constant perspiration, prevent the necessity of more irksome applications; but if the eruption comes out very slowly, and the cough and difficulty of breathing increase, a sinapism to the chest may be of the greatest service; and I have seen it produce the most beneficial effects in less than an hour after it has been applied.

When the fever, cough, head-ache, &c., increase on the appearance of the eruption, it is a sign that the malady will be severe, and means must be sought to relieve the painful symptoms. The feet should be put into a sinapized bath; or, if the child seems weak, they may be fomented with flannels wrung out of hot water, with mustard and vinegar, which may answer the purpose as well as bathing, and be preferable on account of not fatiguing.

If there be reason to suspect a foul stomach at the commencement of the measles, a few grains of ipecacuanha may be given with advantage; and if the bowels cannot be kept free with clysters, a slight cooling purge may be administered; and this treatment will be found to promote rather than check the eruption.

To relieve the cough, there is nothing better than equal parts of oxymel of squills, syrup of poppies, and mucilage of gum-arabic, mixed together and given by a tea-spoonful at a time, now and then, according to the circumstances and the age of the child.

The air of the room inhabited by a child in the measles, should be kept of an equal and moderate temperature. Too much heat might possibly occasion a nervous fever; too much cold, an inflammation of the lungs. The bed coverings should not be increased in this, or in any other eruptive fever; as forcing a sweat either by clothes or medicines is very hurtful. Nothing should be employed for this purpose but plenty of warm drink; and infusions of aromatic herbs (sage, balm, elder-flowers, &c.,) are very suitable, if they can be rendered agreeable to the patient.

About the third or fourth day from the commencement of the eruption, the spots grow pale, in the same order as they first came out, and the skin begins to peel off in little scales; generally on the ninth or tenth day, the cough and other troublesome symptoms disappear: and, in about a fortnight from the first attack of the disease, the skin returns to its natural colour and no mark remains.

Sometimes the eruption begins to appear on the second day, and sometimes not till the seventh or eighth; and either of these deviations from the common course are reckoned unfavourable symptoms.

If the eruption suddenly grows pale and flat, it is a bad symptom, which would probably require the aid of blisters and camphor; but if a physician is to be had, he should be called immediately, as quite a different sort of treatment might be necessary, of which none but an experienced practitioner can judge. Weakness and delirium, (especially of the low muttering sort,) and great difficulty of breathing, are bad symptoms, which require immediate assistance: fomentations or sinapisms to the feet, and a blister to the chest, may be applied in this case, without waiting for the arrival of the doctor.

Sometimes there are *aphthæ* (or small white spots) in the mouth which are very troublesome, and make children unwilling to drink; but this is not an alarming symptom, and only requires the local applications already recommended for the thrush *.

There are cases of measles in which bleeding is of the greatest necessity, and others that require cordials, wine, &c., &c.: but these are remedies which cannot be employed without the advice of a professional man, as they may produce the most fatal consequences, if not used with extreme discrimination.

If the eyes are much inflamed and very painful, and especially if there be a violent head-ache, a child who has not yet been bled may have a leech applied behind each ear; but in case the child has been already bled, it will be better to apply two small blisters to those parts. Bathing or fomenting the feet will also be advantageous on such occasions.

For a violent pain in the chest or side, a sinapism to the part affected may be tried; but if that does not answer the purpose, and the child is very red and hot, with a full strong pulse, one or two leeches † may be applied to the spot where the pain is most acute.

The camphor mixture or julep might be given

---

* See page 78.

† Sometimes a leech will occasion extraordinary and acute pain; in which case it should be immediately taken off, (by putting a little salt on it,) and either that or a fresh leech applied a quarter of an inch from the wound already made.

without danger, by mothers or nurses in case of the eruption suddenly disappearing; but when this medicine is necessary, there are usually many symptoms which require the advice of a skilful physician, so that it is not likely to be administered without the orders of a medical man.

In cases of violent cough with acute pain, (in the chest or side,) excessive high fever, delirium, great difficulty of breathing, extraordinary stupor, or uncommon debility, a physician should be called in without delay, as there are various complications which may render this malady extremely dangerous, and which may be relieved by the immediate application of proper remedies. Sinapized baths, fomentations, or sinapisms may always be applied to the feet on such occasions with safety, and may sometimes keep off imminent danger till the arrival of the physician.

Sometimes children have the legs and hands, and even the face very much swelled, after the measles; for this, the best remedy is oxymel of squills, which may be given with an unsparing hand*: but if there be a cough, which this medicine appears to excite, it may be mixed with equal parts of gum-arabic mucilage, which will prevent

---

* No doubt it will be understood that the quantity should not be such as to excite vomiting. One, two, or three tea-spoonfuls, three or four times a day, according to the age of the child, violence of the symptoms, &c., &c.

this inconvenience and not diminish the efficacy of the remedy.

According to the manner in which a child has been affected by the measles should be the quantity of purgative medicine given afterwards. However, in general, *two* doses will be sufficient unless more be ordered by a medical practitioner. The opinion that "a person who has just recovered from the measles cannot be purged too much," is a dangerous error. A delicate child will be more injured by a purgative medicine too much than one too little; and a few days more of low diet and confinement to the house, is much better than a great quantity of medicine.

Notwithstanding all I have said to assist mothers, in the treatment of a malady which requires so much care, and in which the least neglect might be fatal, yet, I must again urge the necessity of immediately applying to a good physician in case of any extraordinary symptoms in the course of the measles, and still more when it has left after it any remains of indisposition; as it sometimes requires the utmost skill to prevent those chronic diseases, which often result from even the mildest species of this malady.

When a cough continues after the measles, it should not be disregarded as a thing which will wear off, but rather treated like an original disease.

It often happens that children do not regain their health entirely, for several months after recovering from the measles; and great care should be taken to guard against any other malady it may occasion, such as dropsy, scrofula, or pulmonary consumption, which have been known to follow it. If the disease have taken place in autumn or winter, it would be prudent to put on a flannel waistcoat next the skin, and worsted stockings; as the best means of preventing subsequent maladies is to keep up the natural perspiration. But should the weather be warm when the child recovers, the use of flannel might be oppressive, and do more harm than good: however, the greatest care should be taken to avoid damp, cold, and draughts of wind, for a long time after the measles; the feet should be kept particularly warm and dry, and the slightest indisposition examined with attention. Children sometimes look pale and ill, for a considerable time after the measles, without having any real malady; and I have known this sickly appearance continue several months, and then go off without any bad consequence.

Great care should always be taken in returning to the usual habits of life, both with regard to diet and exercise; and it is much better to restrain a child for a few days more than is absolutely necessary, than to run the risk of those complaints which may follow the slightest imprudence after the cure of the measles.

Those parents who can afford it would do well to remove children who have had the measles severely, in the latter end of summer or autumn, to a warmer climate before winter.

CHAPTER VI.

SCARLET FEVER. — SLIGHTER MALADIES OF THE SAME NATURE.

The SCARLET FEVER is an epidemic and contagious malady, which in its simplest state is a complaint of little importance, and requires only care and a strict diet to bring it to a conclusion, without the aid of medicine: but when attended with complicated symptoms, as frequently happens, it becomes a very formidable disease. It is one of those maladies to which the human frame is supposed to be only once liable *, and the younger children are, (after the accidents of teething are over,) the less they suffer from the scarlet fever.

The scarlet fever attacks children (like other maladies of the same nature) with uneasiness, lassitude, peevishness, weight and pain in the head, and frequently vomiting. The eruption usually appears on the second day of the fever, when the skin becomes covered with little red spots, which

---

* I have, however, read and heard of the scarlet fever returning, but have never seen an instance of it, though I have known several of small-pox and measles.

show themselves first on the face, and spread by degrees over the whole body, till it becomes almost entirely of a bright red colour; the arms and legs in general being swelled. Sometimes the fever diminishes when the eruption appears, but more commonly it continues as before. There is sometimes a cough, and great redness of the eyes, at the commencement of this disease, but they are quite different from those of the measles: the cough has not the appearance of catarrh, and the eyes are not much offended by the light.

On the sixth day, the eruption grows pale, and by degrees disappears; and on the seventh or eighth day, the skin begins to peel off in large scales; and, at the same time, there are sometimes profuse sweats or diarrhœa, and much sediment in the urine.

If there is reason to believe, at the commencement of this disease, that the stomach requires cleansing, a few grains of ipecacuanha may be given; or perhaps if there be an inclination to vomit, and the child is old enough to listen to persuasion, some warm drink to encourage the vomiting may be sufficient. There is usually an uneasiness in the throat, from the beginning, which should be gargled or syringed (according to the child's age) with some cleansing gargle.

In general the treatment of this disease is the same as that of the measles, except that, in the scarlet fever, the drink may be more acidulated, as there is not the same danger of exciting a cough. Great care must be taken to keep the bowels free with clysters and aperient drinks; for purgative medicines should not be given, in this malady, without the order of a physician.

The same regulations in regard to the temperature of the child's room should be observed in this disease as in the measles; but, if the weather be warm and dry, a door or a window may be left open for a few minutes once a-day, to change the atmosphere of the apartment; and the greatest care should be taken to keep it clean, a matter of considerable importance in all contagious maladies.

When the scarlet fever is accompanied with a severe ulcerated sore throat, it is very dangerous, and requires the advice of a physician; and, should there be a violent head-ache, or any stupor or delirium, he should be called in without a moment's delay. If, on account of distance or any other cause, the medical practitioner is likely to be retarded, the malady should not be neglected till his arrival. The throat may be gargled or syringed, the feet bathed or fomented: and in case of the head being much affected, a blister may be put on the back of the neck, without fear of reproof from the physician. A sinapism may also be applied to the throat.

Inhaling the vapours of hot water and vinegar, or decoctions of herbs, has been recommended for the sore throat, and may be of use where not attended with inconvenience; but, if a child has a severe head-ache, or is very weak, this may be too fatiguing, and in that case it would be better to syringe the throat and apply a sinapism at once.

Bleeding is sometimes necessary in this malady, and at other times bark and wine; but it requires profound medical knowledge and great judgment to determine when such remedies are to be employed; so that no one but an experienced physician should prescribe them.

When the inflammation of the throat is very great, local bleeding with leeches, or the application of a blister, may be necessary; the former will perhaps give more immediate relief than the latter, but a blister may be more safely employed, without the advice of a medical man, than any sort of bleeding; and as the quantity of blood drawn by leeches is uncertain, and the bleeding sometimes difficult to stop, it is better not to apply them in this disease without the order, or (at least) the permission of a physician. Still less is it to be allowed to those who have not studied medicine to administer wine or any other cordial. There is, however, a remedy frequently prescribed where there is great depression, weakness, and a low pulse, which may in some cases, be given without waiting for the presence of a medical practitioner, and this is camphor. But when this medicine is necessary, the symptoms are, usually, such as to require the immediate advice of a physician: if by any accident he should be delayed, blisters, sinapisms, and camphor julep* may be employed, both in scarlet fever and in measles, and indeed in any feverish disorder, when accompanied with lowness of spirits, weak pulse, stupor, quiet delirium, and other marks of debility; more particularly, if they occur in consequence of an eruption having suddenly disappeared.

When scarlet fever is mild, a little care and attention, a few days' confinement to bed, and plenty of warm acidulated drink, will be sufficient to cure it; but when severe, the greatest medical skill may be required to save the patient's life; and when the malady is quite over, the orders of the physician should be implicitly obeyed, as it is frequently after the scarlet fever that the greatest dangers occur.

When the disease has been so slight as not to have required the attendance of a professional man, the greatest care should be taken for some time afterwards to enforce a strict diet, and to avoid all risk of getting cold. It would also be prudent to give two or three moderate doses of calomel and rhubarb, with an interval of five or six days be-

---

* See Appendix: *Camphor.*

tween them, before the child be allowed to return to its usual course of life. Warm clothing and nourishing food are necessary after the cure of this malady, and some bitter infusion (such as bark or quassia in good white wine) should be given for some weeks.

There are great varieties of scarlet fever as well as of measles, and though I have only thought it necessary to describe the regular form, yet it is right to mention that the first attack is sometimes very sudden, and requires immediate medical assistance. I have known a child of twelve or thirteen years old, with a good appetite, and every appearance of being quite well at dinner-time, who, in less than four hours afterwards, was affected with violent head-ache, sore throat, vomiting, &c., which were followed by the worst sort of scarlet fever. When the symptoms are thus sudden and severe, a physician should be called without delay, as it is a rapid disease; and the distance between perfect health and imminent danger may be only three or four days.

It is easy to distinguish between scarlet fever and measles, at least in their regular form. In the scarlet fever, the eruption usually appears on the second day; in the measles, on the fourth. In the scarlet fever, it is of a bright, in the measles, of a dark colour; also the redness of the former is spread more over the entire skin than that of the latter; and, in the measles, the skin is more rough to the touch than in the scarlet fever. After the measles, the skin peels off in little scales, but after the scarlet fever, it comes off in large pieces. Besides these differences, the appearance of severe cold in the head is peculiar to the measles; and, indeed, the character of each of these maladies is so distinctly marked, that any person who has once observed the progress of the two diseases, is not likely to mistake the one for the other.

In one respect the scarlet fever perfectly resembles the measles; the danger is not over with the disease, the consequences of which are often worse than the malady itself.

Improper treatment in either measles or scarlet fever, such as keeping the patient's room too cold or too hot, giving meat and fermented liquors, &c., may render a disease dangerous which would, otherwise, have been slight.

Swelled legs, and swellings of the glands of the throat, are usual after the bad sort of scarlet fever. They require medical advice and much care, but with proper attention are easily conquered.

There are many more diseases of this nature, but they are comparatively trifling; and I refrain from further details as unnecessary in a work of this sort; the directions already given being sufficient for all sorts of eruptive fevers, (whether chicken-pox, nettle-rash, erysipelas, &c., or one of those maladies which have no appropriate name,) if they are slight; and if they are accompanied with *extraordinary* or *dangerous* symptoms, the advice of a physician should be sought without delay.

CHAPTER VII.

COLDS AND COUGHS.

There is no malady more frequently disregarded (both in children and adults) than a COLD; and there is none which may lead to worse consequences when neglected. The general cause of this complaint is the perspiration being checked, either by exposure to a current of air after exercise, sitting in damp clothing, especially on the feet, or sleeping without sufficient covering.

The symptoms of a cold require no description; they are not doubtful; and those diseases which in their commencement resemble it, viz., measles, hooping-cough, or croup, cannot be augmented by being treated in the beginning as a cold, nor can any bad consequences result from mistaking the one for the other during the first few hours.

There is no better remedy for a recent cold than a warm bath for the feet, composed of salt and water for very young children, and for those who are old enough to explain their sensations, water with mustard and vinegar in it. The best time for using this is on going to bed at night. The heat of the water should be rather more than that of new milk; and when mustard* is used, the bath should be sharp enough to make the feet a little red, after being in it a quarter of an hour. If the child can be persuaded to bear it for twenty minutes it will be better, but no coercion should be used on the occasion; every thing that causes vexation (except in very extraordinary cases) does more harm than good. This remedy is useful in all sorts of colds, as it draws the blood from the head, throat, and chest; and there are various diluting liquors, which, taken hot in bed after it, will carry off a recent cold in four-and-twenty hours. Barley or rice water, with honey and lemon-juice, lemonade, currant-jelly and water, infusions of various herbs, such as balm, sage, elder-flowers, hyssop, sweetened with honey or sugar, and perhaps there is nothing better than (what I have seen used with great success in the south of France) bran-gruel, sweetened with honey, and sharpened with a few drops of good vinegar. If the throat be sore, a bit of flannel should be put round it, which may be cut away by degrees when the child is recovered.

It is much better to clothe children warmly, give them strong shoes, and let them go into the fresh air, when the day is fine, than to shut them up in the house for a slight cold; but this need not

* See Appendix.

prevent the administration of remedies necessary for the cure of that species of indisposition. There is no symptom of a cold which may not be benefited by putting the feet into a warm bath and going to bed immediately afterwards. For head-aches*, sore throat, sore eyes, cough, difficulty of breathing, this is always a safe and a useful remedy; and I have often found it of great service to children both for tooth-ache and ear-ache, which so often proceed from a slight cold, or partially checked perspiration.

In case of a severe cough I know of no better medicine than the oxymel of squills, syrup of poppies, and mucilage of gum arabic†, already advised in treating of the measles. When the sleep is interrupted either by violent fits of coughing, or that slight obstinate cough which sometimes lasts for hours, there is no remedy so efficacious as a clyster of *seven* or *eight* drops of laudanum, in about an ounce of tepid water, which should be given by a small syringe, very gently, so as not to stimulate the bowels to reject it. The quantity of laudanum must be more or less, according to the child's age and the effect that it produces: what I

---

* It is to be observed, however, that if a head-ache proceeds from indigestion, too much bile, or any other foulness of stomach, the bath will have no good effect; and the complaint is not likely to be removed without vomiting or purging.

† See Measles, p. 201.

have specified is for a child of five or six years old; but if it be necessary to continue the remedy long, it must be increased by a drop at a time; and when the cough is cured, the laudanum must be left off by one drop every night; for if it be discontinued all at once, the child will not rest well. I have had great experience of this remedy, and can answer for its beneficial effects. Laudanum administered in this way is perfectly safe, and does not affect the head or stomach.

But with regard to children's coughs, if they occur in winter, or in a cold climate, the first remedy to be tried is *warmth;* and covering the chest and feet with flannel, at the same time that fires are made in the rooms they inhabit, will frequently cure the first autumnal catarrhs of children, which, if neglected, might last with more or less violence during a considerable part of the winter.

Oily medicines should not in general be given for children's coughs, and the white emulsion, which used to be so often prescribed for them, has been sometimes hurtful. There are remedies in abundance without having recourse to oils; and those which strengthen the stomach, such as infusions of aromatic herbs, &c., with plenty of sugar, are to be preferred; especially as it frequently happens that coughs are occasioned or augmented by indigestion or worms. Barley-sugar, refined liquorice, sugar-candy, and many other things which come from the confectioner's shop, are very good for coughs, but they are sometimes attended with inconvenience; for children, finding the remedies given for this complaint very agreeable to the palate, repeat the cough without necessity; and as this may produce bad consequences, it must be put a stop to immediately. The best method I know of effecting this, is for the persons about a child in such a state, to remark that " as the malady seems to be growing worse, it must have some more powerful remedy;" then to make a strong decoction of horehound, and give a table-spoonful, *without sugar*, every time the child happens to be seized with a fit of coughing. It is an excellent medicine, and one which gives no encouragement to force a cough. I have employed this expedient more than once with success.

When a cold is accompanied with fever, the low diet recommended for that complaint is requisite; and for bad coughs the same precaution is necessary; care, also, should be taken that children do not eat too much at a time of any sort of food.

Children are subject to various kinds of symptomatic coughs, which are to be cured by removing the maladies which occasion them. That which belongs to teething, being usually nervous, must be treated as a convulsive malady; that which proceeds from indigestion or worms, requires first a purgative medicine, and afterwards bitter infusions;

and the best remedy I know, when a cough comes on immediately after a rash has disappeared, is sulphur, taken in a very small quantity, every night at bed-time: I have known a cough cured by this medicine in a fortnight without the eruption returning.

CHAPTER VIII.

THE HOOPING-COUGH.

The hooping-cough is a malady both epidemic and infectious; and one of those which do not return a second time. It is right to defend children from it as long as possible; for it is more dangerous the younger they are, and is particularly so to little infants. Though a disease of terrific appearance, yet it is not usually attended with danger to children who are well formed and healthy, unless some accidental cause, neglect, or mismanagement, should occasion it to be complicated with other maladies.

It begins like a common cold; and, after some days or weeks, is first marked by that peculiar sound which distinguishes the disease, and which proceeds from the difficulty of recovering the breath after it has been lost by the prolonged cough. Some medical writers assert that it is over in a month; but instances of that sort must be rare, as it generally lasts from three to six months, and sometimes even a whole year. It is very infectious, and children apparently perfectly recovered, on being removed for change of air, to a distant village, have been known to communicate the disease to the inhabitants of that place. For this reason, great care should be taken to prevent young and delicate children from approaching those who are but lately recovered from this malady.

When the hooping-cough is slight, it requires little medicine; but the diet should always be particularly attended to, as any thing heating or difficult of digestion may augment the disease. The greatest care should also be taken to prevent children who have the hooping-cough from getting cold; but they should not be confined to the house, (when there are no feverish symptoms,) unless the weather be such as to render it absolutely necessary. They should be well covered when they go out; and if the season is not warm they should wear flannel, which, in very cold weather, ought to be next the skin. Their feet should be kept particularly warm; and might be put into a sinapized bath once or twice a week, or at any time that there appears an augmentation of the malady.

If there be any stuffing in the chest, an emetic of ipecacuanha should be given; and a little of the same powder once or twice a week, (oftener if necessary,) in so small a quantity * as not to produce vomiting of itself, but to assist it when excited by the violence of the cough, may be found useful.

* A quarter, or half a grain, (according to the age,) two or three times a-day.

The state of the bowels should be attended to; and, if they cannot be kept moderately free by stewed fruit, honey, broths with vegetables, &c., it would be right to give now and then enough of infusion or syrup of rhubarb to produce one or two evacuations: but a child, who has the hooping-cough, should never be purged without the orders of a physician, as the malady, being in a great degree nervous, is likely to be increased by debilitating remedies.

When there is great redness of the face, difficulty of breathing, or much fever, a professional man should be immediately consulted, as bleeding or blistering may be necessary to prevent dangerous consequences; and when extraordinary symptoms of any sort appear, medical advice should be sought without delay, for a malady which complications often render fatal. The appearances, however, are sometimes alarming to mothers when there is in fact no danger: a discharge of blood from the nose, mouth, or ears, unless violent, is not to be considered as a bad symptom; and vomiting is always a good sign, especially if the child recover immediately after the fit of coughing, and has good spirits and a great appetite. Care should be taken not to indulge the inclination for food too far; and the quality of the child's nourishment should be particularly attended to. When the disease is slight, and no complication threatens, it is not necessary to prohibit meat, though it should be given more sparingly than usual: wine and fermented liquors should in general be avoided; but to children who have been accustomed to such things, a very little wine in water may be allowed; barley-water, however, or currant-jelly and water, &c., would be preferable, if plain water be not thought sufficient for common drink.

Children with the hooping-cough should be kept as tranquil in their minds as possible, for anger or fear are likely to bring on fits of coughing, in a malady which affects the nerves so much. When the patient is very delicate, or of a consumptive family, the first suspicion of hooping-cough should be a reason for calling in a physician, as both the violence and the duration of the disease should be diminished as much as possible; and there are a variety of remedies to which an experienced medical man will have recourse on such occasions.

The violence of the hooping-cough may be diminished by slight emetics and opiates, and its duration shortened by frequent change of air, especially if it be from a cold to a warm climate.

Neither purging nor bleeding should be employed in this malady, without good medical advice, though the latter is sometimes absolutely necessary. Local bleeding is, generally, best adapted to children (and delicate people); and in case of any sudden inflammatory attack on the chest, during the hooping-cough, leeches applied to that part may be of use.

In the absence of the physician, if a difficulty of breathing should occur, a sinapism may be put on the chest*, (as directed elsewhere,) and the feet bathed; but these are temporary remedies, which should not be relied on entirely. There are a great variety of medicines for the hooping-cough, not necessary to be specified here, as the disease, when severe, requires medical advice to adapt them to the particular circumstances. I cannot, however, refrain from inserting (though against a rule I had laid down not to recommend any preparation of antimony) a prescription which I have used in the cure of great numbers of children, with invariable success†. It consists of two grains of kermes mineral‡, and six grains of purified nitre, with an ounce of simple syrup: the powders should be put into a phial with a small tea-spoonful of water, and shaken until they appear thoroughly mixed, when the syrup should be added; and every time the medicine is given, it should be *carefully shaken before pouring it out*. The quantity is from *half a tea-spoonful to a whole tea-spoonful*, three or four times a day, according to the age of the child, the

---

* See page 183.

† I have been induced to insert this remedy by the cure of an infant, lately, who caught the hooping-cough a few days after its birth. Half an ounce more of the syrup was added to the medicine, and a quarter of a tea-spoonful was the quantity given at once.

‡ See Appendix.

violence of the cough, and the effect it produces, which is often imperceptible and evident only by a diminution in the symptoms of disease; and great care should be taken to give very little at first, as the kermes mineral is a powerful and uncertain medicine, which acts violently on some constitutions. It is necessary to pay great attention to the effects of this remedy, as it sometimes affects the bowels more than is suitable for the cure of the hooping-cough, although in general it only keeps them in a proper state.

Young children should sleep with the head very high, and should be raised up and leaned forward whenever they are taken with a fit of coughing: indeed, it is recommended on such occasions, to all who have the hooping-cough, to stand up and bend forward, as the posture in which it gives least pain.

When this malady, after the first week, is accompanied with fever, it is an unfavourable symptom, and would require the advice of a physician; but when there is no fever or other bad sign, there are many harmless things which a mother or a nurse may give to children without asking the permission of a medical man. Asses' milk, when it agrees with the stomach, is an excellent remedy; hyssop tea, or syrup of hyssop, coltsfoot, and pennyroyal, may also be given: decoction, or rather jelly of Iceland lichen, (which may be made very palatable by putting a great deal of sugar and some juice of lemon or orange in it,) is very suitable; as are also fruit, jellies, and jams.

Nourishment is necessary in a disease which lasts so long; but it is of the greatest consequence that the nourishment be adapted to the state of the malady; when that is the case, much medicine may be spared; and in this disease, (I might say in all diseases,) the less that can be given to children the better.

Maladies are not so much under the command of drugs as those ignorant of the science of medicine suppose; and patients are more likely to be cured of their complaints who take too little than too much medicine. When a great quantity has been administered, the sick person has first to recover from the original disease, and afterwards from the debility occasioned by the remedies, in many instances an unnecessary addition.

CHAPTER IX.

SORE THROATS.

THE SORE THROATS of children are most commonly the effects of cold, but not always: they are sometimes the consequences of bile, and sometimes of epidemic diseases. These different sorts of sore throats require different modes of cure, but none of them can be increased by being mistaken for a cold, and treated as such in the beginning; that is to say, with warm baths for the feet, flannel round the neck, and warm diluting liquors. This treatment will generally remove the sore throat proceeding from a cold very speedily; but the others require the aid of medicine.

A sore throat, which is caused by redundancy of bile, will have occasion for emetics or purgatives, perhaps both; and that which arises from epidemic contagion must be treated according to its peculiar nature, of which no one can judge but a physician, who has had opportunities of seeing the effects of the disease on various individuals. For this reason, it would be right to seek good medical advice for both these sorts of sore throats, especially as it might be hurtful to mistake the one for the other, if they should require contrary methods of cure, as is sometimes the case.

The moment a child complains of a sore throat, a piece of flannel should be put round the neck, the feet bathed at bed-time, and some warm acidulated liquor given before the child goes to sleep. Lemonade, currant jelly, or syrup of raspberry, vinegar and water, or honey and water, with a very few drops of good vinegar, would be suitable for this purpose. If the child is not better next day, and has evident symptoms of a cold, confinement to the house may be necessary, and the same remedies may be repeated at night. A little bit of black currant jelly, or a tea-spoonful of honey, with two or three drops of vinegar to sharpen it, may be given four or five times a day; and if the child is old enough to gargle, barley (or plain) water, with honey and a *very* small quantity of vinegar, (if there be much it will irritate and do mischief,) may be used for this purpose as often as appears necessary*.

In any violent or sudden attack of sore throat, the advice of a professional man should be immediately sought for; but in case of his arrival being delayed, and the malady accompanied with head-

---

* There are many other suitable gargles, but I mention this as the simplest and easiest to provide. I have lately heard milk recommended as an excellent gargle by an eminent physician.

ache, flushed face, great heat of the skin, and difficulty in swallowing or breathing, a large blister may be applied to the throat or chest (whichever seems most affected); the feet may be put into a sinapized bath, or be fomented; at the same time, the child should be persuaded to drink plentifully of acidulated diluting liquors. This treatment may sometimes give relief very speedily, but that should not be a reason for neglecting to consult a physician, as other remedies might be necessary to complete the cure, and prevent a relapse.

After a child has recovered from a bad sore throat, it will be prudent to keep the neck covered for a long time, especially at night, and on going out, if the weather be cold; as it is a malady which leaves the part so weak that those who have had it are liable for a long time to slight returns of sore throat, even when the greatest care is taken. Children who are old enough to gargle, may derive benefit from an infusion of bark, with a few drops of vinegar in it, or water with a little brandy; which are to be used cold, merely to strengthen the part after the malady has been completely cured. In leaving off flannel, or any other covering which has been employed to keep the throat warm, care should be taken to do it by slow degrees, and not till the warm season.

For that sort of slight sore throat, in consequence of cold, which occasions a swelling of the tonsils, without any great pain, head-ache, or fever, it is not necessary to teaze a child with gargling, as it will be sufficient to apply a piece of flannel to the part, and bathe the feet at night. The flannel should not be fastened round the neck, but put under the chin, and drawn up over the ears so as to cover them entirely, but not go higher up, as it is very unwholesome to heat the head of a child. By having the flannel of a proper length, and making two holes in each end of it, a bit of narrow ribbon may be used to fasten it, by tying on the top of the head, instead of letting the flannel be so long as to have the two ends of it meet. The external swellings may be rubbed, now and then, with a mild soap liniment *, which will help to cure it speedily; but this is only for swellings occasioned by a cold, as any thing of the nature of scrofulous tumours should have no outward applications, except by order of a physician.

Children subject to sore throats should have the feet kept very warm, and should be particularly guarded against sitting in wet shoes and stockings. Slight sore throats recurring frequently, and lasting

* Prepared by dissolving as much scraped soap as three ounces of boiling water can melt, and then adding to it an ounce of camphorated spirit.

a long time, would require the advice of a professional man, as they may proceed from an inclination to scurvy, or some other chronic malady, which ought not to be neglected.

CHAPTER X.

THE CROUP.

THE CROUP is one of the most formidable maladies to which children are liable: it is not considered a contagious disease by medical writers, (though there seems to exist in some families a predisposition which favours that supposition,) but it is often epidemic, and the state of the atmosphere is usually the principal exciting cause of it. Cold, damp seasons, such as produce epidemic catarrhs, are supposed to occasion the croup; and some physicians have expressed their opinion, that leaving the bosoms and arms of children bare, in cold weather, is likely to cause this malady.

The croup is a violent inflammatory disease, which begins with symptoms of a slight cold a day or two before the extraordinary sound of the voice and cough, which peculiarly distinguish it from all other maladies, is observable; but when once that appears, all the heat and restlessness of fever, with a quick full pulse, and difficulty of breathing (but not of swallowing) come on rapidly. When the disease becomes severe, it is generally recollected that it had been preceded by a cold so slight as to have been disregarded. It is a great error to neglect the least appearance of indisposition in a child, when we consider how rapid in their progress, and how fatal in their effects, are some of those very diseases, which may be prevented or lightened by extreme attention in the beginning.

The slightest cold should immediately bring to our recollection the ideas of croup, quinsey, and inflammation of the lungs, and we should be on the watch to check their progress, or diminish their violence. I do not mean to say that a child should be confined to the house, and treated as if it was sick, for every trifling cold; but it will certainly be prudent to bathe the child's feet before it is put to bed; and after it is asleep, to observe attentively whether the breathing be natural, or whether there be any extraordinary appearance about it.

In case of any difficulty or wheezing sound in drawing the breath, it would be right to give an emetic: if the uneasiness is not great enough to disturb the sleep entirely, it may be delayed till morning: but if the child is wakeful and restless, it should be given immediately. Syrup of squills, with ipecacuanha powder, is a very proper medicine for young children, and if the complaint be slight, may possibly remove it; but if the vomiting occasioned by it does not procure speedy relief, a physician should be instantly called, lest the malady should be the croup, and require more active remedies.

Bleeding, blistering, antimonial emetics, and strong purgatives, are frequently necessary in this disease; but as they should not be employed without the orders of a medical man, I shall give no directions respecting the administration of such remedies.

It is difficult to distinguish, and impossible to describe, the particular sound of the croup, which has been compared to the crowing of a young cock; but those who have once heard it are not likely to be deceived. Those who have not heard it should be on their guard against mistaking for it a sort of hoarse, croaking cough, to which some children are liable on getting even a slight cold, and which is usually of little importance, (requiring only the common remedies,) though it has sometimes been turned into a serious malady by being treated as the croup. For this and many other reasons, the slightest suspicion of the croup should be a motive for seeking the very best medical advice, to avoid the risk of creating disease by injudicious management.

It sometimes requires a great deal of judgment to distinguish between croup and nervous asthma, especially when those about the patient are prepossessed with a notion that the disease can be no other than the croup; and there is no case in which it is more dangerous to trust to persons of little experience, as the debilitating treatment necessary for the croup is very different from that required in nervous asthma.

There is no malady in which it is more necessary to act with implicit obedience to the attendant physician than in the croup, as the rapidity of its progress allows no time to retrieve errors or atone for neglect; and nothing but the most active remedies can preserve the life of the patient.

The slightest uneasiness in the throat or the chest of a child should be immediately attended to, as it is not impossible that this dreadful malady, as well as some others of the same nature, might be checked in the first stage, by bathing the feet, covering the throat and breast with flannel, and diminishing the quantity of food. An emetic of ipecacuanha may be safely administered to a child of any age who appears to be threatened with inflammation of the throat or chest, but antimonial vomits should not be given without the orders of a physician. Children vomit with more facility than adults, but it is difficult to prevail on them to drink sufficiently: this difficulty is much increased when they are required to swallow camomile tea, or other nauseous liquids: but these are by no means necessary, as warm water with sugar in it, or weak tea, will answer the purpose as well, without being so disagreeable to the patient. In this malady (and indeed in all other maladies) children should be teazed as little as possible.

It appears certain that children who have once had the croup are very liable to returns of it, for which reason they would require particular attention. Their throats, chests, and arms, should be protected from the cold air, their feet should be kept very warm; and it would also be prudent to have accurate directions from the physician, by whom they have once been cured, respecting the precautions to be used for preventing a return of the disease, and the mode of treating it, in case of any sudden attack.

CHAPTER XI.

THE MUMPS.

THE MUMPS is an epidemic and infectious disease, supposed to be one of those which do not return a second time: it requires little medical aid, but very great care.

It consists in a swelling of the glands about the throat and neck, sometimes at one side only; but more frequently at both, often increasing to a prodigious size, and being always accompanied with more or less fever. About the fourth day it is usually at the height; from that time gradually decreases, and in a few days more disappears. If not increased by neglect or imprudence, it is a complaint of little importance; but if a child who has the mumps is exposed to cold, the malady may take a very serious turn, and require the aid of a physician, which should be sought without delay, when any *extraordinary symptoms* appear.

The object in the cure of this disease must be to encourage both general and local perspiration; the former by keeping the child in bed, and giving plenty of warm diluting liquors; the latter by covering the parts carefully with soft flannel or fine wool thoroughly heated.

The proper diet is that prescribed for acute diseases in general, and the bowels should be kept moderately free by clysters or the mildest laxative medicines.

After the malady is completely over, it may perhaps be right to give a purgative medicine before the patient returns to the usual habits of life; but this must depend on the constitution of the individual and the manner in which the disease has appeared.

In countries where this malady particularly prevails, a stranger would always do well to consult a physician resident in that place.

CHAPTER XII.

DIARRHŒA.—DYSENTERY.—CHOLERA MORBUS.

A DIARRHŒA or LOOSENESS, in which there is a considerable discharge from the bowels without pain, is often a malady * of small importance, requiring no medicine; but merely strict attention to the diet and general habits of life for a few days. If a child, who is attacked by this complaint, has been accustomed to meat and fermented liquors, the quantity of these should be much diminished; but, as it often happens that indispositions of this nature are accompanied with a very good appetite, such food should be provided as may satisfy hunger, be of easy digestion, and afford sufficient nourishment. Broths, jellies, sago, rice, &c., may be allowed, but vegetables and fruit would be better avoided: should there be wind in the stomach or bowels, lemon-peel or ginger-tea may be given. The greatest care should be taken that the child be not exposed to damp or cold; and the diet should

---

* The looseness which occurs after tedious maladies is of quite a different nature and generally proves fatal: the advice of a skilful physician may, however, be beneficial.

R

still be attended to for some time after the diarrhœa is cured.

In this malady, it is sometimes necessary to give medicines immediately. If a diarrhœa be violent, and continue more than one day; or if it be accompanied with loss of appetite, but especially if there be much pain in the bowels, there should be no delay in administering the appropriate remedies. The least sickness of the stomach indicates the necessity of an emetic, and there is nothing so well adapted for this purpose as ipecacuanha. A dose of rhubarb should be given on the next day; and if that does not entirely remove the looseness, small quantities of rhubarb * and ipecacuanha may be given for a few days. At the same time, the child should drink plentifully of rice water, sweetened with very white sugar, which is one of the best remedies possible in all bowel complaints to which children are liable.

Diarrhœa may be produced by many causes; such as indigestion, cold, worms, bile; and according to the origin of the disease, must be the mode of treating it. That which is occasioned by indigestion will, probably, be removed by the above-mentioned remedies: a diarrhœa brought on by imprudent exposure to cold or damp may be cured by

* One grain of rhubarb and half a grain of ipecacuanha, two or three times a day, may be given to a child nine years old.

lying in bed, bathing the feet, and drinking warm diluting liquors, to recall and promote the checked perspiration; but if that be not sufficient, rhubarb and ipecacuanha (as already directed) may be given. When worms or bile have occasioned the looseness, a purgative medicine should be immediately administered; castor oil, when it can be procured good, is one of the best for this purpose; but when that cannot be obtained, some preparation of rhubarb may be employed. To a child, who is old enough to be reasonable, a dose of powdered rhubarb, with magnesia, may be given; but for little children, probably syrup or infusion of rhubarb would be more suitable.

Some children are liable to have the bowels affected whenever they are vexed: this is occasioned by too much bile; and generally cures itself by the evacuation of that substance; but it requires great attention to the diet, and if accompanied with much pain, some mild purgative. In bilious complaints, which are usually attended with fever, a low diet is necessary; but if there appears to be much nervous irritation, a few drops of spirit of hartshorn or of ether may be administered. It is scarcely necessary to add, that children of this constitution should have their minds kept as tranquil as possible, the frequent recurrence of these complaints tending to weaken the bowels.

If, notwithstanding the treatment here recommended, a diarrhœa continues undiminished for several days, it would be right to consult a physician, who might be able to discover the cause of the disease, and prescribe the proper remedies; for astringent medicines are sometimes necessary, and it is impossible to say when they can be administered with safety and advantage, unless the exact state of the particular case be known. Persons who have the care of children should always remember that there are no medicines so dangerous as those which suddenly stop a diarrhœa.

The DYSENTERY is an inflammatory disease of the bowels, which is frequently epidemic and contagious, but it may be produced by damp clothing or improper food. It is often occasioned by sudden changes of the weather from heat to cold, by which the perspiration is rapidly checked; and this is the variety of the disease to which children are most exposed. In countries where figs abound, it is often the consequence of eating too much of that fruit; but in northern climates, there is not, I believe, any sort of ripe fruit which can produce this effect; though it frequently results from eating rancid food, such as bad bacon, butter, or fish; unwholesome substances, which children, tolerably attended to, are not likely to partake of.

The distinguishing marks of dysentery are fever, pain, and a constant inclination to empty the bowels, with little effect. The evacuation in this malady is of various sorts, more generally blood and mucus than any thing else: sometimes there is a great discharge of blood, sometimes very little; and not unfrequently there is mucus only, without any blood, though the vulgar name of *bloody flux* sometimes leads into error on this subject. There is little or no evacuation of the usual excrements; and when they do appear, it is generally in the form of sheep's dung, mixed with mucus and blood.

In *diarrhœa*, there is great evacuation from the bowels, with comparatively little pain, and seldom any fever: in *dysentery*, the pain and fever are great, but the evacuation small. The pains in *diarrhœa* are severest just before the bowels are emptied, and are relieved by it; those of *dysentery* are sometimes much worse after than before. *Diarrhœa* is often cured without any medicine, a thing which rarely, if ever, occurs in *dysentery*.

When there is an epidemic disease of this sort in the neighbourhood, on the slightest derangement of a child's bowels, it would be right to apply remedies, and, if convenient, to consult a skilful physician.

The dysentery is frequently accompanied with an inclination to vomit, which should be promoted by a few grains of ipecacuanha (a medicine particularly useful in this malady); and the next day it would be right to give some purgative, as this is a disease which cannot be cured without thoroughly clearing the stomach and bowels. Good castor oil*, or some preparation of rhubarb, may be employed for this purpose; and after the desired effect has been produced, the bowels should be kept in a free state, until the pain and other bad symptoms are removed. A drink † made by dissolving cream of tartar in barley water has been recommended, strongly, by one of the best writers on this subject; and as the disease is usually attended with great thirst, it is a remedy easily administered, when made palatable with a great deal of sugar and a little lemon peel. The same author advises that almond milk should be drank plentifully, and when it agrees with the stomach this is likely to be useful, both as medicine and nourishment.

Clysters are of the greatest benefit in this malady, as fomentations to the inflamed bowels, and should be composed of mucilaginous substances, which may blunt the acrimony of the bile, such as rice water, with gum arabic dissolved in it, or the same gum mixed with milk, decoction of linseed, &c. Oily clysters are very useful when there is no discharge of the natural excrements, but only blood and mucus; and they may be given with infusion of

---

* Or oil of sweet almonds, for young children. See Appendix.

† See Appendix, *Cream of Tartar drink.*

camomile, when the patient is troubled with wind in the bowels.

This disease, being of an inflammatory nature, is frequently accompanied with severe pain in the head, for which the feet may be bathed or fomented, as directed for other maladies; and as it is of the greatest consequence to promote perspiration, the child should be kept in bed; and when obliged to be raised up or moved, the greatest care should be taken to guard against any possible impression of cold.

When the fever is high and the discharge of blood great, a physician should be immediately called, as bleeding or blistering (perhaps both) might be necessary to check the inflammation.

Extreme cleanliness, and changing the air of the apartment, is as necessary in this disease as in eruptive fevers; and, by attention to these particulars, the contagious quality of it may be greatly diminished.

When the stomach and bowels have been well cleared, small doses of rhubarb and ipecacuanha (as directed for diarrhœa) may be given; or, if there appears to be much fever, cream of tartar may be used instead of rhubarb.

As there is a necessity for a great deal of drink in a malady of this nature, it should be varied and adapted to the taste of the child. Rice water, sweetened with white sugar and acidulated with a little lemon juice, is one of the best things that can be given; barley water, and thin arrow root or salep, prepared in the same manner, are very suitable; also linseed tea, if agreeable to the patient: currant-jelly and water, and toast and water, may be allowed; and gum arabic may be dissolved in balm tea, and given from time to time.

No sort of animal food or fermented liquor should be allowed in this disease, unless positively ordered, by a physician, on account of some extraordinary symptom. Perhaps there is no malady in which the absolute prohibition of these substances is so necessary as in this, in which there is an internal inflammation, which may easily be rendered fatal by any error in diet.

Rice, sago, salep, arrow root, with sugar and lemon or orange juice, may be given; and various sorts of fruits, such as strawberries, raspberries, gooseberries, currants, apples, grapes, &c., may be allowed, provided they be perfectly ripe, and such as have agreed with the child when in health; but great care must be taken to observe if any sort of food produce wind: and should raw fruit be found to have this effect, it may be stewed with sugar, and a small bit of lemon peel or cinnamon added. Stone fruit, except peaches, would be better avoided; and every sort of food should be given in small quantities at a time.

If any perspiration appear, great care should be taken not to check it; and, therefore, nothing should be given quite cold while it continues; for this reason, any fruit that the patient may eat during that time should rather be stewed or roasted than raw.

When all inflammatory symptoms have ceased, and there is no longer head-ache, thirst, uncommon heat in the skin, nor pain in the bowels; and the frequent necessity for emptying them appears to be merely the result of habit and weakness, laudanum may be given in a clyster, (as directed for a cough*,) from five to thirty drops, according to the age of the child and the effect produced.

A child who has just recovered from a bad dysentery should not be suffered to go out without wearing flannel next the skin; and the greatest care should be taken to keep the feet particularly warm and dry: all cold and damp should be avoided, and the diet particularly attended to for a long time, as the malady is easily renewed, by the slightest neglect or error. Good broths and roasted meat, in moderation, rice boiled in milk with a little cinnamon, sago, salep, &c., with a small quantity of good wine, if the child has been accustomed to fermented liquors: ripe fruit and vegetables, of easy digestion,

* See page 218.

may all be allowed with safety; but all greasy substances, and whatever is heating or difficult of digestion, should be prohibited.

It would be well to give two or three grains of rhubarb every day, for some weeks after the cure of dysentery; and if the child complains of any uneasiness in the stomach or bowels, a purgative dose of some preparation of this medicine should be immediately administered. Moderate exercise, at proper hours, will assist much in restoring the strength; but both morning and evening damp should be carefully avoided.

There are various sorts of dysentery, which it would be superfluous to describe, as the treatment here recommended can do no injury in any; and when extraordinary symptoms or complications occur, a medical man should be consulted without delay.

If a child be attacked by severe vomiting and purging, *accompanied with violent pain*, it may be suspected that the disease is CHOLERA MORBUS, a malady so extremely dangerous, and rapid in its progress, that although not one to which children are liable, yet, as it might occur, I think well to mention it here.

Many causes* may give rise to this disease; but

---

* The eggs of certain fresh-water fish are sometimes capable of producing this effect. I have seen a violent cholera morbus occasioned by those of the barbel.

the most likely cause is indigestion, or excess of acrimonious bile, which unfavourable weather sometimes occasions. Be the cause what it may, the evacuation from the stomach and bowels should, at first, be promoted by drinking plentifully of weak chicken broth or camomile tea, or, indeed, any watery liquor that the child finds easiest to swallow. Clysters should also be administered, of rice water, chicken broth, or linseed tea; and when the stomach and bowels have been well cleared, means must be taken to check the vomiting. Balm tea is sometimes useful for this purpose, or lemonade without sugar; but the most efficacious remedy (allowable without the orders of a physician) is the saline draught*, sweetened with syrup of white poppies, and given in a state of effervescence.

The child should be put into a well-heated bed, have the feet warmed as directed for the ague †, and a piece of flannel dipped in warm camphorated spirits ‡ and laudanum, may be applied to the stomach.

This is one of those maladies in which the assistance of a medical man would be *immediately* required, as there are various remedies which an experienced physician might, on seeing the patient, be enabled to apply with effect.

After this malady is quite cured, the greatest at-

---

* See page 113.   † See p. 186.   ‡ See Appendix, *Camphor*.

tention is necessary to prevent a relapse: the diet should therefore be very strict, and all cold and damp should be carefully avoided, as well as all vexation and agitation of mind.

CHAPTER XIII.

HYDROCEPHALUS.

HYDROCEPHALUS (or Water on the Brain) is one of the most fatal maladies which can affect a child; and it frequently happens that the propensity to it is not suspected till an acute fit of the disease destroys the patient, though there may have been numerous preceding symptoms to give warning of what might be apprehended.

Head-aches in children of any age should never be neglected, especially if violent and of frequent recurrence. Parents get accustomed to this sort of malady, and one often hears people say, "It is only worms," or it is "only an indigestion;" or, perhaps, that "the child inherits the complaint;" which is, therefore, disregarded until dropsy of the head suddenly appears, with all the signs of imminent danger.

When a child is subject to frequent pains in the head, a good physician should be consulted without delay, and more particularly if the head-aches have been preceded by a tendency to maladies of debility, or there is any reason to suspect a scrofulous taint in the blood. The same constitution to which this last disease belongs has, generally, an inclination to hydrocephalus, which has often been developed by blows on the head, or by the imprudent cure of eruptions.

When there is reason to suppose that water is collected in the head, bleeding and purging are generally necessary, and these would require the best medical advice: in fact, hydrocephalus is one of those maladies in which, when once developed, nothing can be effected without the aid of a physician, though much may be done to counteract the predisposition to it.

Symptoms of this disease (especially in very young children) are often mistaken for those of other maladies; and it has sometimes happened that indispositions occasioned by water on the brain have been ascribed to teething or worms, which do, indeed, frequently offer appearances so similar as not to be distinguished but by a very experienced physician.

Languor, sleepiness, heaviness of the head, vomiting, aversion to light and noise, especially if accompanied by sudden fits of screaming, are to be considered as symptoms of hydrocephalus: but a squint* coming on suddenly, or the disappear-

---

* To spare unnecessary alarm to young mothers, I think it right to mention here, that new-born infants frequently squint before they have learnt, by experience, how to use their eyes.

ance of one which has hitherto been habitual; in short, any extraordinary change in the natural position of the eyes, is one of the strongest characteristic signs of water in the head. The best medical advice should be sought without delay, whenever the above-mentioned symptoms appear; as the malady may sometimes admit of a cure, if attempted in time, and with sufficient skill and energy.

The means to be used for preventing this fatal malady are the same which are advised for scrofula* and rickets; and, in addition to these, the sinapized bath for the feet (so many times recommended in the course of this work) should be frequently used. This should be, instantly, resorted to in the case of a child being attacked with acute pain in the head, without waiting for the arrival of the physician; and, if he cannot be expected for several hours, (as so often happens in country places,) a dose of calomel may be given; and whatever evacuations the child has, in consequence, should be kept, as a skilful practitioner may draw much information, respecting the nature of the disease, by inspecting what has passed from the bowels.

The pupils of the eyes being much enlarged, and not contracting in the usual way on the approach of light, is considered as a strong symptom

* See chapters xvi. and xvii.

of hydrocephalus: it may, however, be occasioned by worms; but, at all events, it is a proof that the brain is greatly disordered, so that whatever can draw the blood and humours from that part must be advantageous: for which reason baths and fomentations for the feet should not be neglected.

I do not mention the medical applications requisite for the cure of this malady, as they are not likely to be employed with any good effect, except by a professional man of much experience and sound judgment. It should be remembered, that there is no disease in which the orders of the physician should be more strictly obeyed than this of hydrocephalus; and particular care should be taken that the child's evacuations be not thrown away, when he has desired that they should be preserved for him to see.

Hydrocephalus, though one of the most difficult maladies to cure, is by no means out of the reach of medicine; and the earlier assistance is sought for, the more likely it is to be effectual. This disease is of two sorts, the chronic and the acute; and it is in the former that medical advice is most likely to be of use, and most frequently neglected. In the acute hydrocephalus, the symptoms of disease are so violent, that a physician is sure to be called, though it seldom happens that he can be of any use. However, parents should not quite despair in such cases, as this is one of those maladies in which a professional man will exert all his knowledge, experience, and ingenuity; and of late years some children have been recovered from this dreadful disease.

CHAPTER XIV.

CONVULSIONS.

Convulsions are unnatural and involuntary movements, which may generally be known even by a person who sees them for the first time. They frequently affect the whole body, but are often confined to one part; and any sudden distortion of the head or eyes of a child may be considered as a convulsion.

Numerous and various are the causes which occasion convulsions in children: those who are born with very large heads, as well as those who are extremely delicate, are particularly liable to them. Even the strongest constitutions may be attacked by this malady in consequence of teething, worms, or eruptive fevers; but many other causes may excite convulsions in weak and sickly children; such as fear, cold, and pain, either internal or external. Unless in these latter cases, this disease does not come on suddenly: there are many preceding signs by which an observing person may be induced to suspect its approach. Disturbed sleep, a frightened look, crying in the night, heaviness in the day, momentary changes of colour, grinding the teeth, shutting the hands fast with the thumb inside, stretching the legs out stiff, are some of the signs which should put people on their guard against convulsions.

Sometimes children preserve their senses entirely in a fit of convulsions, and at other times lose all knowledge of every thing around them. This is a malady which has always occasion for the advice of a physician; and the persons about the sick child should be very particular in describing to him every circumstance which has occurred, with truth and accuracy.

The only remedies which may be employed without the orders of a medical man, are the tepid bath, clysters, slight emetics, purgatives, spirits of hartshorn and camphor julep. Bleeding, blistering, bark, wine, opium, &c., are often necessary; but the judgment of a good physician is requisite to distinguish the cases in which such remedies should be prescribed.

The first remedy for all sorts of convulsions is the tepid bath*: those which have been brought

---

* Children from five to nine months old may be put into the warm bath for ten minutes two or three times a day, if necessary; those of a year old, and from that to three years old, may remain in the water a quarter or half an hour at a time.

on by a fright, without any other cause, will require only the bath, and a few drops of spirits of hartshorn in cold water, both of which (but especially the latter) may be repeated three or four times in the course of twenty-four hours, if it should appear necessary.

Convulsions occasioned by indigestion or by worms, would require a purgative medicine as soon as the warm bath has put a stop to the spasmodic movements; and if they seem inclined to return after the stomach and bowels have been well cleared, recourse must be had to spirits of hartshorn.

Sometimes very young and delicate children are thrown into convulsions by wind in the bowels, and for this the best remedy (after the warm bath) is a clyster of camomile flowers, or of water, with about fifteen drops of tincture of assafœtida, more or less, according to the age of the child and other circumstances.

When convulsions are known to arise from some indigestible substance recently taken into the stomach, the best thing would probably be a few grains of ipecacuanha. In very young children, acidities are capable of producing convulsions, and for these magnesia and rhubarb are the best remedies. To cure convulsions perfectly their cause must be discovered; for though the warm bath is the first resource in all cases of convulsions, yet the subsequent treatment of the disease must depend upon the occasion of them.

A violent-tempered, or a drunken wet nurse, may cause a child to have convulsions, and the milk should undoubtedly be changed when such a circumstance is discovered. A mother who has defects of this nature, and cannot command herself sufficiently to overcome them, should not attempt to suckle her children.

Convulsions have often been produced by repelling an eruption; and the proper cure for this species of the disease is, evidently to recall the complaint to the surface of the skin with warm baths externally, and sulphuric medicines * internally. If this cannot be effected, it is probable that a perpetual blister, an issue, or a seton, would be the most suitable remedy; but the advice of a professional man would be necessary to determine in such a case.

Every family of children should be provided with a convenient vessel for the warm bath; and also with one for the feet, of such a size and form that a sufficiency of water to cover them above the ancles may be procured in a few minutes. In all convulsive maladies, the immediate application of

* There are various remedies for this purpose, not necessary to mention here, which a physician would order.

remedies is of great consequence; at the same time, those who are about children on such occasions, should be cautious never to appear in a hurry or a fright: a quiet manner of doing every thing for them is of much importance, and a child subject to convulsions should be always attended by a woman of good sense and presence of mind.

Convulsions sometimes increase at the first moment of the child being put into the warm bath, but diminish soon after, so that mothers need not be alarmed at this appearance. Sometimes children have an extreme aversion to the bath; and in that case they should not be forced into it; but bathing the legs and feet only, or fomenting the whole body, must be substituted.

There is no disease in which the assistance of a physician is more necessary than convulsions; but there is none in which it is more frequently requisite to do something before his arrival. The moment a child of any age is taken with convulsions, all the clothes should be loosened, and (if there be not good reason against doing so) a window should be opened, to let the fresh air into the room: a warm bath should be prepared as quickly as possible, and in the meantime, if so much hot water can be had as is sufficient to foment the feet and legs, that should be done without delay: vinegar may be held to the child's nose, and a bit of linen, wet with vinegar and water, may be applied to the forehead. These are all things which can do no harm, and may help to shorten the fit of convulsions.

Opium should not be given to children, particularly in convulsions, without the advice of a physician; but, in case of any extraordinary delay in obtaining medical assistance, after the stomach and bowels have been well cleared, either tincture of castor, spirits of hartshorn, or camphor julep may be safely administered; four or five drops of the two first, or a spoonful of the last. Ten or twelve grains of camphor, well rubbed with the yolk of an egg, and mixed with a sufficient quantity of water for a clyster, may be given with good effect. But there is no use in tormenting children with remedies for those convulsions which come on at the end of violent or tedious maladies, as the cure of such is hopeless.

Those convulsions which have been occasioned by vexation or terror, require particular attention to the moral feelings; at least as much as medical assistance. The patients should be soothed and tranquillized by all possible means, or they will derive little comparative benefit from antispasmodic remedies.

Convulsions which precede the measles, or other eruptive maladies, are not dangerous, and, in general, only require to foment the feet, and to keep the child very quiet.

Tooth-ache or ear-ache may occasion convulsions: in both these cases, the feet should be bathed: for the former, warm milk and water, with a little nitre in it, or warm water with brandy, may be used to wash the mouth; and for the latter, a few drops of warm milk, or of oil (it should be *rather* more than blood-warm) may be put into the ear, and afterwards a little bit of cotton heated at the fire *. The ear and jaw should be covered either with a piece of hot flannel, or (what I have sometimes found more beneficial) a thick layer of cotton, large enough to cover the whole ear and all the adjacent parts, and tied on with a muslin handkerchief: probably fine wool might be still better adapted to this purpose.

To cure convulsions perfectly, the precise cause of them must be discovered, and this is sometimes very difficult to do, even with the aid of a clever physician; chiefly, because the persons about children are not sufficiently observant of the various symptoms, which may have appeared before the convulsions. If they have been occasioned by the impression of too great a degree of cold, the tepid bath will probably give instant and effectual relief, so as to render the employment of medicine superfluous.

It is not necessary to specify here the various

---

* If this should not be sufficient, two drops of laudanum with three of warm oil may be tried.

maladies of this nature, as they may all be comprised under the head of convulsions; and all require immediate assistance, great attention, and good medical advice. The best mode of preventing convulsions is to give children a great deal of air and exercise, to keep the bowels sufficiently free, to have much regard to the moral feelings, and, in case of any cutaneous disease, to have it slowly and prudently cured, and not driven in by the injudicious application of external remedies. Great care should be taken to avoid all the causes within our power; and to meet those which are beyond our power with proper remedies and presence of mind. It is certain that children, who are treated according to the directions given in this book, will avoid many causes of convulsions.

A child who is threatened with epilepsy has generally a frightened and astonished look, is inclined to be melancholy, and has its sleep interrupted with sudden cries and causeless terrors. Fear, surprise, or anger are capable of exciting convulsions or epileptic fits in delicate children. In the last-mentioned malady they lose their senses entirely, and usually foam at the mouth; and when this is the case, it is still more necessary to consult a skilful physician than in other species of convulsions. The leaves of orange or of lemon plants, made into tea, are considered as very proper for children who are liable to convulsive maladies, especially epilepsy; and may be made very palatable by the addition of a great deal of sugar: but when there has once been an attack of this disease, it would be prudent to have the advice of a professional man with respect to diet as well as medicine.

CHAPTER XV.

WORMS.

In all indispositions of children, after they are weaned *, there may be reason to suspect the presence of WORMS. The symptoms of this malady offer a combination of those belonging to many others; and it sometimes requires a great deal of experience and discrimination, to ascertain the real nature of a disease which assumes such a variety of forms.

Vomiting, diarrhœa, sharp pains in the stomach and bowels, swelled belly, irregular appetite, the face pale but sometimes flushed, fetid breath, difficulty of breathing, head-aches, coughs, pains in the limbs, disturbed sleep, extreme peevishness, running at the mouth, hiccough, itching of the nose, swelling of the upper lip, grinding the teeth and starting in sleep, convulsions, and fevers of various kinds, are amongst the symptoms occasioned by worms.

* It sometimes happens that children have worms before they are weaned, but as this is not a common occurrence, the malady cannot be considered as one belonging to sucking infants.

A very red tongue, or a red stripe down the middle of the tongue with the sides foul, is a sign of worms; as is also the point of the tongue being very red. Children subject to worms have generally the pulse more or less intermittent, the pupils of the eyes are sometimes much enlarged, and the skin under the eyes is of a dark colour; the bowels are irregular, and the urine often appears as if it was mixed with milk.

A certain number of these symptoms united together gives great reason to suppose the existence of worms; but it sometimes happens, that many of them are to be met with where there are no worms, and at other times where worms do exist, several of these signs are wanting. Children have passed worms without shewing any of the most decisive symptoms previous to their evacuation: the fetid breath, which is considered as one of the most positive and universal signs of worms, has sometimes been wanting; and I recollect to have known an instance of a child, about a twelvemonth old, passing one of the long round sort, without ever having lost the very sweet breath which belongs to sucking infants in health.

After the time of dentition, it becomes easier to distinguish the indispositions which proceed from worms; but while children are cutting their teeth, those about them should beware of ascribing every morbid symptom to that cause, as many are afflicted with worms before two years old.

It has been said by many medical writers, that whenever a child is ill, there is reason to have suspicion of worms, which is very true in regard to some constitutions; but it is necessary always to keep in mind, that the same symptoms, which arise from worms, are also frequently the indication of more dangerous diseases. Many children have died of water on the brain, whose pale faces, constant head-aches, want of appetite, disturbed sleep, &c., have been ascribed to worms; and others, suffering under that debility which proceeds from a scrofulous constitution and mesenteric obstructions, have had their complaints disregarded, because nothing was supposed to be the matter with them but "worms, which their elder brothers and sisters had also suffered from and outgrown." For this reason, it would always be right to consult a good physician when such symptoms appear.

Improper food, or too great a quantity of even what is wholesome, may be generally considered as the cause of worm diseases; and were the diet of children, during the first four or five years of their lives, more strictly attended to, such complaints would be much less common than they are. Worms are easier to prevent than to destroy, and one means of doing this is to take care that infants do not eat fruit or vegetables till they are weaned.

It is probable, that by unremitting attention to the food of young children, worm maladies might be altogether avoided; but as this is seldom paid, and as most children are liable to such indispositions, it is very necessary to know how to treat them.

The mode of curing these complaints is, first to expel or destroy the worms, and then, by strengthening the stomach, to prevent their re-production. A variety of remedies for the former purpose have been recommended; but after repeated trial of a great number, I have found calomel the most simple, active, and easy to administer. The quantities must be proportioned to the age and the constitution of the patient, but *in general* till eight or nine years old, as many grains as a child has years may be given with safety: however, those parents who have the means of consulting a good physician, should not fail to seek his advice on such an occasion.

The time I have found best for giving calomel is at night on going to bed; and some children require a purgative medicine next day to make it pass off by the bowels: castor oil is very suitable for this purpose, but perhaps some preparation of rhubarb might be still better. *Neither acids nor vegetables should be given for several hours before calomel, lest it should occasion pains in the stomach and bowels; nor, for the same reason, should food of that nature, nor even cold drink, be allowed the next day, until the medicine has been worked off; and great care should be taken that a child to whom calomel has been given, be not exposed to damp or cold for the next four-and-twenty hours.* It is of little consequence, in the first instance, to ascertain whether the symptoms of a foul stomach, &c., &c., which appear to be the effect of worms, are really produced by that cause, the object being to clear the stomach and bowels of something which deranges the system: be that what it may, a dose of calomel is the best remedy that can be administered.

I have sometimes had occasion to observe, that there are cases in which calomel is more effectual for destroying worms when it does not purge; and therefore, where the nature of the malady is perfectly known, and purgative medicines have been tried without entire success, I would recommend to give a *small* dose of calomel two or three times, at intervals of three or four days, and afterwards castor oil or rhubarb: but what *is* a *small* dose can only be known by experience, as three grains will have more effect on one child than double that quantity on another of the same age. It often happens that the dead worms are not expelled till several days after the medicines have been taken, and then possibly without being observed; so that their destruction is to be inferred only from a cessation of the symptoms occasioned by them.

The same debility of stomach which gives rise to violent worm diseases may possibly be the cause of others of a different sort; and I have sometimes suspected it to have occasioned glandular obstructions when they have appeared in children who had no hereditary title to scrofulous maladies. Fevers are often produced by worms; but worms are also produced by fevers, being the effect instead of the cause; so that a malady is not to be called a worm fever, because in the course of it worms have been evacuated. I mention this as it has sometimes happened, that in consequence of a child having passed worms, in a fever to which the attendant physician has given another name, the parents have lost all confidence in the man of science, and placed their dependence on quack remedies and the prescriptions of the ignorant. An indigestion will sometimes assume the appearance of a worm fever; and I have seen all the most positive signs of this malady removed by a dose of calomel, which produced an evacuation of the undigested substances that occasioned them.

When by the use of calomel, or any other medicine, the worms have been destroyed, and all symptoms of their presence have ceased, the object must be to strengthen the stomach, and by that means to prevent their reproduction. This is to be effected by every thing that can fortify the constitution of the child: bark, iron, rhubarb, and infusions of bitter and aromatic herbs, (hyssop, wormwood, pennyroyal, camomile, &c.,) also animal food and wine, much air and exercise, in some cases sea-bathing; and in short every thing necessary to conquer debility: at the same time, the diet should be strictly attended to, and no excesses of any kind permitted.

Even the ripest fruit and best vegetables should be given in smaller quantities to children who have suffered by worms than to those who have not; and the greatest care should be taken that they do not eat too much of any thing at one time, or at irregular hours. It sometimes however happens that children, who are greatly afflicted with worms, have sudden fits of hunger at extraordinary times, and on these occasions it would be dangerous to prohibit food. I have known a child of two years old scream dreadfully for something to eat in the middle of the night, and at the same time complain of a pain in the stomach, which was immediately appeased by food. When this symptom appears, a piece of bread should always be kept in the child's bed-room, to give in case of necessity; but if worms produce such an effect, the malady must be so severe as to require medicine, and a few grains of calomel will probably suffice to remove this troublesome symptom.

Sometimes a child appears to be almost choaked by worms rising in the throat; and for this, a simple and secure remedy is cold water with as much salt as can be dissolved in it, two or three spoonfuls of which will immediately drive down the worms. Indeed, common salt is an excellent vermifuge, and if children could be persuaded to take it in sufficient quantity (dissolved in broth) to produce the effect of a purgative, it would often answer that purpose as well as any other medicine.

Sulphur, camphor, and assafœtida are all useful in maladies produced by worms; and there are above a hundred remedies advised, which may all have good effects at various times and in various circumstances; but there is none so sure, and so well adapted to most cases of worms as calomel.

In some coughs occasioned by worms, I have found sulphur beneficial*: it may be given in honey after the child is in bed for three or four nights, even if it should slightly affect the bowels. There are, however, other coughs produced by the same cause, but arising from irritation of the nerves, which would require antispasmodic remedies; and for these assafœtida is well adapted, being a vermifuge as well as a nervous medicine. Clysters of assafœtida are often useful for complaints produced by worms, especially when they have excited convulsions.

Convulsions occasioned by worms ought, in the

* See Appendix.

first instance, to be treated like all others, that is to say, with the tepid bath; afterwards calomel and assafœtida may be given together, in equal quantities, proportioned to the age of the patient. Clysters of warm milk have been found very useful in pains of the bowels caused by worms; and indeed, for the small thread-like worms, (*ascarides*,) which belong to the lower bowels, these sort of remedies are particularly adapted. I have known instances of children of nine or ten years old having derived benefit from salad oil and lemon juice mixed together, in the quantity of a table spoonful of each, given, on an empty stomach, for ten or twelve mornings; and I have seen the camphor julep of use in slight spasmodic maladies produced by worms.

In giving strengthening food to children, care should be taken that neither the quality nor the quantity be such as to occasion fever, an effect likely to produce or augment that debility which is one of the chief causes of worms. There is a vulgar prejudice against the safest of tonic remedies and most agreeable of nourishing substances, *sugar*, which is very commonly believed to promote the formation of worms in the human body; but that it can do no harm is evident by the impossibility of producing an indigestion with plain sugar; and, since the middle of the last century, many experiments, made by eminent physicians, have proved it to be *an admirable remedy for worms*. Had I not been already convinced by their assertions, the following instance, which has fallen under my own observation, would go near to establish the truth of their opinions in my mind. A child of eleven months old, attacked by an epidemic dysentery in the midst of a very difficult dentition, was reduced to such a state of debility that her powers of digestion seemed to be lost, as every thing she swallowed passed through her unchanged. To procure her some sort of nourishment, she was allowed to eat as much sugar as she pleased, for which her instinctive propensity was so strong that she used to consume many ounces both by day and night. The malady continuing for several weeks, the child acquired such a habit of devouring sugar that it was a long time before she could be broke of it; indeed it continued in a great degree for several years, and in case of illness her favourite drink has always been sugar and water. She is now a healthy child, about seven years old, and never has had the slightest appearance of worms, though others of the same family have suffered much by them. This instance may serve to corroborate the opinion of those physicians * who have ascribed an

---

* By the information of a friend (whose veracity as a man, and skill as a physician, are both of the highest class) I am enabled to give another example of the advantages of sugar, in the case of an elderly man, afflicted with worms to a great degree, who, after every other remedy had been tried in vain,

anthelmintic power to sugar; and is at least a tolerable proof that this substance, so agreeable* to the palates of children, is not likely to produce worms.

There is no malady for which a greater variety of remedies are recommended than for worms: but mothers are earnestly entreated to avoid *all patent medicines, old women's secrets, and prescriptions of quacks.* If the advice given here produces no diminution of the complaints, or so little as not to afford consolation, a good physician should be consulted immediately, who may point out the mode of treating that particular case, and distinguish the nature of those maladies with which the worm disease may happen to be complicated, and in which either neglect or the use of quack remedies might be fatal.

In treating of the cure of worms, I only mean the long, round worm, (*lumbricus,*) which in shape and size resembles the common earth-worm, and the small worms like threads (*ascarides*); for when the tape-worm (*tænia*) exists, the aid of the most skilful professional men is absolutely necessary; as well as for all those uncommon worms the descriptions of which are to be met with in medical books.

when reduced to a desperate situation, was restored to health by the use of that substance in large quantities.

* I never saw but one child who disliked sugar, and he was a miserable looking being, thin and yellow, and suffered much from worms.

CHAPTER XVI.

SCROFULA.

There is no disease in which so much can be effected, by early and unremitting attention, as Scrofula; and it is of the utmost importance for mothers to be aware of the first symptoms of that malady, and acquainted with the means of preventing its approach, and checking its progress.

Diseases considered as hereditary, and therefore not feared by those who know that they are not in the blood of their families, may easily be acquired, and sometimes come on suddenly without any apparent cause*. Scrofula is one of those

---

* I cannot refrain from making some observations here on the strange prejudices which many inhabitants of the British islands entertain on the subject of a malady for the cure of which there are so many resources, and which is not more an hereditary disease than others less within the reach of medical assistance. Persons who make no scruple of confessing that they have lost a number of near relations by pulmonary consumption, would yet be capable of leaving a physician in a dangerous state of ignorance, rather than acknowledge that they had any reason to suspect a scrofulous taint in their blood. There are other maladies equally to be dreaded, which are also hereditary; but this one appears to have an unreasonable and absurd mark of ignominy annexed to it, which some-

maladies which may appear spontaneously in any delicate child, under circumstances favourable to its development, and of which the slightest symptoms should be combated without delay.

Scrofulous complaints usually appear between the ages of two and seven years: delicate, relaxed constitutions, and those which have been debilitated by previous maladies, (difficult teething, worms, measles, small-pox, &c.,) are most liable to be attacked by them. Fair, fat, light-haired children, with blue eyes, are generally supposed to be subject to scrofula; but this indication does not appear to be so sure in the northern parts of Europe, where many of the strongest individuals come under that description; though with respect to southern climates, it seems to be a just remark; as, however, the assertion has been made (without any exception) by medical writers of authority, children of this complexion should be particularly attended to; at the same time that parents should not be lulled into security, by seeing their offspring with dark eyes and dark hair, and without that delicate skin which is generally supposed to belong to the scrofulous constitution. I have seen the disease

---

times occasions parents to deceive even themselves, and neglect complaints that are more to be assisted by the preventive part of medicine than any others, and therefore more in the power of a mother to conquer by early and constant attention to her children.

make great ravages in families where there was not one member of them with a fair skin, light hair, or blue eyes; and, in fact, it may be produced in almost any child by mismanagement; by low, damp, and dark habitations, food not sufficiently nourishing, a sedentary life, and privation of the amusements and open air necessary to the happiness of children. To these, perhaps, may be added another cause, in the too frequent administration of purgative medicines, especially mercurial preparations*, which are often given to children by persons entirely ignorant of their nature and ultimate effects.

The best mode of preventing the development of a disease which requires the greatest attention to the physical education, is to take care that children inhabit dry and airy rooms; that they have warm clothing, nourishing food, and a great deal of exercise in the open air: they should not be debarred from the light and heat of the sun, except in cases of weak eyes, or for other substantial reasons; and they should be indulged in every thing that can exhilarate the mind, as there is nothing more likely to prevent glandular obstructions than that quick circulation of the blood which is produced by gaiety.

When there is any reason for suspecting an ori-

---

* Almost all the *patent medicines* and *quack remedies*, which are prescribed for *worms*, contain *mercury* in one form or another.

ginal taint of scrofula in the constitution, or any acquired propensity to the disease, the slightest appearance of debility should be a reason for resorting to the use of tonic remedies, such as sea-water baths, (tepid or cold, as may be most agreeable to the child's feelings,) infusions of bark, bitter and aromatic herbs, and the different preparations of iron. Children who are liable to scrofula, should be allowed meat as soon as they can digest it, and also wine and spices, which would otherwise be unsuitable to their age.

If a child of any age is observed to grow dull, languid, and indolent, the cause should be immediately enquired into, and these symptoms ought not to be neglected, as is too often the case: for it not unfrequently happens that the persons who are about children find them less troublesome at the commencement of chronic maladies than when in perfect health; and do not discover, till too late, that what conduced to the convenience of their attendants was only the sign of a disease, productive in its progress of far more uneasiness to them than the most boisterous vivacity. The moment a lively child begins to grow quiet, the greatest attention should be paid to find out whether this quietness does not threaten indisposition; and every means should be employed to exhilarate the mind and excite to bodily exercise.

At the beginning of scrofulous maladies, children

usually grow pale, and often complain of being tired without cause; the appetite and the general functions of the body become irregular, the spirits variable, the face, and especially the upper lip, appears swelled, and the jaws are more than naturally full. On perceiving any of these symptoms in a child of three or four years old, it would be right to examine whether there is any enlargement of the glands under the jaws and chin, under the arms, or about the groins; and if there be, no time should be lost in applying the proper remedies. The chief of these is the sea-water warm bath. Should it, however, be inconvenient or impossible to procure this immediately, a bath of common salt and water (of which any one who has ever tasted the sea can judge) may be substituted; and though many of the component parts of the sea-water are wanting, yet, from the effects produced by this remedy, there is every reason to believe that common salt is the most efficacious. I particularly wish to recommend this artificial sea-bath, because it often happens that, when a physician orders something for a child, which the parents cannot procure, they give up the case as lost, and totally disregard his advice, when it might be possible to substitute a remedy almost as good as that which he has prescribed.

The bath prepared with common salt may be had every where, and does not require to be changed so often as the sea water; once in five or six days is sufficient, whereas the sea-water should be fresh twice a week. The temperature should be about that of new milk, a little more or less, according to the difference of constitutions; as that which might be too warm for one might be too cold for another. It should, however, be as cool as the child can bear with satisfaction; but great attention should be paid to suit it to the particular feelings of the individual. Too hot or too cold a bath might occasion debility and also the risk of catching cold, either by causing too much perspiration, or by giving a chill; but when the temperature suitable to the child is once ascertained, it would be right to mark it by a thermometer, and always have the water heated exactly to that degree. The directions which I have already given about the precautions * required in warm bathing are not necessary to be repeated here, but should always be attended to. The child should begin with a bath of ten minutes, and increase by degrees, so as to remain at least three quarters of an hour in the water, if it be found to agree; but great care should be taken that the length of time does not fatigue or vex the child, which might counteract the good effects of the bath. Children of all ages generally like going into tepid water, and if they happen to be impatient of staying in it the necessary time, means should be found to amuse them, by singing, telling stories, or making

* See page 68.

paper boats to swim in the bath. If *the moral feelings of children were more attended to, medical prescriptions would be seldomer necessary and oftener efficacious*. Every thing that depresses the spirits or irritates the temper must be injurious to constitutions inclined to maladies of debility.

Children disposed to scrofulous complaints require little medicine; but strict attention should be paid to their manner of living; they should have as much air and exercise as they can bear without fatigue, and the most strengthening and nourishing food. The greatest attention should be paid to their digestive powers, which are sometimes very weak, and it frequently happens that things which would appear the best adapted to them, do not agree with the peculiar state of their stomachs. Strong broths and jellies are amongst the aliments one would be most inclined to recommend; but they will sometimes disagree and occasion fever. Sago, salep, arrow-root, &c., which are prepared with wine, sugar, and lemon juice, where they agree with the stomach and please the taste, are excellent food for children inclined to debility. Eggs are generally suitable to children, and coffee and chocolate may often prove medicinal to those of a relaxed, delicate constitution*. Chocolate in substance will agree with stomachs which cannot bear it mixed

---

* I must explain that the chocolate meant here is that which is made with sugar, and without any mixture of fat, flour, &c., in short, such as is usually to be met with in Italy.

with hot water, and a piece of this with bread, and a glass of cold water after it, is by no means a bad breakfast for a weak child. Good bread, well fermented and well baked, is considered, by many eminent physicians, as more proper food for children inclined to scrofula than unfermented farinaceous substances, such as barley, oatmeal, &c., &c.: but I am convinced that if they take sufficient exercise, this last-mentioned sort of food, in moderation, will not hurt them.

The irregularity of bowels to which children threatened with scrofula are liable, should, if possible, be remedied by changes in the diet, &c.; but, when medicine is found to be absolutely necessary, the various preparations of rhubarb are preferable to any other. In case of worms or indigestion, a dose of calomel may be occasionally administered; but rhubarb is the only substance of a purgative nature which can be given frequently without injuring the stomach. Magnesia is also a safe medicine, and in case of acidities, may be joined to rhubarb with advantage. And here I must observe, that when a child is subject to habitual constipation of the bowels, it is by no means sufficient to apply the temporary remedy of an opening medicine; but the cause of this indisposition should be sought after, as it may proceed either from some error in the child's food or habits of life, or from some incipient malady which would require medical advice.

Children who are inclined to scrofula, are generally very subject to acidities, for which rhubarb and iron are the best remedies. Small quantities of magnesia will usually relieve this symptom immediately, but the others are more efficacious in preventing the return of it; indeed, they are the medicines chiefly to be relied on at the commencement of this disease and when it is not hereditary. The irregular fever and white tongue will generally be removed in a short time by the proper use of these medicines; and the nervous irritation, which sometimes prevents children in this state from sleeping, may be calmed by a few drops of spirits of hartshorn or of æther, in sugar and water, after the child is put to bed: but these last are remedies which should be only occasionally resorted to.

Among children who are inclined to scrofulous maladies, some are very intelligent, and others quite the contrary: the former should not be encouraged to learn too soon, and the latter should be taught late and slowly. Amusing exercise should be the great object of both, but care should be taken to avoid fatigue. They should have all those toys which excite children to use their limbs, and in dry weather should be as much as possible in the open air. Swinging is an exercise particularly adapted for them, especially as it may be so contrived, by fixing a seat with a back to it on the rope, that a very weak child may have a great deal of motion without fatigue, and in the house as well as out of doors.

When delicate children cannot have much exercise, or are obliged to live in climates where bad weather often confines them to the house, their bodies should every day be rubbed all over with flannels which have imbibed the fumes of frankincense, benzoin, amber, &c. In summer, their beds should be exposed to the sun, and in winter heated by a warming-pan, in which a little of one of the abovementioned aromatic substances have been burnt. Scrofulous children should never be allowed to suffer from cold, (indeed it is injurious to all children,) and particular care should be taken to change their clothes according to the season.

With regard to the instruction of children threatened or afflicted with diseases of debility, it is of the greatest consequence that they should be taught by persons who will treat them with gentleness, and neither irritate nor terrify them, but especially the latter. There are no painful moral sensations so injurious to children of this constitution as *fear* and *shame*. Anger irritates the nerves, and promotes the morbid secretion of bile, but does not depress the spirits and check the circulation, like feelings of terror and shame; and for this reason it is more hurtful to children inclined to glandular obstructions to be frightened and mortified than to be enraged. They should be guarded as much as possible from every sort of moral pain, but more especially from such as retard the course of the blood: for this reason they should never be left with persons likely to treat them with contempt, or to frighten them with severe threats or practical jokes.

There is a scrofulous disease which does not shew itself in swellings of the external glands, though it has all the general symptoms already mentioned, and requires the same treatment; I mean that which particularly attacks the *mesenteric* glands*, and is often disregarded until too late, the large belly which belongs to it being common to many maladies of children, and, in fact, if not accompanied by other corroborating symptoms, being no proof of a scrofulous complaint; but if a child eats a great deal, and yet grows thin and weak, there is reason to suspect *mesenteric* obstructions, and it should be observed what other morbid symptoms may be present.

There are cases in which scrofula attacks the bones before it affects the glands; but the preceding symptoms of general debility and indisposition are

* The *mesentery* is a membrane which covers and contains the bowels.

usually the same, and wherever such symptoms appear, the best medical advice should be sought, being often more necessary on such occasions than in acute diseases.

One thing to be particularly remembered in these sort of maladies, is, that although much may be hoped from the preventive part of medicine when they threaten or first appear, yet when (through neglect or any other cause) they have already made some progress, there are none more difficult to cure, nor which require more knowledge, attention, and judgment in the physician. Very strong medicines are sometimes necessary, and if these are not administered with the greatest skill and caution, the consequences may be fatal. When, therefore, the advice given in this chapter, after three or four weeks' trial, produces no change for the better; and that notwithstanding the use of salt-water baths, a tonic diet, sufficient exercise, rhubarb, iron and bark, the symptoms of weakness, pallid and puffed face, swelled upper lip, irregular fever, &c., do not diminish, some clever physician should be immediately consulted, as remedies of the most active nature may be required to conquer the disease.

There is no malady in which delay, or the use of quack medicines, is more dangerous than in scrofula; for though the steps of this dreadful disease be slow, and the stages in which its progress may be arrested numerous, yet when neglected, there is none more distressing or fatal. I must, however, again repeat, for the consolation of mothers, that a constant and minute attention to the prevention of scrofulous complaints will generally meet with success *.

* People should not obstinately doubt of the existence of scrofula amongst children who have no hereditary right to it, as it is sometimes produced spontaneously, without any apparent cause, except that complexion and form which are supposed to mark a predisposition to it. I have known one individual of a family (where there were no hired nurses) afflicted with this disease to a great degree, though a number of brothers and sisters, by the same father and mother, (themselves free from the malady,) had not the least appearance of it.

CHAPTER XVII.

RICKETS.

This is one of those maladies which are easily acquired by children who are neglected or mismanaged, and more difficult to cure than to prevent. Errors in the physical education may excite this disease even in children who have no predisposition to it; but in those families where it has appeared to be hereditary, the greatest care is required to prevent its development. The same causes which produce scrofula are likely to give occasion to rickets, and the preventive method employed against the one malady is equally proper for the other, though the medicinal treatment of the two diseases be not exactly the same; so that, in general, all which has been recommended in this book to prevent scrofula, is applicable to the rickets, as it remains to the physician to prescribe what the peculiar circumstances of the case may require.

Rickets generally begin between the ninth and the twenty-fourth month, but the commencement of the malady is not absolutely confined to that period, and it has been known to make its first appearance at various ages. It comes on by slow degrees: the first symptoms are the flesh growing soft and flabby, and the strength diminishing; in a short time the child becomes unnaturally grave and quiet, and shews a dislike to motion; the face appears bloated, and has sometimes a high colour; the head and belly increase to a great size; the wrists and ancles grow too large; the legs become crooked, as indeed do all the bones by degrees, if means be not found to check the progress of the malady. The face changes, and the child acquires either a sharp, cunning look, or a silly expression of countenance; the faculties of the mind are in general superior to those in healthy children, but sometimes they are inferior. When the disease has made any progress, the pulse is usually quick and weak, the appetite, digestion, and evacuations are irregular; teething is late, and the teeth are apt to decay soon. All these symptoms appear, by degrees, as the malady advances, and some of them are common to other diseases; but they should not be disregarded for this last reason, as they always mark the presence of some malady which would require good advice and great attention.

The means of preventing rickets (when a predisposition to that disease is suspected) are the same which are necessary to prevent the development of other chronic diseases: good air, much exercise and amusement, strengthening food and warm clothing; high, light, and cheerful habitations, apartments fronting the midday sun, baths, frictions, &c., &c. Medical writers are also of opinion that children inclined to this malady should be weaned early for the purpose of being nourished with tonic food.

On the very first appearance of symptoms which may threaten rickets, a good physician should be consulted, as the earlier the disease is combated by judicious medical treatment, the more likely it is to be conquered; but if permitted to make any progress, it is with the greatest difficulty that it can be stopped, and even if cured, it usually leaves those who have suffered from it more or less disfigured. When it has been neglected too long for medical skill to have any power over it, it either ends in death by consumption and diarrhœa, or in excessive deformity, for which there is no remedy.

In this malady, the air which is breathed should be light and elastic, without being very cold; the mattresses on which the patient sleeps should not be either very hard or very soft, and great care should be taken that there be no lumps which can make them uneasy*. Tepid baths, with infusions of aromatic herbs, may be useful; also baths of brandy and water, or of sea water, either warm or cold;

* Those of horse-hair are preferable to wool; but many physicians have advised that the mattresses of rickety children be stuffed with dried fern, mixed with aromatic herbs.

spunging the body all over with cold water, (which is recommended by some in preference to immersion,) and rubbing it dry with flannels, and frictions of various kinds. Iron, bark, and rhubarb have been used with good effects; and the last mentioned substance is undoubtedly one of the best medicines that can be given to a child affected with rickets, to keep the body sufficiently open, to strengthen the stomach, and to prevent diarrhœa, all which are necessary in this malady.

But little advantage is to be derived from medicine, or suitable diet, baths, &c., if there is not a sufficiency of air and exercise; and for this last purpose artificial aids are necessary to rickety children, as they cannot move like others: they will not learn to walk of themselves, and therefore must be taught; but this ought to be done very late, with great caution and by slow degrees. They should be exercised in swings, riding-chairs, and little carriages, with springs, to be drawn about on smooth roads or fields; but it must be remembered that a jolt, a fall, or a blow is particularly dangerous to children affected with this disease.

To prevent rickets, a great deal can be done by the physical education; but when the malady has once begun to develop itself, the advice of an experienced medical man is absolutely necessary; for though in general it is improper to give much medicine for rickets, yet the skill of a clever physician is required to discriminate what ought to be done. Many persons consider cold bathing as a specific in this disease; but I should not recommend any one to try it, without good advice, as there are cases in which it might be very hurtful. If a strong, healthy child shews a tendency to rickets, (which happens now and then, in consequence of a lazy nurse letting it sit on the floor, or lie in the cradle, when she should carry it out or dance it on her knees,) the cold bath will, probably, prove an excellent remedy: but even in this case, those who have it in their power would act prudently by consulting a good physician.

Medical writers strenuously recommend that the clothes of children who have this disease should be *extremely dry*; but I consider that as an essential point for *all* children, healthy or unhealthy: what should be particularly attended to for those who have this or any other chronic malady, is, to expose their bedding to the air and sun every day, as well as their night-shifts, or any other part of their clothing which is to be used a second time before it is washed; and it would also be good to burn a little frankincense (or some other aromatic substance) in a chafing-dish, for the purpose of fumigating such things. The greatest part of the year, children afflicted with this malady should wear flannel next the skin; but much precaution is necessary in leaving it off; indeed, in climates where the heat is never very intense, it might be better to keep on flannel all the year round, and only to change to a thinner sort during the summer months: but this must depend on the feelings of the child and other circumstances of the case.

For a child threatened with rickets, who inhabits a great city, perhaps one of the best remedies would be immediate removal to the country; and those parents who have the means would do well to try the effects of a warmer climate.

CHAPTER XVIII.

CUTANEOUS DISEASES.—ERUPTIONS ON THE HEAD.
—ITCH.—HERPETIC ERUPTIONS.

GROWING children are subject to various sorts of ERUPTIONS, unaccompanied with fever or sickness, which sometimes continue a long time, and are very troublesome, but of no serious consequence to their health, unless suddenly or imprudently repelled from the surface of the skin.

The strongest children are frequently those most liable to rashes and eruptions, which they outgrow as they advance in years. Sometimes these are so slight, that, were it not for the impatience of the children, they would be scarcely visible: half-a-dozen spots like flea-bites on the face, and fifteen or twenty scattered over the body, would probably escape notice; but as they generally itch, children are apt to scratch them, so as to make sores, by which they become more visible and durable than they otherwise would be; and mothers, vexed at seeing the beauty of their children spoiled, are sometimes induced to employ remedies the pernicious effects of which they do not know.

No medical treatment of the slightest eruption should ever be undertaken without the advice of a *skilful* physician: but, if the itching be troublesome, the tepid bath may be safely used, and the child put into it for a quarter of an hour, just before bed-time. The diet may also be changed for one of a more cooling nature than usual; and fruit, either raw, stewed, or dried, and vegetables (if they agree with the stomach) may be given, in preference to meat or eggs: milk and whey are very proper for drink, but all sorts of fermented liquors should be avoided: and if the child who is *broken out* happens to be delicate, and to require nourishing food, sago, salep, arrow-root, &c., made palatable with lemon or orange juice, rice boiled to a jelly, and oat-jelly (*flummery* *), will probably be found suitable. Fruit-jellies and jams, with bread, may also be allowed, and, in short, every thing that usually comes under the denomination of cooling diet. The state of the bowels should be particularly attended to, and if the sort of food above mentioned, combined with a proper quantity of exercise and air, does not keep them sufficiently free, (as, however, it generally will,) a little magnesia, or magnesia and sulphur †, may be given, in such a quantity as to procure one or two evacuations: but purgative medicines should not be habitually

---

* See Appendix.   † See Appendix.

employed without the orders of a physician. I mention this especially, because many persons suppose that cutaneous diseases are to be cured by continual purging, which on the contrary, in many cases, is more likely to increase the complaint.

Children are very liable to eruptions on the head, and sometimes a small pimple which has been accidentally scratched, if not immediately attended to, may become a spreading and obstinate disease. The slightest appearance of this sort would require great care; and many of these complaints might be cured in a few days, by cutting the hair quite close round the inflamed spot, and washing it three or four times a day with warm water and soap, continuing to do so for at least a week after the part appears to be perfectly cured. A pimple or a scratch, of no importance in any other place, may easily become a bad sore on the head.

If an eruption on the head be not cured by cutting the hair and washing the part with soap, it would be right to consult a physician, lest the complaint should prove to be one of the various species of tinea (*scabbed head*) which are so difficult to cure, and for which the appropriate remedies can only be known by seeing the eruption.

As there is some reason to suppose the tinea a contagious disease, children should be cautioned against putting on the hats or caps of those they do not know.

Extreme cleanliness is of the greatest importance, both in the prevention and cure of cutaneous diseases; and though it may not entirely keep them off, yet it will always be of use in diminishing their violence, as well as in greatly conducing to the comfort of children afflicted with them.

If a child has the misfortune to be infected with the ITCH, a disease which cannot be removed without the application of external medicines, a good physician should be consulted, as the cure ought to be effected with great caution, it being dangerous to apply repelling ointments to too great a portion of the skin at once: but it should be remembered that the sooner the cure is commenced, the easier it will be. It is necessary to observe here, that young children have sometimes slight eruptions so strongly resembling the itch, that even a physician, unless he be a man of much experience, may be deceived by them; and the use of ointments for this malady is by no means safe. The best mode of ascertaining the nature of the disease is to give a little sulphur, on going to bed, for three or four nights together, a remedy which can do no injury in any case; and, if the eruption be the itch, will throw it out sufficiently to prevent mistakes.

Those violent HERPETIC ERUPTIONS (vulgarly called *scorbutic*) which torment and disfigure children for a length of time, require the greatest care: it would always be better to let them remain on the surface of the skin, than repel them without the positive orders of an experienced medical practitioner; as the internal diseases which may follow are far more to be dreaded than any temporary ugliness or inconvenience caused by the eruption *.

The only safe, and probably the only efficacious remedies, are to be found in the various kinds of warm baths; and these should, in many cases, be accompanied with the use of certain internal medicines, which a judicious physician would know how to adapt to the particular circumstances. There are several springs in England, of which the efficacy in the cure of such complaints is well known, and there are, besides, many ways of composing artificial baths for this purpose. On the Continent, there are numerous sulphureous and other hot baths, beneficial for these sort of diseases; and, no doubt, when the additional advantage of a warm

---

* It should be remembered that these sort of eruptions are sometimes, though not generally, contagious; and the requisite precaution of not using the towel of one afflicted with them, nor drinking out of the same vessel, &c., should be attended to.

climate can be obtained, it must conduce much to the efficacy of the waters.

Great care should be taken that the skins of children affected with herpetic eruptions be not irritated; for this reason, they should never wear any thing of cotton next them, and their linen should be as soft and fine as may be convenient. When any part of the skin is so moist as to make the linen stick to it, a young leaf of lettuce or beet should be applied and changed frequently: when these cannot be had, a little clean suet or spermaceti ointment, spread on soft linen, may be employed for this purpose, taking care not to leave it long without changing.

These being maladies which give a great deal of trouble, the attendants of children afflicted with them are always in a violent hurry to have them dried up; but a skilful, prudent, and conscientious physician will not easily be persuaded to gratify them; and mothers should themselves see that nothing is neglected which may relieve their children's uneasiness. An extraordinary degree of patience is required in the persons who are about children in this state, as *the slow cure is the only one likely to be safe and permanent.*

When properly treated, these complaints diminish by degrees, without producing any bad effect on the child's general health; but if they are rapidly cured, that is to say, repelled from the surface of the skin, the disease is transferred to some other part, and not unfrequently some fatal or incurable malady is the consequence. Consumption, dropsy, asthma, epilepsy, palsy, &c., &c., may be brought on by the sudden cure of a cutaneous disease; whereas by slowly removing it, these dangerous effects are avoided, and in the course of time the skin becomes clear and smooth.

Children suffering under maladies of this nature should be warmly clad, as it is of great consequence to avoid all danger of checking the perspiration; and though it be impossible they should wear flannel next the skin, yet the cold of winter may be guarded against by putting it over the linen, (which should be very thin,) and when the children go out, worsted may be put over thread stockings.

There is always hope of a cutaneous disease being thoroughly cured when the subject is a growing child; and even those which in adults prove inveterate, may be removed by proper treatment of children: but again I must repeat—let those who value the health and happiness of their offspring beware of hurrying the cure of diseases which shew themselves on the surface of the skin only, as irremediable maladies, or even death, may be the consequence.

Children are liable to many other maladies which

do not belong peculiarly to them; but as the cautions I have given are sufficient to prevent some of these, and the others positively require the attendance of professional men, I do not think it necessary to treat farther on these subjects, in a work which is designed for an essay on physical education only, and not a manual of medicine.

PART THE FIFTH.

GENERAL OBSERVATIONS RESPECTING CHILDREN OF ALL AGES.

CHAPTER I.

FOOD. — PURIFICATION OF WATER. — CHILDREN SHOULD NOT BE PRESSED TO EAT. — IRREGULARITY OF APPETITE. — SWEET THINGS. — CHILDREN NATURALLY GLUTTONS. — DO NOT REQUIRE FOOD IN INFLAMMATORY DISEASES.

To preserve the existence of children, and promote their physical and moral welfare, constant attention is necessary to a variety of circumstances, many of evident importance, others apparently trifling, but none of which can with safety be neglected.

Their food, clothing, exercise, amusements, repose, &c., &c., also their learning and mental discipline of every sort, conduce to their health or the contrary according as they are well or ill directed.

In regard to the mode of feeding children, it is impossible to give any precise rules, as the powers of digestion vary in different stomachs, and even in the same stomach at different periods. Generally speaking, their food should be light, nourishing, and agreeable to the palate: they should not be forced to eat any thing they dislike; and the offspring of parents accustomed to the constant use of animal food should never be confined to a vegetable diet, unless ordered by a physician. The human stomach seems to be adapted for variety of substances; and therefore it would be injudicious to habituate it to one species of nutriment; but sudden transitions should be avoided, and all the changes of diet which the growth of children require should be made by slow degrees. For those who are in health, it is not good to make any strict prohibitions, and, in general, it is better that their food should be too tonic, than not sufficiently so. A person who has been accustomed to children will soon distinguish those who require a cooling diet; and it is safer, in our days, to err on the other side than on this. Children in whom there is any reason to suspect a tendency (either natural or acquired) to scrofula, or any other malady of debility, should have the most strengthening food that their stomachs will support, and (as has been already advised in treating of those diseases) more wine and other fermented liquors than would be proper for children of a different constitution.

It is unnecessary to mention, that great care should be taken to procure good bread for children, and that all such as can be suspected of being made white by any unwholesome substance should be avoided. People are generally aware of the necessity of attending to this point; but it does not appear that the qualities of the water they drink is considered of equal importance. It is, however, perhaps of still greater; for the injury done by bad bread being soon discovered, in consequence of its immediate effects on the stomach and bowels, remedies are sought, and the cause quickly removed: whereas the mischief incurred by drinking bad water is not likely to shew itself by any instantaneous effects, (water so unwholesome as to occasion sickness never being in common use,) but slowly hurts the constitution.

When there is any doubt respecting the salubrity of water*, that which is given to children (or very delicate persons) should be boiled and left to stand till it cool, that any sediment contained in it may fall to the bottom of the vessel; and when it is taken off clear, it should be poured from one vessel into another three or four times (as is done in making punch) that it may imbibe the air, which is

* When water is known to be *bad*, it should be purified by distilling.

supposed to render it lighter for the stomach. Persons extremely nice in this respect would do well to have the water boiled in glass or earthenware vessels, which are less likely to give a bad taste than those of metal. This mode of purifying water at least secures those who drink it from swallowing any live things, as well as from some other unwholesome substances.

For healthy children, there is no better drink at their meals than good water. Fermented liquors should rather be reserved for medicinal purposes; and tea, or any warm diluting liquors, unless in case of illness, should never be given to children: they weaken the stomach, and lay the foundation of many maladies.

Except in some very extraordinary cases, one should never entice children to eat, by offering them any thing they particularly like, when they do not appear hungry. It is not the quantity of food that is swallowed, but the quantity that the stomach can easily digest, which nourishes and strengthens the body; and whatever more is added, rather diminishes than increases the nourishment, by giving the stomach more to do than it is capable of performing. Any substance that is digested with difficulty produces a certain degree of fever, which is always followed by proportionate weakness. For this reason, we may observe, that some children who appear strong, and well nourished, are very small eaters; whilst others, who swallow large quantities of food, appear weak and half starved. But the fact is, that the former have in reality had the largest portion of nourishment, though they have appeared to take the least, because all they have eaten has been well digested, and the nutritive part completely extracted; whereas those who have consumed the largest quantity of food have had but little nourishment, on account of their stomachs being able to extract nutriment from but a small part of what they have eaten, and the large portion remaining has only produced indigestion, fever, and consequent debility. The quantity of food which each child requires, can only be ascertained by observation, as well as the quality adapted to each particular stomach.

Children require food much oftener than adults; and I have frequently observed in them a great irregularity of appetite, according to their irregular starts of growth. A child will sometimes have an inclination to eat a great deal for three or four months together; and then, for a similar space of time, appear to have scarcely any appetite: but neither of these changes should ever occasion uneasiness to parents, if accompanied with no symptoms of indisposition.

When people choose to give children sweet things out of meal-times, (which by the by is a very bad custom,) the nearer they approach to plain sugar the better. There is but one injury sugar can do, (and even that doubtful,) which is to the teeth. To the stomach it can never be otherwise than beneficial, and the common prejudice respecting its being unwholesome has originated in the combinations with which it has been given. Sweet cakes, puddings, pastry, &c., have often encouraged children to load their stomachs with more than they could digest; and the mischief resulting has been ascribed to the sugar, which, had it been extracted from the other substances and given alone, would probably have produced beneficial instead of injurious effects. I have heard of its causing an acid in the stomach, but am inclined to think that this is rarely (if ever) the case; and that, when such an effect has been observed, the sugar has been mixed with some greasy substance, which was the real cause of the complaint. I am the more particular in treating of this subject, because there are mothers who will permit their children to devour quantities of meat, butter, cheese, &c., and drink beer and tea in abundance, who would not suffer them to taste a morsel of plain sugar.

All children are more or less gluttons, (and perhaps they ought to be so,) but whether to such a degree as can injure their health, depends on those about them. If the faults of children are to be punished by making them fast, they will learn to consider eating as the first of privileges, and indulge it to excess whenever they have an opportunity; and if they are only to be deprived of certain meats which they particularly like, it is still worse, for they are thus taught to consider luxury in food as one of the greatest blessings, and prepared for unnecessary misery should circumstances happen to prevent their enjoyment of it. A child should never suffer any privation in regard to eating by way of punishment, except when it is appropriate to the fault that has been committed: if the child have eaten too much of any particular thing, or have cried for it, then it is perfectly right to prohibit what has been the cause of offence; but to deprive a child of pudding or of pie at dinner, because he has been disobedient, or ill-humoured just after breakfast, can answer no purpose but to make him doubly a glutton; which should be carefully avoided by all those who are anxious to preserve the health of their children.

Great care should be taken that the attendants of children, who are suffering under acute maladies, do not urge them to eat when they have no inclination for food, or give them improper things when they are beginning to recover. It is difficult to persuade the vulgar that existence can be prolonged without solid food, and nothing is more common than to hear servants and nurses say of a child, in the height of an inflammatory disease, " Poor thing! he must be very weak—he has not eaten a morsel these five days—he can never hold out without some nourishment," though most probably, on enquiry, one finds the child has drunk great quantities of diluting liquors, sweetened with sugar, which in itself contains a great deal of nutriment; quite as much as is suitable to the situation of the sick child.

CHAPTER II.

CLOTHING.—COVERING THE BOSOM AND ARMS.—ORNAMENTS INJURIOUS TO HEALTH.—BEAUTY TO BE ACQUIRED.—LIGATURES OF ALL SORTS BAD.

In regard to the clothing of children, there are different opinions; but all persons who know any thing of medicine must agree, that in cold weather they should be warmly and at the same time lightly clad. For this purpose there is no substance so proper in the winter season as flannel; but the greatest caution should be used in changing the clothing after the cold is past, and it should not be done (especially when children are very delicate and have worn flannel next the skin by medical advice) until the weather be perfectly settled. It would be well to have some clothing for them less warm than flannel, and yet not so cool as their usual summer habiliments, to wear for a few days; for example, thick calico or some sort of cotton cloth; and flannel next the skin might be left off by putting it over the linen, and then cutting it away by degrees.

Some physicians have recommended that boys should be put into trowsers as early as possible, and that girls should wear a similar dress, (which, with the addition of a short petticoat, seems to be much the fashion at present in England,) whilst others have given exactly the contrary advice; desiring that even boys should be kept as long as possible without the confinement of trowsers. These various opinions are founded on the same physical reasons, and the partisans of each have much to say in support of their different ways of thinking. For my own part, I confess myself to be against the modern custom: preferring to keep boys in petticoats at least until they are four years old, and never to put trowsers on girls at all. But these are matters of comparative indifference, and therefore not of sufficient consequence for me to explain the causes of my adhering to the one opinion rather than the other. What I do consider of great importance is, that the breasts[*] and arms of young children be constantly covered, at least during cold weather, until the period of dentition be quite over. Children who have the bosom and upper part of the arms exposed to the cold while they are cutting teeth, are much more subject to coughs and inflammations of the lungs than those who have them covered; and no one can guess at how early an age

[*] Some medical men have considered the exposure of the arms and bosom as one cause of the croup.

a malady of this nature may occasion some organic defect, which may prove fatal by the production of pulmonary consumption fifteen or twenty years afterwards. The exposure of the upper part of the arm has been supposed, by some eminent physicians, to have a great part in producing those rheumatic pains in the jaws, which destroy the teeth of many young people; and there is no doubt that cold caught in that part is very likely to occasion the tooth-ache. I have never heard any reason assigned for stripping children in this imprudent manner, except that " it makes them look pretty; " and what reasonable and affectionate mother would run such risks from so absurd a motive? But to this love of " looking pretty " great sacrifices are often made; and even medical men have sometimes been persuaded to become accomplices in this folly.

Besides being light and warm, the clothes of children should always be plain. All kinds of ornaments and finery are injurious to their health; for, however regardless the parents may be of the damage done to such useless matters, this will rarely be the case with the servants, who are to mend and wash the embroidered flounces or lace trimmings with which the children are encumbered; and therefore they will not be allowed to run amongst the bushes, or roll upon the grass, or even to skip carelessly along the smooth pathway, without being continually reminded of the respect due to their fine clothes; and whilst the robust courageous child will ever forget this matter of importance, and incur daily reproaches and chastisements for an unworthy cause, the delicate and timid, impressed with the fear of spoiling its dress, will refrain from taking that exercise which the instincts of nature direct, and at the same time acquire an habitual veneration for the object of its constant care; which thus becomes an injury to both body and mind. No expense which can conduce to the health of children should ever be spared; but that belonging to fine clothes, being absolutely detrimental, might be saved with great advantage; and yet we frequently see parents who would not spend money on battledores, skipping-ropes, wheel-barrows, &c., &c., lay out ten times the sums that these would cost on flounces and trimmings, and lace and trumpery of all sorts.

Pretty children never look so well as when they are plainly dressed, and it is a pity to draw attention to those who are not so, by foolish ornaments; especially as ugliness in children is always the effect of bad health, and consequent ill temper. A healthy, good-humoured child (who has no strange defect or deformity) cannot be ugly; and, indeed, I have long thought that human creatures might be educated into beauty, by strict attention to their physical and moral welfare.

Great care should be taken that children have nothing too tight on any part of the body. Unnecessary ligatures are hurtful both to health and beauty, and should therefore be prohibited. Garters, either above or below the knees, should never be allowed to growing children: they are likely to spoil the shape of the leg, and must, in some degree, interrupt the circulation of the blood, which can never be done without more or less injury to the health; but the stockings may be fastened to some article of clothing, whose point of support is on the shoulders, which precludes the necessity of squeezing any part of the body. Tight shoes occasion corns, by which even very young children often suffer; and such impediments thrown in the way of one just beginning to walk may occasion awkward movements, scarcely possible to be corrected during the rest of its life. But the worst of all pressures is what is frequently inflicted on the bodies of female children, by that most detrimental of fashions, the use of stays, — the origin of a thousand deformities and diseases, and the cause of many fatal accidents. Were it even true that an excessively small waist was a necessary part of beauty, and that great sacrifices ought to be made for the acquisition of it, we should first consider how far this mode of squeezing the stomach and bowels is likely to have the desired effect; or whether it is worth while, for the doubtful chance of obtaining this end, to run the risk of producing certain ugliness, by crookedness and bad health. I have very good reason for believing that this mode of acquiring a slender shape does not always succeed; and, on the contrary, I have known many instances of clumsy girls, whose forms were entirely left to nature, growing up with much smaller waists than others who had been subjected to the tortures of fashion.

I well recollect in my youth to have heard certain individuals blamed, extremely, for their very injudicious and careless conduct towards their daughters, who were doomed, by many prophetic voices, "to grow up as thick round the body as kitchen maids;" and I have afterwards seen those very young women, who had been so pitied for the cruel neglect of their parents, with more slender waists, and (what were then called) finer shapes than any of their neighbours, who had enjoyed all the advantages of being squeezed and tormented from their infancy.

Beauty is by no means to be neglected; but it cannot exist without proportion; and if a girl be so formed as to have broad shoulders and broad hips, (as many handsome women are,) surely nothing is so calculated to destroy the symmetry of her shape as to pinch in her waist until it is as small as her arms. Besides, let it be remembered, that whatever hurts the health must produce ugliness in a greater or less degree; and all persons who know any thing of medicine, can have but one opinion on the subject of *tight lacing*.

CHAPTER III.

EVACUATIONS. — EXERCISE. — AMUSEMENTS. — WARMTH. — CHANGE OF AIR.

No person can enjoy perfect health in whom the natural evacuations are deficient. It is not, however, necessary that they should be always equal: difference of seasons, of food, and a variety of other accidental causes, may produce temporary irregularities, which should not be subjects of uneasiness, and still less of medical treatment, unless they are accompanied with evident marks of indisposition.

To develop the forms of children, and give to every part its proportionate degree of growth and strength, a great deal of exercise, of various sorts, is required; and when they are in health, nature (if not counteracted) will always lead them to continual movement. This should be encouraged, by giving them all those toys which promote activity; for the more exercise is united with amusement, the more it will conduce to the well-being of body and mind.

Mothers need not be afraid that their daughters should acquire masculine habits, or rough manners, because, as growing children, they are permitted to have the free use of their limbs: for there is no doubt that those girls are likely to be most graceful, as well as most healthy, who have been active in their infancy. It is a great improvement in the modern education of females, that they are allowed such plays as promote strength of body; and nothing is a greater acquisition in this respect than the *skipping-rope*, which was formerly the exclusive property of school-boys. Dolls are useful to girls for the purpose of making them acquire the necessary knowledge of needle-work with pleasure, (for when instruction can be united with amusement, it is always advantageous to the health,) but as a constant employment in the hours of relaxation, they are too apt to lead to sedentary habits, which must invariably injure the physical welfare.

Nothing can be more false than (what is asserted by several respectable male authors) that female children have a natural propensity to amuse themselves with dolls. I never saw a robust, healthy girl who did not prefer those plays usually appropriated to boys; and I have known sickly, delicate male children as much diverted with dolls as females could be. The truth is, that weak children like sedentary amusements, whilst the strong prefer those which are active; and, besides, girls are early taught that a doll is a very reputable companion, whilst boys are ridiculed if they look at one. These sort of prejudices often produce effects injurious to the moral and physical welfare of children, and therefore I think it right to point them out here.

So far as air and exercise are concerned, there ought to be less difference made (at least till nine or ten years old) between the physical education of boys and girls than usually is. It is a great disadvantage to females, that, at thirteen or fourteen years of age, they are often obliged by the persons about them, or induced by their own vanity, to relinquish those active sports which are necessary to the health of growing creatures, and which instinct would lead many to continue to a much later age, if art or affectation did not put a restraint on their movements, extremely injurious to both their physical and moral welfare. The longer those childish, sportive feelings, which tend to active amusements, can be preserved, the more healthy in body, and innocent in mind, are young females likely to be; and mothers would do well to cherish rather than suppress such propensities.

Male children, as they grow up, should be inured to more violent exercise than females: they should be more strengthened by muscular exertions: but both sexes ought to be equally accustomed to the open air.

Though, generally speaking, children are inclined to be ever in motion, yet, there are many who can be easily induced to remain quiet, and those sometimes of the most active dispositions. Either a very dull or a very clever child may be taught to sit still too much; the former for the pleasure of doing nothing, the latter from taking a strong interest in some sedentary amusement; but, by judicious management, without any appearance of coercion, these hurtful propensities may be counteracted before they have become habitual.

When children are forced to walk out against their inclinations, and without any object of amusement, the discontent, which depresses their minds, prevents the benefit of exercise to their bodies. For this reason, children should have their walks diversified, or rendered agreeable by the accompaniment of some of the many toys which induce them to take exercise; such as balls, skipping-ropes, kites, wheel-barrows, rolling-stones. The last-mentioned, when adapted in weight to the strength of the individual, is an excellent means of opening the chest, and throwing back the shoulders; and when the child has the pleasure of thinking itself of use in smoothing the walks of a garden, for the accommodation of those it loves, the effects on body and mind will be far more beneficial than any which can result from the employment of *dumb-bells* and *back-boards*, with which so many girls have been obliged to pass long melancholy hours of dulness and discontent.

Playing in the open air is much better for children than taking long walks; but those parents who are obliged to inhabit large towns, and have no gardens to their houses, should make it a rule to send their children to some square, or open place, every tolerably fine day, either on some errand of amusement, or under some pretext which may induce them to go with pleasure. Every thing that renders children happy, (improper indulgence of course excepted,) conduces to make them healthy, and they are never so happy as when in motion, in the open air. Children of all ages should be out as much as possible, that is to say, while it is agreeable to their feelings; but the persons about young infants should particularly observe whether it gives them pleasure, which when the weather is fine and they are in health, it never can fail to do: but it is quite impossible that the fresh air can afford them any advantage, if they are not sufficiently clothed to prevent them from shivering and looking so unhappy as I have sometimes witnessed. All extremes must be injurious to body and mind; and there is nothing to be more carefully avoided, in both the physical and moral education. Children who are guarded against every breath of air, and not allowed to stir out in the warmest weather without being wrapped up, are equally liable to get cold with those who are sent out in nankeen dresses, when the north wind blows, and not permitted to change their shoes when they have got wet. I scarcely know which is the worst extreme, for they both tend to debilitate, and to produce disease. If children complain of cold, when they are on foot in the open air, it is a proof that either they are ill, or their clothes not sufficiently warm for the season. When those of four or five years old are in perfect health, and warmly clad, they usually delight in running against the wind, and playing in the frosty air: but such as do not, should never be forced to remain in the cold, which is very hurtful to sickly, delicate children.

Children should not be obliged to take exercise directly after a full meal; nor should they be prevented, if naturally inclined to do so: they ought to be allowed a certain portion of time after dinner for relaxation, which they should be permitted to pass either in motion or repose according to their feelings. Either instinct or experience will soon teach them what is suitable in this respect; for exercise after eating agrees perfectly with some stomachs, and not at all with others: therefore it is not expedient to send children out to take a long walk immediately after dinner. In general, the best time for taking exercise is before meals; but little children should not be prevented from following the impulse of nature, which leads the greater number to be constantly in motion.

Though the health of children is sometimes so invincible, and the force of habit so strong, that they exist and flourish in atmospheres apparently far from wholesome; yet whenever there is the slightest symptom of debility, a change of air should, if possible, be contrived; and a child who is growing sickly or crooked whilst shut up in a small house, in the narrow street of a large town, will be more likely to recover if sent into the country to run about the fields, than through any medical or mechanical aid.

On the first symptoms of chronic diseases in children who inhabit a great city, they should be removed into the country; and many a child will be sooner cured by sporting in meadows, or climbing hills, than by swallowing drugs, which are, perhaps, not less expensive in the end, than a few months' lodging in some small village or farmhouse.

Persons of restricted incomes (especially in large towns) are often deterred from giving their children a sufficiency of air and exercise, because they are unable to take them out themselves, and fear they might be injured by being with the common sort of servants; but of two evils we should always choose the least, and the *mere chance* of learning vulgar ways, or even to tell falsehoods, &c., are less to be dreaded than diseases, or weakness of constitution, which *must* be the consequence of confined air and a sedentary life during childhood; as the former are far easier to be remedied than the latter. Those whose occupations prevent them from accompanying their children in their walks, should choose the least exceptionable person they can find to send with them, and trust to Providence for the rest. Once in fifty times a child may learn some disagreeable or vicious habit by going out with servants; and forty-nine times out of fifty, the health will be destroyed by staying at home.

Parents, who have occasion to employ their children at an early age in any sedentary occupation, will find it greatly their interest to assign a certain portion of the day for exercise in the open air, and to see that it is so disposed of; for (besides the expense attendant on sickness, in a country where so much medicine is used as in England,) health is always advantageous to industry; and a brisk, animated child will be able to work much quicker and better, than one oppressed with the indolence which attends the commencement of chronic maladies. The baneful effects of a too sedentary life may be seen in manufactories where children are employed, whose sallow looks and sunk eyes the heart shudders to behold. I only allude to this evil, for the purpose of convincing the minds of those who may happen to think that the advice above given is unnecessary; for it is one too painful to reflect on, being out of the power of such a work as this to remove.

CHAPTER IV.

HEAT OF ROOMS.—CROOKEDNESS.—ROUND SHOULDERS. — UNWHOLESOME POSTURES. — SLEEP. — BEDS.—NOCTURNAL TERRORS.

The atmosphere of apartments inhabited by children, should be moderately heated in cold weather; but they should never be allowed to approach a fire, as there is nothing more likely to occasion them many troublesome maladies, such as tooth-ache, chilblains, inflammation of the eyes, &c., &c. They should always be encouraged to warm themselves by running and jumping; and, as partial cold is very hurtful, if they complain of suffering much in the hands and feet (as very young children sometimes do) these should be well rubbed, and then covered with shoes or gloves which have been made hot; but on no account should they be brought near the fire.

When children are of an age to sit still at their studies for any length of time, care should be taken that the air of the rooms they occupy, on such occasions, be sufficiently warm, and their clothes such as may be necessary to their comfort. Some children are much more sensible of cold than others; and differences should be made according to their years and constitutions.

Children who have been judiciously educated from the beginning of their lives, and allowed to enjoy a sufficiency of air and exercise, are not liable to become crooked from weakness; in their rapid fits of growth, however, they should be watched attentively, and not induced to walk or to stand too much at a time, lest fatigue should occasion awkward habits, which might injure the form. As most crooked persons have been straight during their infancy, and many of them acquired their defect of shape without apparent cause, it is not improbable that this misfortune may be the consequence of some temporary and local debility, which with timely attention could be remedied: mothers, therefore, who have reason to dread an hereditary crookedness in their families, should be particularly careful to watch the slightest commencement of weakness, and oppose its progress by the use of salt-water baths, iron, bark, &c. They should guard the child from fatigue of either body or mind; and not fail to examine from time to time the appearance of the hips and backbone. After all that has been said in other parts of this book, it is hardly necessary to recommend amusement and agreeable exercise. Above all things, back collars and other violent mechanical remedies are to be avoided, as there are few cases in which they will not be likely to augment the defects they are employed to cure. Children are often made to sit on seats without backs, on purpose to prevent them from leaning; but this is a mistake: on the contrary, to keep them straight, they should rather be encouraged to lean; and for this purpose should have chairs exactly proportioned to their size, made with sloping backs in such a manner, that when they lean against them, the chest may have full space to expand, which cannot be with straight-backed chairs. Obliging children to stand when they are tired, is very likely to cause a crookedness in the hips, as they usually stand on one leg to rest: when they wish it they should be permitted to lie down; the well-known boards, which were sanctioned by fashion till they became ridiculous, are excellent things to allow (but not to force) children to lie down on. The floor, however, or a hard bed or a sofa, may answer the same purpose for those who have not this convenience.

If a child be observed to be growing round-shouldered, the cause should be examined into; and should it prove to arise from a careless habit of sitting to write, draw, &c., a piece of stiff leather, about three inches in breadth, and of a length sufficient to cover the shoulder-blades, may be applied over the shift, (or shirt,) and by having a case of linen, it may be fastened to the waistcoat with pins, in such a manner that they cannot hurt. This answers the purpose of reminding the child not to stoop; and in a few weeks it may remove the defect. If, however, it be ascertained that bringing forward the shoulders in this manner is occasioned by weakness in the chest, in consequence of outgrowing the strength, the proper remedies for debility must also be employed, and the child persuaded to lie down when fatigued.

It would be a great advantage for children to have the habit of using both hands equally; but this is not allowed, and those who are naturally inclined to do so are reproved for it: when, however, by exercising the right arm more than the left, the shoulder on that side becomes larger than the other, the proper remedy is to use the left arm entirely, and to leave the other in repose.

Kneeling is a very unwholesome posture, in which children should never be suffered to continue long. I am particular in mentioning this, as I have known of some being put on their knees for a punishment, which is very dangerous, as crying and sobbing in that situation is likely to occasion ruptures *.

Children should be cautioned against lifting

* I have been assured that the inhabitants of convents, who sing aloud in this posture for hours, are particularly subject to ruptures.

weights too heavy for them, or carrying each other, by which disagreeable accidents sometimes happen.

The repose of children is not, always, sufficiently attended to. Their comfort, in respect to hours of sleep and arrangement of their beds is often too much disregarded, though perhaps of even more importance to their strength and growth, than the quality of their food. Extremes should be equally avoided in nourishment, clothing, and beds; and there is no greater mistake than supposing that children are to be made robust, by allowing them but little covering at night. The sleep of a child who suffers from cold will be broken and unrefreshing, whilst that of one whose bed is too warm, will be prolonged and debilitating. In this the feelings of the individual should be consulted, (and an attentive mother will soon discover how far,) as it must be remembered that children, like grown people, differ in this respect; and that one will require a heavy covering, when the lightest is almost too much for another.

In regard to the beds of children, they should neither be very hard nor very soft. Feather beds are generally denied them, and with great propriety; but the contrary extreme of making them lie too hard, is by no means uncommon, though capable of producing equally bad consequences. A bed which is too soft is injurious, from being relaxing; but one too hard may induce a child to sleep in unnatural postures, and thus occasion crookedness; besides, when the rest is broken by painful sensations, it cannot bestow all the benefit which ought to be expected from it.

The best bed for a child is a thick, well-stuffed mattrass, (of either wool or horse-hair,) on a tight drawn sacking bottom; and care should be taken that the mattrass be re-made frequently, lest it get into lumps. In regard to the height of the bolster, as well as the warmth of the coverings, the children's own feelings should be the only rule: for one child, in perfect health, will desire to have the head high, while another, equally well, will prefer sleeping without any bolster; in the same way that one will feel too warm with a light blanket, while another will suffer from the cold without a heavy one. While children are under four years old, those about them must endeavour to guess at their feelings: after that age, they are able to explain their wishes, which should always be attended to; for when instinct can be consulted, it is probably our best guide. Children who are not sufficiently warm at night cannot sleep quietly, and usually grow pale and thin; and those who have too much covering, become weak from unnatural perspiration. All these things deserve great attention, as they may be remote causes of disease.

Growing children should be allowed to sleep as long as they please; and if properly treated in other respects, there is no danger of their lying in bed too late. Those who take as much exercise as they ought in the day, will require to go to rest early; and great care should be taken that their sleep be not interrupted: should it on any occasion be necessary to call them before their usual hour, it ought to be done in the gentlest manner, as there is nothing more hurtful to delicate nerves than to be suddenly wakened. Some children require a great deal more sleep than others; and in this they should be allowed to follow the dictates of nature.

Children should always be allowed to divert themselves, but not with any violent exercise, for some time before they are put to bed, that they may go to sleep with cheerful impressions on their minds. When they are extremely restless at night, it should be ascertained whether this proceeds from any error in the time or the quality of their eating, or from indisposition, that the proper remedies may be sought; but, as there are individuals who, in consequence of a particular organization of nerves, are, from the beginning to the end of their lives, subject to disturbed sleep, even when in perfect health, this should be carefully distinguished from the restlessness that proceeds from indigestion, worms, or any other morbific cause. What is a mark of disease in one person is not so in another; and, in children of this constitution, quiet sleep should be rather an object of attention, as an unaccustomed thing, which may be a symptom of some malady. Any change from the usual state should always be suspected as a sign of indisposition.

All children should be carefully observed during the time of sleep; for many are subject to frightful dreams, against which (as being prejudicial to the health) precautions should be taken. When a child of any age appears uneasy in sleep, it should be turned, or the head raised higher, or even wakened, if nothing else be found sufficient to break the chain of disagreeable ideas which interrupts its tranquillity. The constitutions of lively children are sometimes much injured by nocturnal fears; and the persons about them are not, in general, so careful as they ought to be, in guarding them against impressions of this nature. I have known children of strong imaginations suffer agonies of terror in dreaming of ghosts, witches, and devils, after having listened to stories on those subjects, just before they were put to bed; and who, having no soothing voice to console them when roused from sleep by the excess of their fears, have suffered very unnecessary indispositions in consequence. People should not be deceived in this respect by the robust appearance of children, or be convinced that their nerves are strong because their minds are not cowardly; as it not unfrequently happens that the greatest sensibility of nerves is united with uncommon strength of body and boldness of spirit; and that without particular attention, a being so constituted, and capable of enjoying the highest degree of health, may become weak and sickly, by the workings of a lively imagination, and consequent agitation of nerves.

CHAPTER V.

PAINTED TOYS. — INDEPENDENCE. — PRAISE. — WONDERFUL CHILDREN. — INDOLENCE. — DEFORMED OR DISCONTENTED PERSONS SHOULD NOT BE ABOUT CHILDREN.

THE numerous painted toys which are made for children are, probably, injurious to the health of many; and I have often suspected temporary maladies, of which the causes were not evident, to be occasioned by these poisonous play-things. Very young children always put every thing into their mouths; and those who are older are by no means careful on this subject, but will readily eat bread or cake, with the white, and red, and green paint of their toys adhering to their fingers; which, though not in sufficient quantity to occasion an immediate or violent effect, must always be hurtful in a greater or less degree. Painted toys should be banished from the nursery, until children arrive at an age to understand, not only that their playthings will be spoilt by being put into the mouth or touched with wet hands, but also that the coloured paint is poison, which, by being taken into the stomach, may produce pain, and even death. At five or six years old, they are capable of knowing their interest in this respect; and, being aware of these dangers, they may then be left to their own discretion.

Children should be made independent as soon as possible: too much care in preserving those who have passed the first weakness of infancy from lesser dangers, is likely to throw them into greater. Show them the evils they have to dread, and how to guard against them by their own prudence, rather than give them the habit of being constantly protected. Tell them to take care of themselves, and they will do so. Let them climb upon chairs, and go up and down stairs, without assistance, as soon as possible, and they will meet with fewer accidents, than if they have always a servant to watch them; and even if the mother's eye, with trembling anxiety, follows their steps, let them not know it. Teach them early to be proud of courage, and let them feel the pleasure of independence. Nothing conduces more to the well-being of children than having a good opinion of themselves; and from the cradle to the grave, nothing creates such an exhilaration of mind, as the consciousness of being able to stand alone. By teaching children to be proud of not being afraid, you give them a sense of their own worth, and guard them against numerous physical and moral ills.

Few things are more detrimental to children than excessive praise; and parents who, from not having observed those of others, imagine their own to be miracles, are apt to injure them by admiring every infantine trick in presence of the children themselves, and forcing indifferent spectators to join in their absurd praises. In this manner, they do infinite mischief to their offspring, by exciting that restless vanity, which renders them unhappy when they are not the chief objects of attention. Children should be taught to amuse themselves without incommoding others, and never to expect the notice of strangers. Let them always consider themselves of importance to their parents, as objects of present affection, and future esteem; but not of admiration to any one, much less to unconcerned visitors; and they will thus be spared many of those mortifications, which, even during the first seven years of existence, may produce the worst effects on both their minds and bodies.

Wonderful children are by no means common; nor are they to be desired. In such instances, what the mind gains the body loses; and these unnatural infants generally grow up deformed, or die early. No prudent mother will ever desire to see her child either prematurely wise, or uncommonly tranquil: these are usually morbid symptoms, which end in positive disease. For the first, there is no remedy; and distempered nature must take her own course: but the latter (especially if it be a new appearance) should be watched, and counteracted; not by forcing the child to take exercise against its will, but by offering every sort of amusement which can exhilarate the mind, and quicken the circulation of the blood.

Females of thirteen or fourteen years of age are sometimes liable to that excessive indolence of body which is the forerunner of disease; and I have known mothers make it a point of obliging girls in this state to rise from their seats every moment, to go on some message, by way of counteracting this morbid propensity. But such is not the proper mode of curing this sort of laziness: on the contrary, the ill-humour excited by continual interruptions serves only to increase the indisposition; and, in fact, exercise seldom produces beneficial effects, when not occasioned by some agreeable motive. Amusing occupations should be found, which might break through the inclination to sit still: companions of lively dispositions should be sought; dancing parties, and active plays might be encouraged, and country excursions or short journeys resorted to. Such methods are the best adapted to correct that indolence, which if not occasioned by disease, at least tends much to produce it.

No persons who have any great natural defect, or acquired deformity, should be placed about children, either as attendants or instructors. Servants who squint, or have but one eye, or walk lame, or have particularly harsh voices, or rough manners, or indeed any thing that can offend the feelings of infants, (however great may be their merits in other respects,) are unfit to have the care of children. It is unnecessary to mention the impropriety of letting them be with persons who stutter, or have any impediment in their speech; but I wish, also, to caution against any extraordinary sort of ugliness, as the nerves of very young children are usually so delicate, that it is probable they suffer much which they cannot explain.

I remember once to have heard of a poor country girl, whose face (in consequence of her having fallen into the fire when a child) was disfigured in a frightful manner, both by distortion of features and unnatural colour of the skin. On her going to serve as nursery-maid in a neighbouring gentleman's family, it was observed that every time an infant of nine months old looked at her, he began to scream violently; but this was at first ascribed to her being a stranger. One morning, however, after she had been about a fortnight in the house, the child, on first waking, and beholding her at his bed side, was taken with a violent fit of convulsive crying, which lasted so long that it was thought necessary to send for the family physician; who, on enquiring into the circumstances of the case, recommended that the servant should be parted with. His advice was followed, and the child had no more fits of screaming afterwards.

Few things can be more hurtful to the health of children, than to see dismal countenances, and hear constant lamentations around them; for this reason parents should take especial care that the servants who are chiefly about their children be cheerful, free from envy and malice, and rather of a careless than thoughtful temper; and fathers and mothers who have troubles to talk over, should never allow their children, during infancy, to know any thing of the matter. The cares of the world always come too soon; and parents should prepare their children to struggle with them, by giving them that strength of body which so much conduces to fortitude of mind. This is to be done by keeping misfortunes out of their sight, rather than by studying to make disappointments for them, as I have sometimes heard people boast of doing. Prepare children for adversity, by fortifying their bodies and minds; but do not give them habits of discontent by unnecessary displeasures. Many chronic diseases are to be developed by whatever depresses the spirits; and in families where there is any reason to suspect a scrofulous taint in the blood, the greatest pains should be taken to keep the children constantly cheerful. It is generally known that strengthening and exciting food is necessary for children of this constitution; but it does not seem to be as generally known, that fretting is still more injurious to them than low diet. All those who really desire that their children should grow up healthy, ought to protect them as much as possible from every painful moral feeling; should treat them with constant kindness, and procure for them every exhilarating amusement that may be within their reach.

CHAPTER VI.

SENSIBILITY.—JEALOUSY.—PUNISHMENTS.—
COURAGE.—PEEVISHNESS.

THERE is no greater error than that committed by persons who like to exercise what they call the sensibility of children, and commend them for proofs of feeling. When they really have that excessive sensibility, which ignorance of its true nature leads so many to admire, a prudent mother will use every means to moderate it, as a quality which tends to injure the health and debilitate the mind. It is, in reality, a defect; and there are few things more detrimental to the well-being of individuals than that extreme sensibility which, by some strange error in judgment, has been generally considered as a meritorious quality, and admired as a virtue, when it ought to have been cured as a disease. Because this moral malady is frequently found in persons of the most amiable characters, we are not to cherish it as a necessary component part of a good disposition, any more than we should cherish the itch as a beauty, because those most liable to it are persons of a fair and delicate complexion. As in most people the body influences the mind, we should, in the work of education, consider health of body as the first object, and every moral feeling which tends to disturb the physical welfare as a defect. This is a subject on which a great deal might be said; but to develope it at full length, and display all the dangerous consequences of a cherished and cultivated excess of sensibility, would lead me away from the object of my present work.

Parents who sincerely desire to see their children healthy and happy will never play upon their feelings, nor suffer others to do so. It is very common for thoughtless persons to amuse themselves by exciting the jealousy of a child, without considering the train of evils, present and future, which appertain to this pernicious sentiment. Besides the feelings of hatred to which it infallibly leads, and which lay the foundations of moral depravity, there is nothing more likely to occasion maladies of a most dangerous nature. It deranges the stomach, bowels, nerves, liver, and brain; producing, according to the habits of the different subjects, indigestion, diarrhœa, convulsions, jaundice, and various sorts of fevers. It, also, by the general depression of spirits which it occasions, augments any predisposition which may exist to scrofula, and other diseases of debility; and instances have been recorded, by eminent physicians, of children who have been brought to the grave by the effects of jealousy.

This, like most other bad feelings, is entirely the consequence of mismanagement. The persons about children develope their faults by their own imprudent conduct, and then complain of the bad dispositions of their victims. By judicious attention, children the most inclined to jealousy may be prevented from feeling those painful sensations to which they are liable; and, in the course of time, from not being exercised, the baneful propensity will cease to exist. Jealousy proceeds from weakness; and in proportion as the physical and moral strength increase, the inclination to it diminishes: but if continually excited by the malicious or the foolish, it augments with years, and may perhaps at last end in that most detrimental of all feelings, envy, which poisons the sources of happiness, and forbids the well-being of mind and body. It is the duty of those who are concerned in the education of children, to remove every cause of jealousy far from them, and to watch over such as are inclined to this defect with the most unremitting care; by which means it may be completely removed, before it has acquired any dangerous influence on the character.

No expression of contempt should ever be made use of towards children. If it produce the effect desired, it degrades the child in its own opinion, and makes it feel that most painful and depressing of all sensations, shame: if it fail of this effect, it fills the mind with indignation and resentment, and is in every way injurious to both the physical and moral welfare. The high-spirited child will hate the person who appears to despise it; while the timid will be awed into mean servility, and become contented under a degree of mental debasement, which is sufficient to destroy every virtuous feeling. Excessive flattery may be hurtful to children, but looks of scorn are a thousand times more so; and vulgar minds are apt to use expressions of contempt, and exhibit disdainful airs, by way of recovering that level which their ignorance denies them. Parents should therefore be extremely particular respecting the manners and dispositions of those to whom they entrust the care of their children's education; for many, who would think it a dreadful thing to have them beaten, will yet (perhaps unconsciously) subject them to treatment far more hurtful to body and mind, by suffering them to live with scornful persons.

It is a palpable absurdity to say that all children are to be educated without coercion, and that punishments are never to be resorted to. As well might it be asserted that health is to be preserved without restraint, and that medicines should never be employed. Undoubtedly the less they are used the better; and neither the one nor the other should be administered without positive necessity. Punishments should be, like medicines, adapted to the particular constitution and circumstances; if not they may prove more injurious than beneficial; and there are some sorts of both which should never be employed in the treatment of a child. Generally speaking, the punishments inflicted on children should be immediate and of short duration, (as any thing which occasions fretting is hurtful to body and mind,) and whenever it can be so contrived, they should appear to be the natural consequence of the fault, or at least be so connected with it by some link of relationship as to unite the two ideas in the child's mind. It is difficult to give examples, without trespassing too much on the space allotted to other subjects; but a judicious parent will easily infer what the author wishes to recommend. All changes and privations which regard the quality or quantity of food, by way of chastisement, except they be directed to the express purpose of correcting some fault derived from that source, are to be deprecated as injurious to both body and mind. Such also are those which respect dress; a species of punishment frequently exercised on female children, and which, when much felt, is of very bad consequence.

All punishments which call forth the sensibility of children are to be employed sparingly and cautiously, lest they should lead to hypocrisy or debility. A child, who is not to have a kiss from mamma whenever it has been disobedient or cross, will, perhaps, either fret extremely or totally disregard it; and a cunning child will soon learn to feign great uneasiness about a species of chastisement, which it is unnatural should make any very durable impression.

No faults of children should, ever, be punished in such a way as to make them think themselves objects of contempt. Teach a being to despise himself, and you prepare his mind for the reception of every vice and every baseness. Self-respect is necessary to the existence of virtue, and without it, there can be no hope of establishing either physical or moral welfare.

The injudicious way in which young children are usually treated, makes them more unreasonable than they would otherwise be, and often occasions them to cry for things which they cannot have. It should be established, as a general rule, in all nurseries, that the children are to have immediately whatever they ask for with good-humour and civility, if it be possible to give it to them: what they cannot have, should be refused, mildly but positively; and, on no account, should they ever obtain any thing by crying for it. They would soon learn by this, that it was their interest to be good-humoured; and thus, would be removed a great source of that peevishness and discontent which is so detrimental to the health of body and mind in the first years of childhood.

At two or three years old it sometimes happens that children of great vivacity will cry and scream without well knowing why for a length of time together. No doubt this proceeds from some error in the treatment of them; but let the origin be what it may, it is necessary to seek a remedy, and (when perfectly secure that it proceeded from no malady*) I have usually found the best to be three or four smart slaps with the open hand, applied on that part subjected of old to this kind of discipline. The child's attention is immediately attracted by this new misfortune; it screams perhaps a little more loudly for the moment, but as soon as the smarting ceases, the crying is at an end. This is, however, a remedy, which can only be administered with advantage by a parent, or some person of high authority in the family, and should no more be left in the hands of nurses or servants than any other medicine: besides, it must be observed that it does not agree with all dispositions, and when it does not, immediately, produce the beneficial effect above mentioned, should not be persisted in. Punishments should always be employed to cure, not to irritate; and those which are found to exasperate rather than to correct, should at once be relinquished. And here I should wish to impress in the strongest manner the danger of indiscriminate blows. There

* This is of great consequence to ascertain, as children troubled with the long round worm (lumbricus) are very subject to violent fits of screaming, which might lead to vexatious mistakes.

is but one part of the body on which a child may be struck with perfect safety; and I am afraid since birch-rods have gone out of fashion, children have been more subject to blows in other places. I am no advocate for birch-rods, or any other instrument for inflicting pain, but there are cases in which I know that two or three slaps on the part formerly submitted to the government of the rod, may have a very good effect on children *under* four years old. But nothing should ever induce any one to give the slightest blow about the head or neck: what is called a box on the ear may be the occasion of incurable deafness, and an unlucky slap on the back of the neck may cause a serious injury to the spinal marrow. Blows on the head from harsh instructors, have been suspected to produce water on the brain; and the mode in which some people gratify their anger towards children, by violently shaking them, might also lead to serious consequences [*].

Locking up children in dark rooms, or inflicting any other punishment which may strongly affect their nerves, should be prohibited. Terror is a sensation against which they should be protected

[*] Since the first edition of this work was published, I have witnessed the progress of a complicated disease, terminating fatally by water on the brain (after many months duration) which there are the strongest reasons to suppose originated in a severe beating and fright given by a violent tempered schoolmaster to a boy eleven years old, with a robust constitution but great sensibility of nerves.

with the greatest care: the injuries done by fear, to the physical and moral health, are incalculable; and a child who is frequently exposed to such debilitating feelings, can never become so robust in body, or so virtuous in mind, as he might otherwise have been. *Courage is the first quality that should be cultivated in children;* it is in every way beneficial to them, and in passive courage they may be exercised at a very early age. They should always be commended highly for bearing pain well; and when violently affected by a trifling hurt, means should be sought to draw off their attention from it, and make them ashamed of their cowardice. I remember once to have seen a child, (under three years old,) who was crying bitterly for the scratch of a pin, instantly suppress his tears on seeing his mother give her arm a similar scratch. He looked up in her face, shewed great surprise at seeing her smile, examined the hurt on his own arm, then that on hers, (which was the worst of the two,) and ceased his complaints.

There is no quality more in the power of education, and none more beneficial to ourselves and others, than courage, which by no means depends so much on the nerves as those imagine who suppose that all women have a right to be cowards. This opinion is extremely injurious to the health of young girls, who would often try to conquer their fears, if they were not taught to believe it a thing impossible, and that they even appear more amiable as helpless than as independent beings.

Children should never be allowed to continue whining and fretting, as there is nothing worse for the health than the prolonged sensation of discontent; but it is not always by soothing and caressing that this is to be remedied. Something which excites a stronger feeling may be necessary, and a sharp reproof, a threatened punishment, an additional task, or a disagreeable* medicine, is sometimes required. Habits of discontent develop chronic diseases, and a peevish child has little chance of growing up healthy or happy. The causes of peevishness should be attentively studied, on its first appearance, and the appropriate remedies, moral and physical, immediately employed for the cure of it.

* See page 368.

CHAPTER VII.

PRAISE.—FORGIVENESS.—RELIGION.—LEARNING.
—ACCOMPLISHMENTS.

GREAT caution is necessary in bestowing praise on moral qualities, and a child should seldom, if ever, be commended for any act which is the spontaneous effect of a naturally good disposition. Nothing should be applauded which does not require exertion; but efforts of industry, instances of self-denial, command of temper, correction of faults, should be applauded. It is dangerous to commend children for proofs of affection, sympathy, or benevolence: let it suffice for them to perceive that they are loved the better for those qualities; but, if they are praised for them, they may learn to place too high a value on mere propensities to good, and content themselves without the principles of virtue; they may learn to admire show, and affect prettiness instead of acquiring worth. How many women are there who, had they been prudently educated, might have been just and estimable, yet have become weak and useless from having in their early years heard their great tenderness and excessive sensibility (the effects perhaps of physical infirmity) cried up as virtues of the first magnitude! and how many men have turned out spendthrifts, because they were admired as children, for their great generosity in giving away money, of which they did not yet know the value! If praise and blame were more judiciously bestowed, and the exciting causes more accurately weighed than they usually are, they would have far better effects in the physical and moral education of children.

Persons who are fond of forgiving children, should be careful to make their punishments conditional, that they may leave themselves some fair pretext for change. The condemnation being once absolutely pronounced, by remitting the punishment, they confess themselves unjust, either in their first or their last act, a thing which should never be allowed in any sort of education. The punishment having been decreed, should be inevitable; for the hope of ultimate pardon often encourages errors; and (what more concerns the subject of this work) the suspense and disappointments which uncertainty occasions are extremely detrimental to the health of children.

The first principles of religion conduce much to the physical welfare of children, and should be taught them as soon as possible. Those who are not accustomed to observe them, can scarcely believe how early children are capable of understanding and rejoicing in the notion of a Supreme Being, on whose protection they rely; and whom they feel satisfaction in endeavouring to please. But it is of the utmost consequence to the health of children, that all gloomy and terrific ideas connected with this subject should be concealed from them ; for as much as may be the benefit derived from the consoling thought of a protecting Providence, so much injury may they receive from the fear of an evil spirit, wandering about on the face of the earth seeking whom he may devour. In truth, the more that every thing can be represented under a cheerful aspect to children, the better for their health of body and mind.

It is extremely difficult to determine, with respect to the physical welfare, at what time a child ought first to learn to read; and, indeed, it should depend entirely on the constitution and character of the individual. Lively, healthy children are more likely to find occupation for themselves, and therefore have less necessity for being taught early, than those who are indolent and inclined to chronic diseases: yet these latter are more injured by coercion of any kind, and *all* children cannot be taught *in play*. The moment a child of any age or disposition appears to be at a loss for employment, it should begin to learn; and those of delicate constitutions should, perhaps, be taught earlier, that they may advance by slow degrees. Generally speaking, when children do not appear at a loss for something to do, it is by no means necessary that they should begin to learn till after four years old; and with proper management, during the first year or two, it ought not to occasion them any uneasiness. Strength of body should be the first object of our care, and whatever can interfere with that should be avoided: but the instruction of children, if conducted with discretion, will increase rather than diminish the physical welfare, as habits of regularity and the alternation of labour and amusement must ever promote health and happiness.

In summer-time children should be encouraged to rise early, by allowing them to begin the day with exercise in the open air; indeed at all times of the year they should get up with the prospect of some agreeable exercise for the first quarter of an hour; and for this purpose, some large hall or unfurnished room should be allotted by those who can afford it, for their children to play in, where, in bad weather, they may divert themselves with skipping-ropes, battledores, and shuttlecocks, and other active sports. A child who gets up, in a cold morning, with the dreary prospect of sitting down to study immediately, will not leave his bed with the same cheerful alacrity as one who knows he can warm himself by play for a quarter of an hour before he goes to his books. It is very unwholesome for children to study in a morning by candle-light, and likely to occasion inflammations of the eyes, especially if the time of sleep has not been so long as is necessary for those who are still growing.

Moral virtue and physical welfare are so nearly connected, that they must unavoidably be cultivated together; but the improvement of mere talents should always be considered as a secondary pursuit, by those who esteem health of body and purity of mind the most important objects of education. Female children, particularly, are often made very unhappy for the purpose of acquiring what are called *accomplishments;* and one of the most valuable of social qualities, a cheerful temper, is sacrificed to the doubtful chance of being able to excel in some fine unnecessary needle-work, or to display astonishing skill on some useless instrument of music. The utmost success in these, (even when cultivated for the laudable purpose of obtaining a livelihood,) is but a poor compensation for the loss of good health, or good temper: and if the physical and moral well-being of children be counted the most desirable attainment, I have no hesitation in asserting, that whatever makes them miserable in the acquirement of it, is better not learnt at all.

At the same time that I appear averse to the cultivation of *accomplishments,* (the general meaning of which comprehensive term is a smattering of ornamental, but useless arts,) it is only when they are held in more than their due estimation: on the contrary, considered as a means of filling up the time of children, and giving them habits of regular employment, it must be acknowledged that they conduce much to their physical and moral welfare. The mechanical exercise of the hands on the pianoforte may be taught as early as four or five years old with great advantage: the position is not unwholesome, the variety of sounds amuses the imagination, and the exercise of three of the senses at once assists the memory of children: so that if the teacher be gentle and judicious, great progress may be made in that art, at a very early age, without injury to the health or temper.

It is a great and most hurtful error to oblige children to devote those hours to study which ought to be employed in exercise in the open air; and so far from confining them against their will, even those who desire to continue beyond the regular hours appointed for labour, should not be permitted. Nothing should interfere with air and exercise; and it will generally be found that the child whose body is strengthened by a proper physical education, although less time be daily given up to study, will, at the end of the year, have done more than one whose constitution has been rendered weak by too much confinement and application, and whose studies have been, consequently, interrupted by frequent indispositions.

In writing, drawing, or doing any sort of needlework, constant attention should be paid to prevent children from sitting crooked, leaning the chest against a table, or acquiring any other awkward positions equally detrimental to health and beauty.

The greatest care should be taken to prevent children from learning those vicious and destructive habits, which are sometimes unfortunately acquired by indiscriminate and careless intercourse with strangers. For this reason, a prudent mother will not allow her children to be with others whom she does not perfectly know, without the presence of some grown person, who can be relied on to pay them strict attention; as the most innocent child might learn, during the momentary absence of an attendant, what would be of the utmost injury for years. Indeed, when children are at play together, the more they can be in exercise in the open air, the greater benefit and the less harm will they derive from the number and variety of their companions. It is very probable that all unnatural and unwholesome practices are the consequence of errors in the physical education, the chief of which is not permitting children to enjoy a sufficiency of fresh air and active amusement.

CHAPTER VIII.

PHYSICIANS.—MEDICINES.—TREATMENT OF CHILDREN WHEN ILL.—CONCLUSION.

When a physician is called to a sick child, it should be with a full reliance on his skill, and a determination to follow his advice. Be sure that he is a clever man before you consult him, then give him all the information in your power on the subject of the malady which has required his presence, and afterwards obey his orders accurately. If, however, he should happen to prescribe any thing that the child particularly dislikes, or which has before disagreed with it, explain all this, and a judicious practitioner will either substitute another mode of treatment equally applicable, or tell you if the case be such that no other than the medicines already directed can benefit. If it should happen, on any occasion, that unexpected resistance on the part of the child may have prevented you from doing exactly as the physician has ordered, fail not to inform him at his next visit: a man of good sense will hardly blame you for not having used violence with a sick child; but you may do the greatest injury by deceiving the medical attendant, in letting him suppose that medicine has been taken when it has not: still worse is it to give the prescriptions of old nurses, or of quacks, privately, when a professional man is consulted: these are sometimes perfectly harmless, and if the permission of the physician can be obtained, may be given for the gratification of relations; but they are often composed of active substances, whose administration is by no means a matter of indifference. Above all things, no patent medicine should ever be given to a child, without the special leave of a medical man.

There is nothing I am more anxious to impress on the minds of mothers, than the injury done to children by giving them too many and too strong medicines. It is not uncommon to hear ignorant people blame the doctor for not ordering what they suppose a sufficient quantity of physic; but this accusation, especially in regard to young patients, should always give a favourable impression of a physician: if he be a man of no eminence, he at least shews good sense in not being persuaded to give much medicine; and if he be a man of established reputation, it is most probable that whatever plan he pursues is that best adapted to the case before him.

Although I positively assert, that children ought to have much less medicine than is usually given to them in the British Isles, I must point out a contrary error of fatal tendency, which sometimes occurs. There are extraordinary cases of inflammatory disease, which require the employment of remedies that appear too violent for the state of the sick person: but when a physician deserving of confidence is called to a child in an acute malady, his orders should be obeyed with the most scrupulous attention; and no fear of weakening the patient should cause the omission of any purgative, emetic, or bleeding which he prescribes. It frequently happens, that where there is an appearance of the greatest debility, an abundant evacuation will relieve it; and what ignorant by-standers have supposed would be sufficient to put an end to a being in so weak a state, has been ordered by the judicious physician on purpose to remove that very appearance of weakness. A child has been seen to gain strength immediately on the administration of some active remedy, which the attendants were convinced must occasion instant death.

There are persons sometimes found so unreasonable as to blame the physician when the patient dies. No doubt the cleverest of men are likely to err; but not once in a hundred times does it occur to a man of learning and experience to mistake the nature of a disease so far as to order improper medicines; and if the malady should have been of such a very extraordinary and occult nature as to have deceived a man of eminence in his profession, it is not likely that persons without knowledge should have discovered the truth. There is no science less understood by the multitude than that of medicine, and yet every one thinks he has a right to judge of the conduct of a medical man. I only mention this for the purpose of cautioning mothers not to be led astray by the assertions of the unlearned, either in regard to giving medicines unknown to the physician, disobeying his orders, or blaming him for events beyond his power to control.

In the cure of all maladies, great attention should be paid to the particular constitution of the child, as the same treatment is not equally adapted for all; and nothing is more likely to lead into dangerous errors, than for ignorant persons to medicate one child in the manner they have heard of another being cured by some eminent physician; when perhaps the same physician, if consulted, would employ a quite contrary method, required by a total difference of circumstances, not evident to persons of less discrimination.

It is to be observed, in regard to all medicinal substances, that they do not agree equally well with every constitution, nor produce always the same effects: but on this subject the judgement of those about children must be exercised, as it is impossible to give any but general directions. One rule always to be observed is, that no strong dose of any remedy should ever be tried without the authority of a medical man: in small quantities, all those prescribed in this work may be employed without danger; and the effects will shew whether the dose can be increased with hope of advantage.

I have sometimes known physicians of the first eminence order remedies for children, which it was not possible to persuade them to take; and in certain cases, the being forced to swallow a disagreeable medicine may be as dangerous to an infant as the malady for which it has been prescribed. On such an occasion, it would be right to inform the physician of this circumstance, and inquire from him whether, at all risks, the remedy must be administered, for sometimes this cannot be dispensed with; as for instance, with respect to bark, in certain maladies, when the life of the patient depends on taking a large quantity of that particular medicine. In lesser matters, and especially on unforeseen occasions, a mother must sometimes use her own judgement; and when it is possible to save a sick child from the pain of crying and agitating its nerves, it is always better to do so; this may frequently be effected by changing the form of the medicine prescribed, which a judicious physician will always be willing to do, if it be in his power.

I recollect an instance of a child, who was suffering under a severe attack of inflammation in the chest, being ordered sinapisms to the feet. This child was about fifteen months old, and of a very quick temper; the sinapisms were no sooner applied than they were kicked off; fomentations of the same nature were then attempted, but with as little success. At length the mother, taking the child out of bed, placed it on her knees, and (as if in play) contrived to get its feet into a sinapized bath, in which she continued to rub them with her hand for twenty minutes; this produced the good effect expected from the sinapisms, and occasioned the child no agitation or displeasure.

Children are frequently induced to make too much of their maladies, with the hope of indulgence and relaxation from their studies; or to conceal them, through fear of confinement and medicine; and it requires great judgement and moderation to treat them properly, when such is the case. While they are very young, it is much safer that they should be inclined to exaggerate their indispositions, and as they grow older, the persons about them must observe that they do not hurt their health by refraining from expressing what they feel. A child should never be accused of pretending to be ill: if the reproach be unjust, the vexation of a false accusation may augment the child's disease; and if it be just, a punishment ought to follow, which would be better avoided. But when a child assumes an appearance of malady where there is none, or greater than that which does exist, it is very easy to render the circumstances attendant on the supposed or exaggerated indisposition so disagreeable, that they may prevent a continuance or repetition of the fault. In all cases of real illness, I should recommend, as part of the cure, that the medicines be as little nauseous, and the confinement as little irksome as possible: whereas if there be any reason to suspect that a child affects to be ill, medical substances (of no active operation but) very offensive to the taste, such as a little powdered rhubarb in water, or a small glass of infusion of wormwood, camomile, or quassia, may be administered without any attempt to disguise their disagreeable qualities; and at the same time the child may be kept in bed with little light, and no company. I will answer for it, that this mode of treating the assumed indisposition will speedily remove all wish to appear ill, and prevent the necessity of resorting to harsher measures. The greatest care should, however, be taken to distinguish the assumed illness of a cunning child from the languor and uneasiness of one who is on the brink of chronic diseases, such as scrofula, hydrocephalus, &c., or suffering under that irregular fever which sometimes proceeds from extremely rapid growth; as it is a far less dangerous error to treat a feigned malady for a real one, than to mistake the indisposition of a delicate child for mere artifice.

Care should be taken that the attendants of children do not find means to persuade them (for the purpose of sparing themselves some slight inconvenience) that it is a great merit to conceal and disregard indispositions, as such a notion has sometimes been followed by dangerous consequences, in rendering maladies severe which might have been removed by a little attention in the beginning.

It would be a great advantage if the minds of youth could be early impressed with the value of good health, as one of the chief ingredients of happiness. Cheerfulness, activity, usefulness, depend much on the possession of physical prosperity; a blessing which many lose by not being aware of the means of preserving it, and which few would disregard, if it were represented to them in the important light it deserves.

―――

A firm conviction that the most delicate infants may grow up healthy, with constant and judicious attention, while the most robust may become sickly, through either neglect or ill-adapted care; and a strong belief, that if all children had the benefits of sufficient air, exercise, and amusement, good moral discipline, habits of moderation, and regular occupations, great care, but little medicine in slight maladies, and strict obedience to skilful physicians in severe diseases, the happiness of mankind would be much augmented; have led to the composition of this work, in which, it is hoped, will be found *such instruction and advice, as may enable young mothers to direct the physical education of their children with success.*

APPENDIX.

The following medicines should always be kept in a house where there are children, and ought to be procured from some eminent chemist and druggist, as much depends upon their being of the best quality.

RHUBARB.—This root is one of the most useful remedies in the diseases of children. It should be kept in pieces, for the purpose of preparing the infusion, &c., and in powder, for immediate use. In the former state (when good) it is compact, rather heavy, and yellow on the outside; but, when broken, is streaked with red, white, and yellow. The brown and spongy is bad. The powder is also yellow, and has a strong smell and taste: it should be kept in a bottle well corked. The quantity of this last, for a purge, is from *two* to *four* grains for an infant under two months old; *five* or *six* for a child of a year old; *eight* or *ten* for a child of five years old; and one of twelve may take *fifteen* or *twenty**. When mixed with magnesia, less is required. A child who has a great disgust to the powder, may take the *infusion;* which can be prepared either by pouring three ounces of boiling water on thirty grains of powdered rhubarb, and after letting it stand in a covered vessel two hours, strain-

* These quantities (as well as those of the other medicines) must be varied as experience shews to be necessary for different constitutions.

ing and sweetening it; or by putting a drachm of the root, a little pounded, into two ounces of cold water, for four and twenty hours before it be strained and sweetened. To infants, either of these preparations may be given by *tea-spoonfuls;* but a child of seven years old may take a *dessert-spoonful,* and a child of twelve, a *table-spoonful:* sometimes double that quantity is necessary.

The syrup of ENDIVE recommended in this book is prepared in the following manner: six drachms of endive roots and two of the herb, one ounce of rhubarb pounded, and seven grains of alkaline salt of tartar, must boil in a quart of water down to three half pints; then strain with strong pressure, add eighteen ounces of fine sugar, and make a syrup in the usual manner*. If this be found troublesome, a syrup of rhubarb, to be used in place of it, may be prepared by taking half an ounce of the root pounded, two scruples and eight grains of cinnamon, the same quantity of carbonate of soda, and four ounces of boiling water: this must digest for six hours, be strained, and have eight ounces of fine sugar dissolved in it; and then be strained again. Either of these syrups may be given to little infants by *tea-spoonfuls,* and to children of four or five years old, by *table-spoonfuls:* after that age, powdered rhubarb must be mixed with them, or they will have little effect. The spirituous tincture of rhubarb may be given in doses of from *three* drops to *half* a tea-spoonful, in any convenient liquid, as a strengthening medicine for the stomach and bowels, but never as a purge, to children.

MAGNESIA† is one of the best remedies for those

* The syrup of endive so much used for young children in Italy is made in this manner.

† The easiest way of taking this medicine is in barley or rice gruel.

acidities to which young children are so subject; and a very safe one, as it carries off the offensive matter by the bowels. This powder should be perfectly white, smooth, and free from all taste and smell. It may be given to little infants (either alone or with rhubarb) in doses of from *three* to *ten* grains, and in much larger quantities to children advanced in age. It should be kept in a bottle well corked.

CALOMEL is the only preparation of mercury that may be given to a child without the orders of a physician; and the person from whom it is bought should be asked for *the mildest preparation*. This powder may be given at first, in the quantity of *half a grain* for every year of the child's age, (so that a child of six years old would take three grains,) and if the effect be not found sufficient, the dose may be increased to a whole grain for every year until after *eight* years old, when it must not be augmented without the advice of a medical man. If too little medicine has been given, it is easy to repeat it; but the mischief done by giving too much at once, is difficult to remedy*. Acids and vegetable food should be prohibited for some hours before calomel be administered; and also for the whole day after it has been given at night, lest it should occasion pains in the stomach or bowels: for the same reason, cold drink is better avoided till after it has worked off; and care should be taken that a child is not exposed to cold or damp after taking this medicine. It is best to keep calomel in a bottle.

CASTOR-OIL, when *really good*, has little taste or smell, is of a light colour, and thicker than salad-oil; to pre-

---

* When calomel and rhubarb are given together, half the usual quantity of each is sufficient.

vent it from growing rancid, it should be kept in a cool, dark place, in a bottle well corked and covered, so as to prevent all possibility of the air getting to it: but, even with these precautions, it is better not to keep it long. It is an excellent remedy for many complaints, as it usually operates quicker than other mild purgatives. A child of a year old may take *one small tea-spoonful;* one of three years old may take *two;* one of six, *half a table-spoonful,* and a child of ten years old may take a *whole table spoonful;* the spoon being more or less full according to the age and the facility of being purged. This medicine may be given in various ways; but it is less nauseous in warm liquids than in cold, as heat diminishes the thickness of the oil. Broth, lemonade, or mint-water may be used, according to the different tastes of the sick; and it is better to pour the oil on the top of the other liquid, than to attempt mixing them together. Little children may be induced to take castor-oil, by mixing it either with lemon juice, or with the yolk of an egg. The lemon juice should first have a sufficient quantity of sugar dissolved in it, and then be put into a phial with the oil, of which it should be nearly double the quantity; these should be well mixed by shaking, and swallowed before they begin to separate. If given with yolk of egg, the latter must be rather more in quantity than the oil, which is to be beat up with it, and then warm, sweet, lemon-peel tea must be mixed with it, in the quantity of a table-spoonful to every tea-spoonful of the oil, which forms an emulsion not at all disagreeable.

OIL OF SWEET ALMONDS is in general to be preferred to castor-oil for little infants, and may be given in larger quantities; twice or three times as much. It is too mild a purgative for children past three years old, except in particular cases. It easily grows rancid, and should be

APPENDIX. 375

kept with great care, in the same manner directed for the foregoing, if it cannot be had fresh made at the moment it is wanting, which would be always preferable.

N.B. In case of sudden attack of cholic, *good* salad-oil may be used in the place of either castor-oil or almond-oil; and is to be preferred to them when they are not of the best quality. The quantity necessary is rather more than double that of castor-oil.

IPECACUANHA is, next to rhubarb, the most useful medicine for children. There is no occasion to keep any preparation of it except the powder, which should be preserved in a well-corked bottle. It is not extremely nauseous, and may be given to young children in any sweet drink. It is a mild and safe emetic, of which *two* or *three* grains may be given to children under a year old; and from *five* to *fifteen*, according to the age and facility of vomiting, may suffice for those between two and thirteen. Sometimes much larger doses are required to produce this effect. In modified doses, ipecacuanha produces perspiration; and is beneficial in many diseases, without acting as a vomit.

KERMES MINERAL is a powerful and valuable medicine in hooping-cough and catarrhs, and is frequently ordered by physicians for cutaneous diseases. It is a dark red powder, which should never be got from any but a very good chemist. Being a substance of very unequal strength, it should always be tried on some adult before it is given to an infant; as half a grain of one preparation of it will have as much effect as two of another. It should be given at first in very small doses: the *eighth part of a grain* to a child of seven years old, two or three times a day, will be sufficient until the effect be observed. Both this and calomel are very dangerous if given in too large quantities; and kermes mineral is a violent emetic. This medicine will remain good for years, if preserved from air, light and damp.

SULPHUR. Washed flowers of sulphur (a medicine hardly necessary to describe) is a fine powder of a beautiful light yellow colour, which has little taste. The quantity of this for a child of one year old, is from *two* to *ten* grains; for one of three, from *three* to *fifteen* grains; and a child of seven or eight years old may take from *five grains* to *half a drachm*. For a cough, or to ascertain whether an eruption be the itch, the smaller quantity may be given; the greater, when intended for a purge; in which last case it may be mixed with a little magnesia. The lesser dose may be given in honey or conserve; the larger in barley or rice water, or in milk.

OXYMEL OF SQUILLS, an excellent remedy for catarrhs and many other complaints, may be given in doses of from a *quarter* of a *tea-spoonful* to a *whole tea-spoonful*, several times a day, to young children; and, in larger quantities, according to the age and malady for which it is prescribed. It occasions vomiting when in a sufficient dose, but is seldom given with that intention, except to little infants.

GUM ARABIC should not be bought in powder, but kept in lumps, to be pounded when it is wanted to be dissolved in any liquid, or to prepare the *mucilage*, which may be made by pouring gradually three ounces of boiling water on two ounces of the gum reduced to powder, and stirring it till well mixed.

SYRUP OF WHITE POPPIES is a mild opiate for young children, and may be given in doses of from a *tea* to a *table-spoonful*, according to the age and circumstances. When mixed with the two foregoing for a cough, they should be all in equal quantities.

Nitre is a white pure salt, which any one who has once tasted it good cannot mistake. It may be given in the quantity of *three* grains to children of two years old, and from that to *ten* as they advance in age; and may be dissolved in water, or any other insipid drink. With warm milk and water, in the quantity of a *tea-spoonful* to *six table-spoonfuls*, it is good to hold in the mouth for the tooth-ache of children; and with cold water, as an application for bruises.

Camphor should be kept for the purpose of preparing the julep, &c., in a bottle, with a glass stopper. To make the camphorated spirit, one ounce of camphor may be dissolved in three ounces of rectified spirit of wine. The camphor julep is prepared as follows :— one drachm of camphor must be well rubbed in a glass mortar, first with ten drops of rectified spirit of wine, and then with half an ounce of white sugar, on which must be poured, by degrees, fifteen ounces of boiling water; and when well mixed, it should be put into a bottle and corked. This medicine may be given in the quantity of *one* or *two table spoonfuls*, three or four times a day, to children from one to four years old, in those maladies which require it: the quantity to be increased for those who are older. *Camphorated spirit* with *laudanum;* a table spoonful of the former to a tea-spoonful of the latter is a good *external* application for the stomach and bowels, in case of great pain or obstinate vomiting.

Spirit of Hartshorn should be kept in a bottle, with a glass stopper, which ought never to be left long open.

From *two* to *six* drops may be given, in any watery liquid, to children under five years old, and increased, in proportion to their age, to *ten* or *fifteen* drops. Volatile liniment may be made, by shaking together in a phial, two spoonfuls of salad-oil with one of spirit of hartshorn. To a table-spoonful of this may be added a tea-spoonful of laudanum, to rub the stomach in obstinate vomiting.

Æther should be preserved in the same manner as the foregoing, and care should be taken not to approach too near a candle with either of these liquids, especially the latter, which is particularly inflammable. From *two* to *ten* drops may be given in some sort of convulsive maladies, several times in the day.

Tincture of Assafœtida.—A small quantity of this should be kept to give in clysters. From *ten* to *thirty* drops, according to the age of the child.

Laudanum.—A small quantity of this should also be at hand, in case of being required for external application, or for clysters.

Opodeldoc and vegeto-mineral water for bruises, and Ceruse to prepare ointment for burns, should be amongst the medicines kept for the use of children.

The following are the best preparations of iron for children. Chalybeate wine, which may be given from *five* drops to *twenty* once a day, (in a spoonful of any convenient liquid,) to those between the ages of eighteen months and ten years. The iron in substance, *reduced to a powder as fine as magnesia*, of which so much may be given as equals *a pinch of snuff*, in a spoonful of thick soup or bread and water, just as the child is going to dinner, when it will have a better effect than if the stomach were to remain empty after it. The quantity must be a *little* more or less, according to the child's age; and no preparation of iron should be given till after children are weaned. The use of this medicine gives a black colour to the evacuations from the bowels, which mothers ought to be aware of, to prevent their being alarmed.

I have not mentioned any of the purging salts in this list of medicines, as children usually dislike them extremely, and it is easy to procure them when ordered by a physician. Common salt, in rather a less quantity than is usually given of Epsom salt, dissolved in a sufficient quantity of broth to be swallowed without disgust, will not fail to purge mildly.

In weighing medicines, it is always right to lay a piece of paper in the scales under them, as many imbibe a degree of poison by coming in contact with brass; and be the quantity ever so inconsiderable, it is better avoided.

CLYSTERS should generally be a little warmer than milk, just drawn from the cow. The quantity for infants under two months old, is from *two* ounces to *two and a half*: children of four or five years old may take *three* or *four* ounces; and those who are older, *five* or *six*. A common table-spoon contains about half an ounce, and for these purposes, *very* exact measure is unnecessary. Oil, coarse sugar, salt, or honey, are the proper ingredients to mix with water, for common clysters, intended only to empty the bowels; but some children require them much stronger than others, and for these a double portion of the above-mentioned substances must be employed; and sometimes castor-oil must be used instead of salad-oil. In general, three tea-spoonfuls of oil may be put to every ounce of water: salt should be used more sparingly than the other ingredients. For the cholic, oil may be mixed with a light infusion of camomile flowers; and if the pain proceeds from wind, three ounces of this infusion, and ten drops of tincture of assafœtida, is a proper clyster for a child of a year old.

BATHS FOR THE FEET of children should be somewhat warmer than new milk. The MUSTARD bath may be prepared with a table-spoonful of coarse mustard to every gallon of water; that of VINEGAR, with rather less than half a pint to that quantity; and when both mustard and vinegar are used, half the quantity of each will be sufficient. To make a SALT-WATER bath, three or four spoonfuls of kitchen salt to a gallon of water will probably be enough. The use of all these baths is to draw the blood from the head and body to the feet, and they are often of the greatest advantage.

FOMENTATIONS, of the same ingredients, and for the same purpose, may be employed; but the liquid must be much hotter; twenty minutes, or half an hour, will be sufficient for fomenting the feet, and the flannels or clothes should be changed four or five times.

There are many ways of preparing SINAPISMS; but the simplest and surest is by mixing coarse mustard with good vinegar, in sufficient quantity to form a paste, and applying it in a piece of thin gauze, which prevents unnecessary dirt and inconvenience. A sinapism cannot be kept long on the hollow part of the foot without causing great pain, which renders walking disagreeable for some time after: this may be avoided, by making them in two parts for the sole of each foot, and removing that next the hollow as soon as it gives pain, which will be some time before the front part of the foot is sufficiently affected.

Gargles should be in general of an emollient nature, such as barley-water, decoction of marsh-mallows, honey and water, &c.; but a few drops of vinegar, or a little red wine, may sometimes be added. When a sore-throat is bad enough to require more active gargles, the advice of a physician should be sought; and therefore it is unnecessary to give directions about them here.

To prepare the *cream of tartar drink*, recommended by an eminent medical author for bilious dysentery, half an ounce of this powder must be boiled with an ounce of barley, in rather more than a quart of water; and when the barley is as soft as in the usual way of making barley-water, it must be strained through a cloth, and sweetened or not, as may be agreeable to the taste of the sick child. This drink must be given from *one* to *four* ounces at a time, according to the age of the patient, very frequently, as it is intended to purge off the bile. It might be found useful as a mild purgative in other maladies also.

Barley and rice-water, chicken-broth, whey, almond-milk, &c., every one knows how to make; and therefore I shall give no directions about them here, but only recommend the greatest attention to *cleanliness*, as children have often refused drink, in diseases where it was of the greatest importance to them, in consequence of having been disgusted by some accidental nasty taste, occasioned by negligence. All these drinks should be made fresh, at least once a day; and such as have remained in a warm room all night, can scarcely be wholesome for a child in the morning, especially as they soon turn sour in a hot atmosphere. In making broth for the sick, care should be taken to skin the chicken completely before it is put to boil; and in making almond-milk, to watch that no part of it turn to oil.

Lemon-peel should not be left to infuse in any sort of

drink more than two or three hours, or it may give a disagreeable taste. *Lemon-peel,* as well as all sorts of herb, tea is to be made, by pouring on it boiling water, and leaving it in a covered vessel by the fire for about twenty minutes. *Ginger* tea should not be made with the powder, but a piece of the root bruised with a hammer. All these infusions are better, when strained a couple of hours after they are made.

No sort of drink should be forced on a sick child, however wholesome it may be considered. When there is a dry, burning heat in the skin, every thing may be given *cold;* and in many cases, *good cold water,* which instinct leads the patient to desire, is of great benefit.

A good way to make *jelly of Iceland lichen* is, to wash an ounce of the herb with tepid water on a sieve, and then to boil it very slowly in a quart of water, down to three quarters of a pint, and strain while it is hot. This may be given by ounces, three or four times a day, mixed with a sufficient quantity of lemon or orange-juice and sugar to make it palatable, to children who are weak, and have a cough after measles, &c., &c.

To prepare *oat-jelly,* (*flummery,*) take a quart of grits, rub them well with your hands in warm water, and leave them to steep for some days, till they are quite sour; then add about two quarts of hot water, and strain through a hair sieve. Let this stand till the water grows quite clear, and then pour it off gently: add to the sediment as much hot water as is necessary to make it boil, and stir it the whole time it is boiling. In short, it should be made like *starch;* and if it becomes too thick before it has formed a sort of jelly, boiling water must be added to it. The vessel in which *flummery* is made ought not to be of tin; and a little butter must be first rubbed on the bottom of it. This *jelly* may be eaten with milk, wine, or sugar; and being very easy of digestion, and extremely nourishing, is particularly good for convalescents when they happen to like it: I give the directions for making it here, because, though very common in some parts of the British islands, it is not known in others.

N.B. All medicines should be kept under lock and key, and no persons be permitted to have access to them, but such as are well aware of the dangerous consequences of any mistake in their management or their administration.

THE END.

G. Woodfall, Printer, Angel Court, Skinner Street, London.

www.ingramcontent.com/pod-product-compliance
Lightning Source LLC
Chambersburg PA
CBHW080050190426
43201CB00035B/2152